Minotaur Press, a Top Cow Productions company, presents...

ECHOES™

Published by
Top Cow Productions, Inc.
Los Angeles, CA

Minotaur Press, a Top Cow Productions Company, presents...

ECHOES

written by: **Joshua Hale Fialkov**

art by: **Rahsan Ekedal**

letters by: **Troy Peteri**

For this edition, cover art by: **Rahsan Ekedal**　　　　Original editions edited by: **Filip Sablik & Phil Smith**

For this edition, book design and layout by: **Vincent Kukua**

IMAGE COMICS, INC.
Robert Kirkman - chief operating officer.
Erik Larsen - chief financial officer.
Todd McFarlane - president
Marc Silvestri - chief executive officer
Jim Valentino - vice-president

Eric Stephenson - publisher
Todd Martinez - sales & licensing coordinator
Sarah deLaine - pr & marketing coordinator
Branwyn Bigglestone - accounts manager
Emily Miller - administrative assistant
Jamie Parreno - marketing assistant
Kevin Yuen - digital rights coordinator
Tyler Shainline - production manager
Drew Gill - art director
Jonathan Chan - senior production artist
Monica Garcia - production artist
Vincent Kukua - production artist
Jana Cook - production artist
www.imagecomics.com

TOP COW PRODUCTIONS, INC.
Marc Silvestri - CEO
Matt Hawkins - President & COO
Filip Sablik - Publisher
Bryan Rountree - Assistant to the Publisher
Elena Salcedo - Sales Assistant
Betsy Gonia - Intern

To find the comic shop
nearest you, call:
1-888-COMICBOOK

ECHOES HARDCOVER. JULY 2011. FIRST PRINTING.
ISBN: 978-1-60706-215-8 • $19.99

Want more info? Check out: **www.topcow.com**
for news & exclusive Top Cow merchandise!

TABLE OF CONTENTS

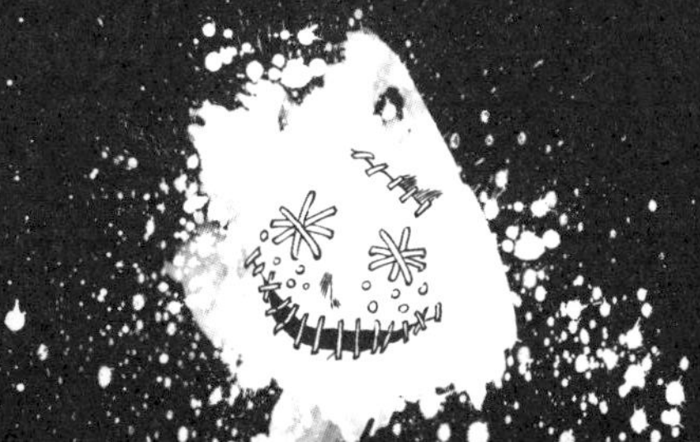

INTRODUCTION
by Steve Niles

Don't let Joshua Hale Fialkov fool you. He might seem like a normal guy, a nice guy, a dad even. But Josh knows something a lot of writers don't know…he knows how to crawl under your skin and dig his claws in.

In other words, Josh Fialkov knows how to scare you.

When most writers take on subjects like serial killers, they place them in urban settings, but Fialkov knows scary is best served with a healthy dose of comfort and reality. *Echoes* is set in the most normal of settings, the 'burbs, and that's what makes the creepy so much creepier. This could be your backyard, your neighbor…your father.

Another thing Fialkov knows is characters. The key to any good horror tale is caring about the characters. The more you care, the scarier it is when terrible things happen to them. The characters in *Echoes* are your neighbors and friends, each with an individual voice and motivations for surviving the story.

Which brings me to the look of *Echoes*. The black and white art by artist Rahsan Ekedal evokes memories of classic horror films, and adds to the tension beautifully.

I love well-rounded, well-thought out horror, and *Echoes* delivers. The scares come out of the slow descent of the lead character into madness as he discovers his life is not what he thought…and the people he loves are not what they seem.

The only thing I love better than a great scare is telling some good news. Well, I have some good news for you. You're about to read a great book.

Steve Niles
Los Angeles, CA
2011

Steve Niles is a comic, novel, and film writer; often credited with helping to bring horror comics back into prominence in the mainstream US comic market. He is best known for his top-selling original series, *30 Days of Night*, which spawned numerous comic series, novels and two feature films. Writing for every major comic publisher in the US, Niles has also created series including *Criminal Macabre*, *American Freakshow*, and *Bad Planet*. In 2005, Niles co-founded the production company, Raw Entertainment, with actor Thomas Jane to produce comic and film projects.

ECHOES™

CHAPTER ONE

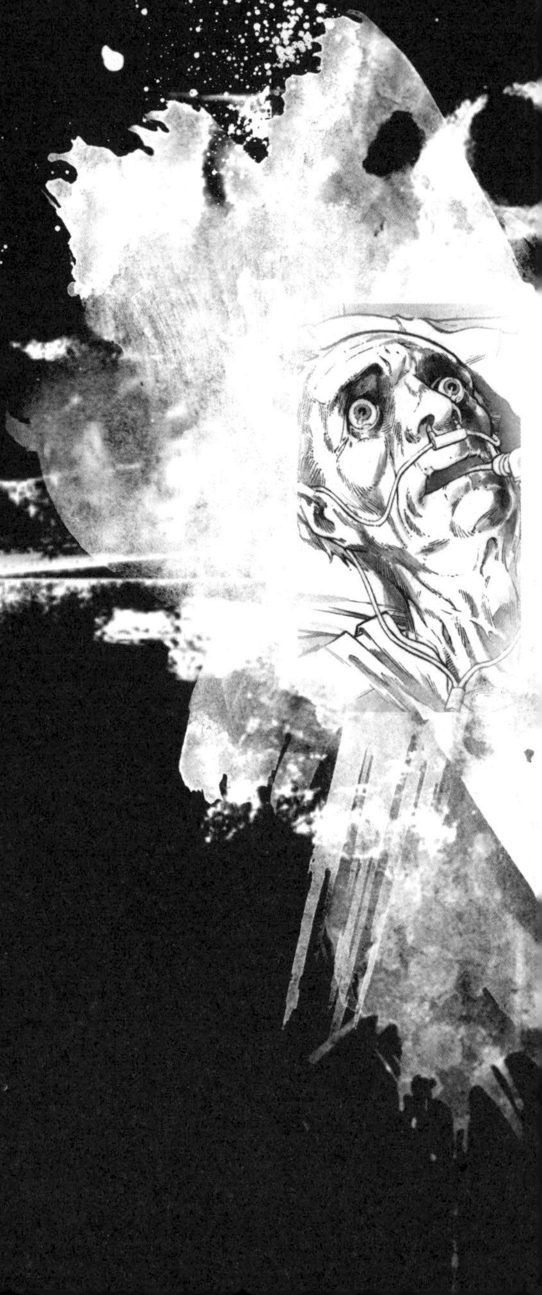

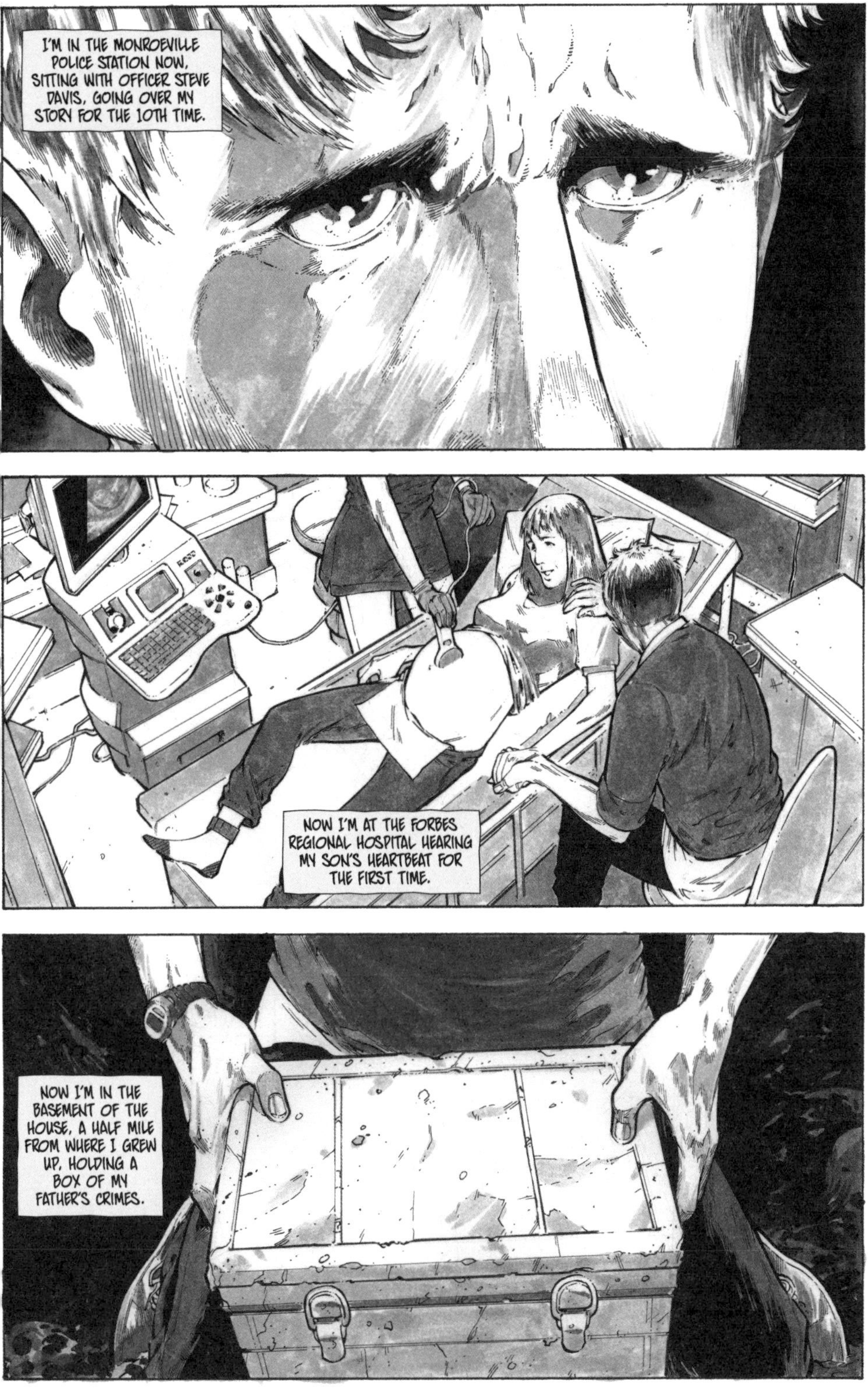
I'M IN THE MONROEVILLE POLICE STATION NOW, SITTING WITH OFFICER STEVE DAVIS, GOING OVER MY STORY FOR THE 10TH TIME.
NOW I'M AT THE FORBES REGIONAL HOSPITAL HEARING MY SON'S HEARTBEAT FOR THE FIRST TIME.
NOW I'M IN THE BASEMENT OF THE HOUSE, A HALF MILE FROM WHERE I GREW UP, HOLDING A BOX OF MY FATHER'S CRIMES.

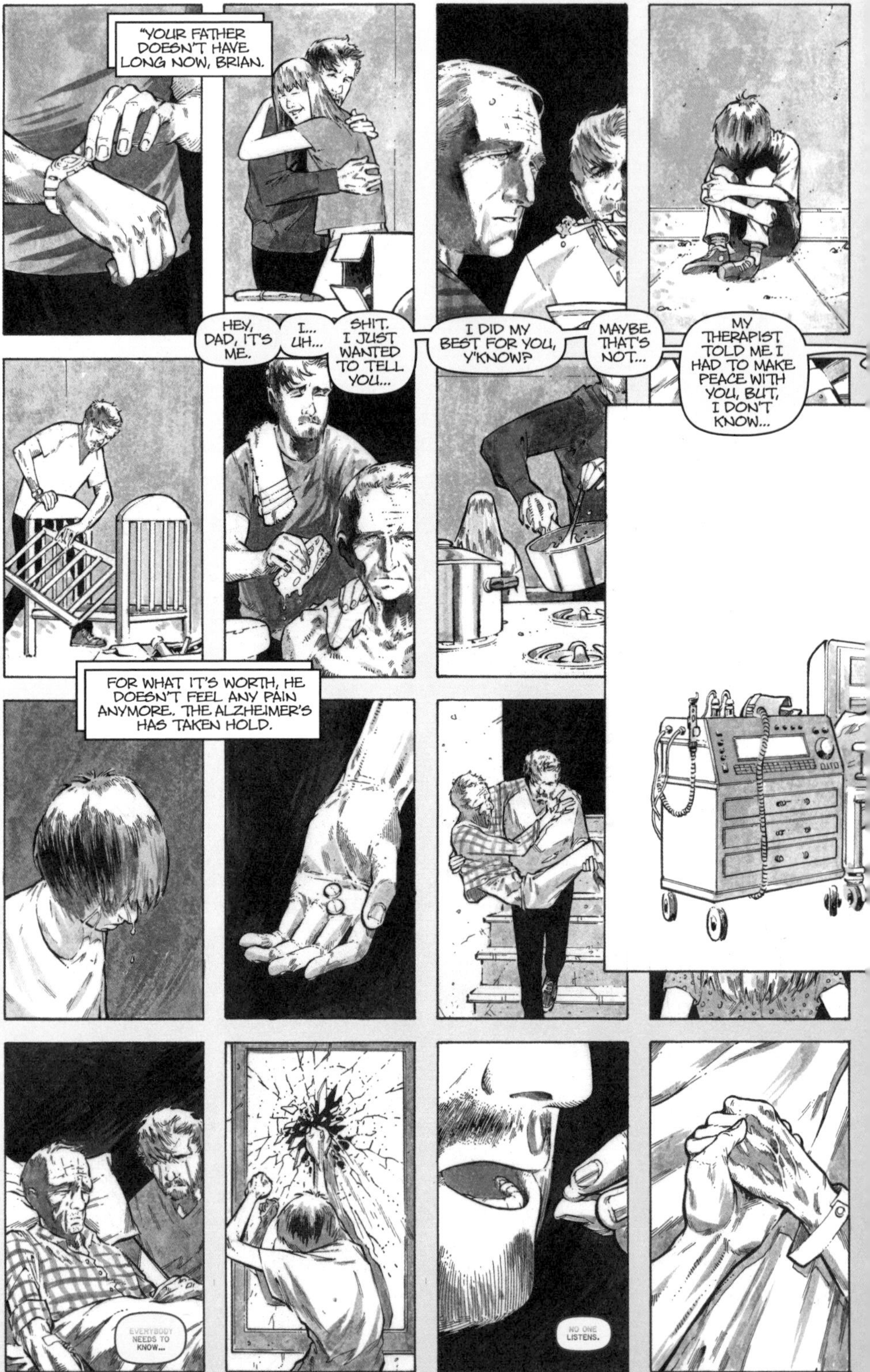
"YOUR FATHER DOESN'T HAVE LONG NOW, BRIAN.
HEY, DAD, IT'S ME.
I... UH...
SHIT. I JUST WANTED TO TELL YOU...
I DID MY BEST FOR YOU, Y'KNOW?
MAYBE THAT'S NOT...
MY THERAPIST TOLD ME I HAD TO MAKE PEACE WITH YOU, BUT, I DON'T KNOW...
FOR WHAT IT'S WORTH, HE DOESN'T FEEL ANY PAIN ANYMORE. THE ALZHEIMER'S HAS TAKEN HOLD.
EVERYBODY NEEDS TO KNOW...
NO ONE LISTENS.

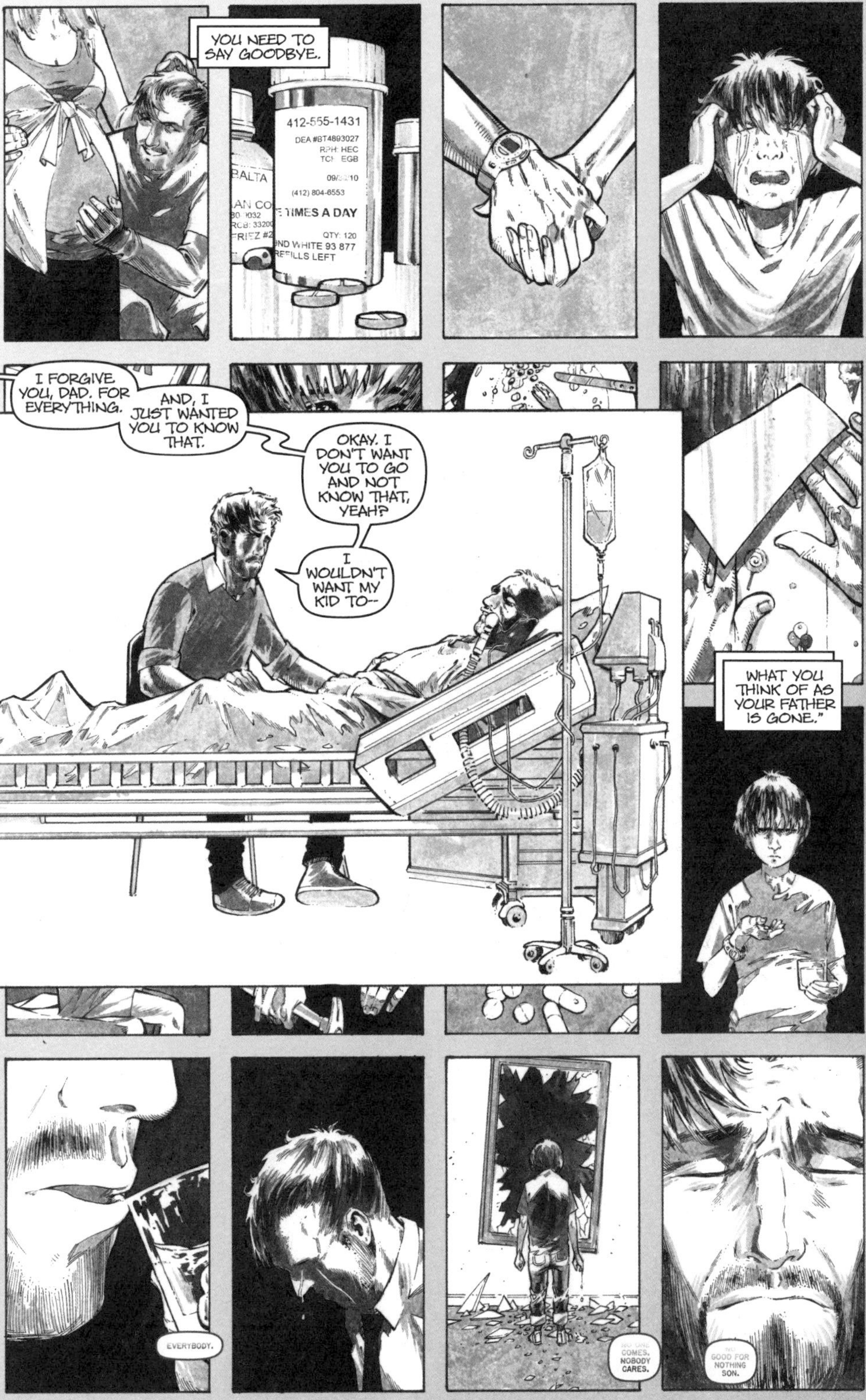
YOU NEED TO SAY GOODBYE.
412-555-1431
DEA #BT4893027
RPH: HEC
TCH: EGB
(412) 804-6553
TIMES A DAY
QTY: 120
REFILLS LEFT
I FORGIVE YOU, DAD. FOR EVERYTHING.
AND, I JUST WANTED YOU TO KNOW THAT.
OKAY. I DON'T WANT YOU TO GO AND NOT KNOW THAT, YEAH?
I WOULDN'T WANT MY KID TO--
WHAT YOU THINK OF AS YOUR FATHER IS GONE."
EVERYBODY.
NO ONE COMES, NOBODY CARES.
NO GOOD FOR NOTHING SON.

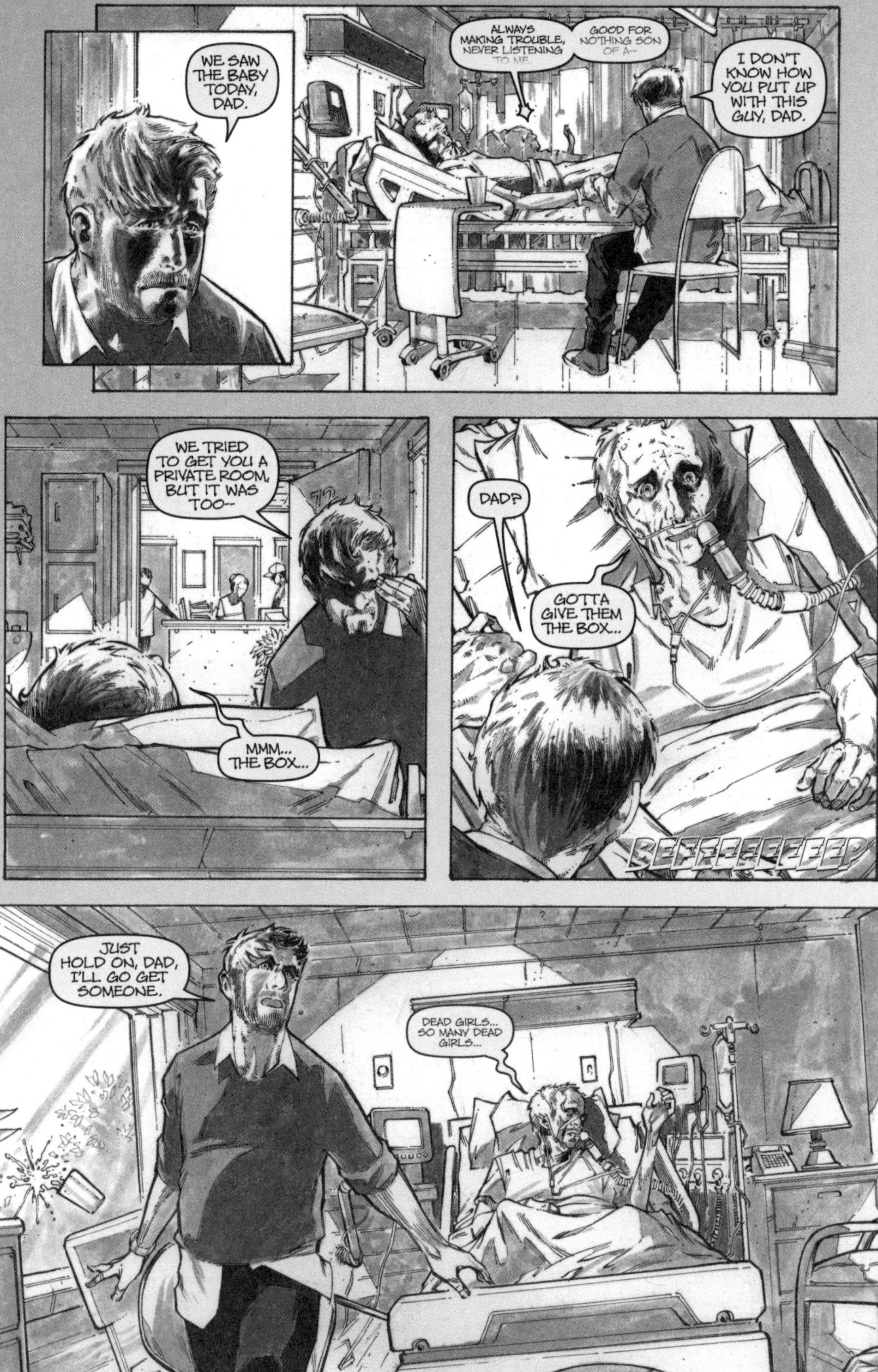
WE SAW THE BABY TODAY, DAD.
ALWAYS MAKING TROUBLE, NEVER LISTENING TO ME...
GOOD FOR NOTHING SON OF A--
I DON'T KNOW HOW YOU PUT UP WITH THIS GUY, DAD.
WE TRIED TO GET YOU A PRIVATE ROOM, BUT IT WAS TOO--
MMM... THE BOX...
DAD?
GOTTA GIVE THEM THE BOX...
BEEEEEEEEEP
JUST HOLD ON, DAD, I'LL GO GET SOMEONE.
DEAD GIRLS... SO MANY DEAD GIRLS...

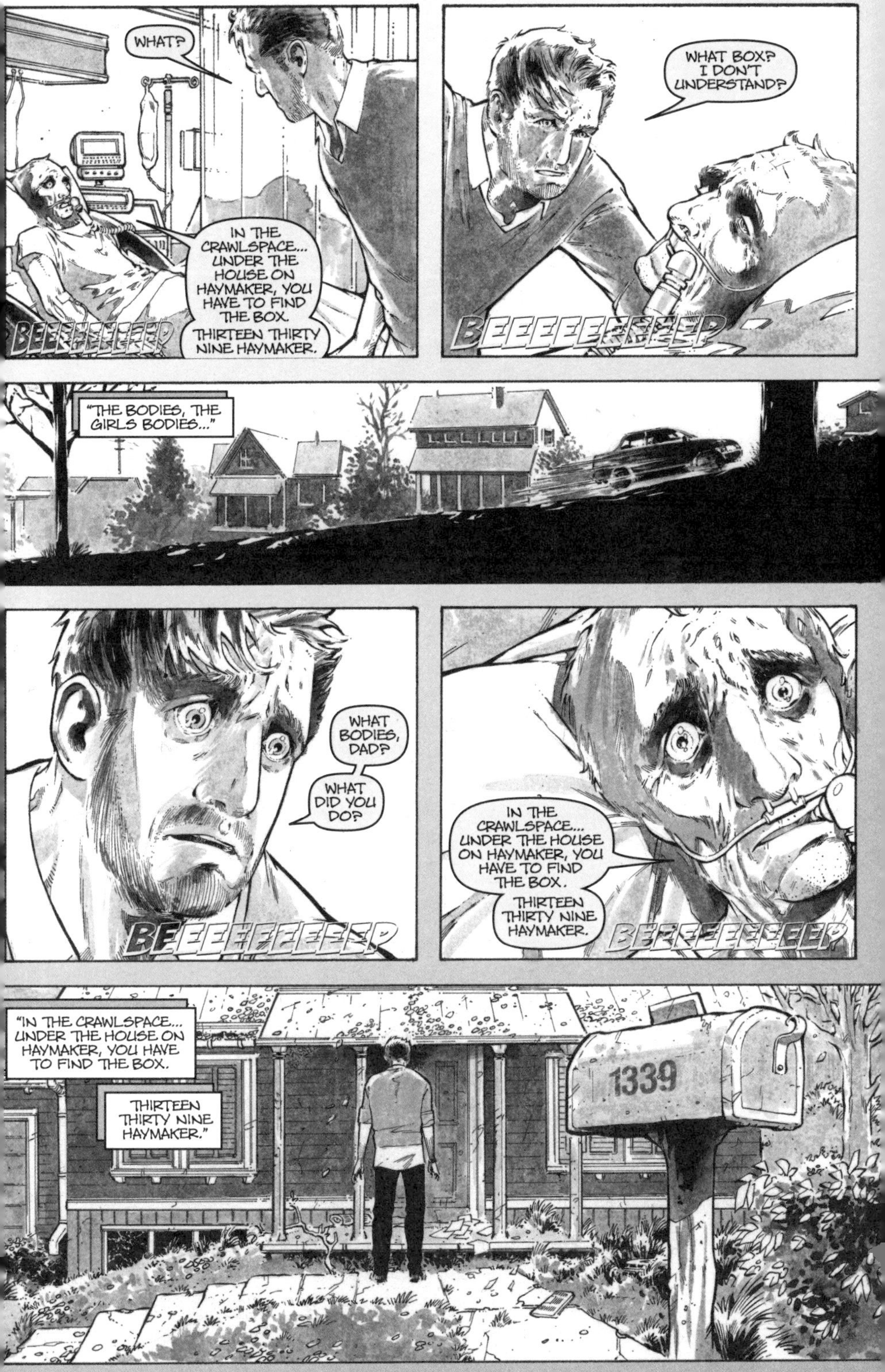
WHAT?
IN THE CRAWLSPACE... UNDER THE HOUSE ON HAYMAKER, YOU HAVE TO FIND THE BOX.
THIRTEEN THIRTY NINE HAYMAKER.
BEEEEEEEEP
WHAT BOX? I DON'T UNDERSTAND?
BEEEEEEEEEP
"THE BODIES, THE GIRLS BODIES..."
WHAT BODIES, DAD?
WHAT DID YOU DO?
BEEEEEEEEEEP
IN THE CRAWLSPACE... UNDER THE HOUSE ON HAYMAKER, YOU HAVE TO FIND THE BOX.
THIRTEEN THIRTY NINE HAYMAKER.
BEEEEEEEEEP
"IN THE CRAWLSPACE... UNDER THE HOUSE ON HAYMAKER, YOU HAVE TO FIND THE BOX.
THIRTEEN THIRTY NINE HAYMAKER."
1339

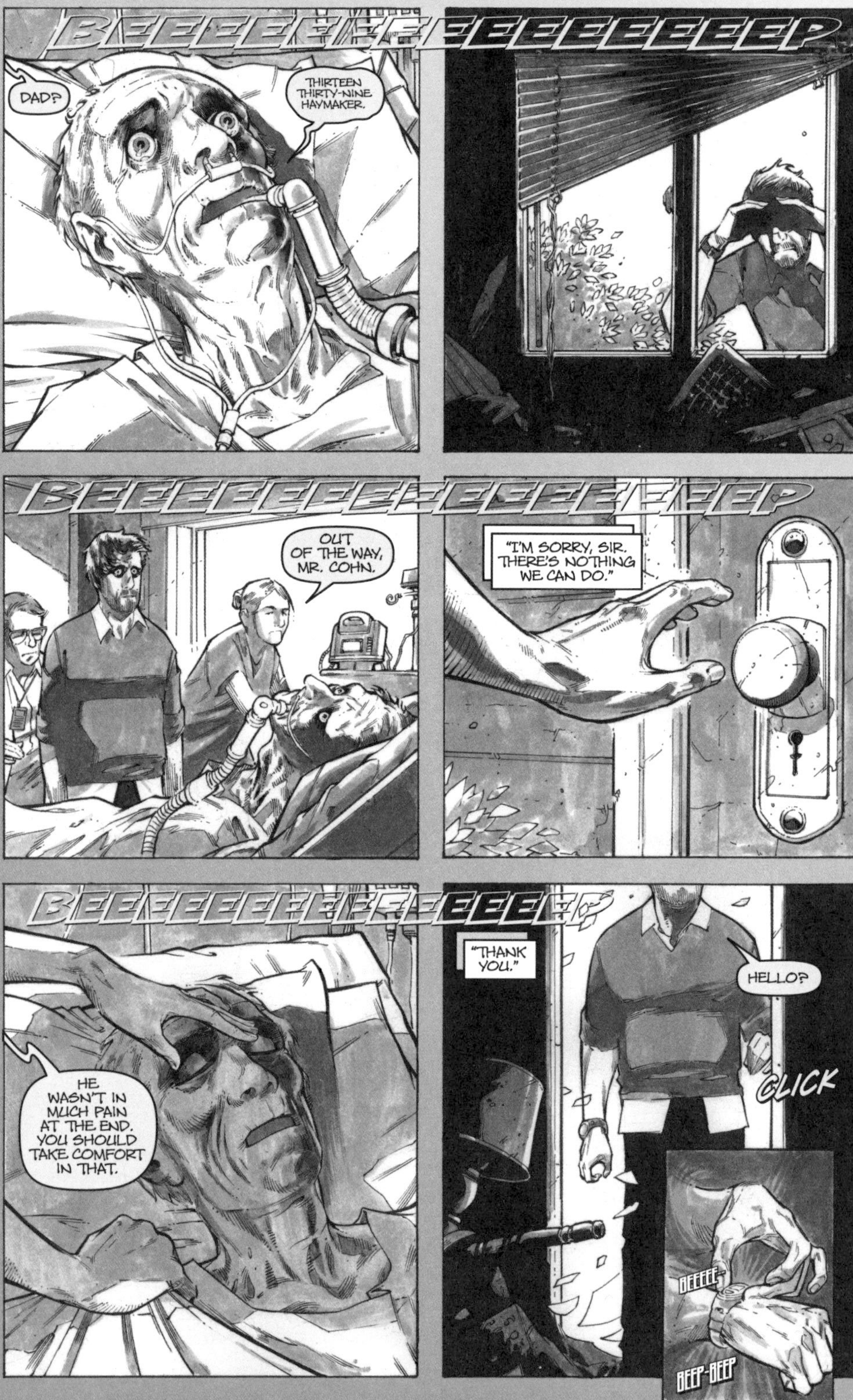
BEEEEEEEEEEEEEEEEEP
DAD?
THIRTEEN THIRTY-NINE HAYMAKER.
BEEEEEEEEEEEEEEEEEEEEP
OUT OF THE WAY, MR. COHN.
"I'M SORRY, SIR. THERE'S NOTHING WE CAN DO."
BEEEEEEEEEEEEEEEEEP
HE WASN'T IN MUCH PAIN AT THE END. YOU SHOULD TAKE COMFORT IN THAT.
"THANK YOU."
HELLO?
CLICK
BEEEEE-
BEEP-BEEP

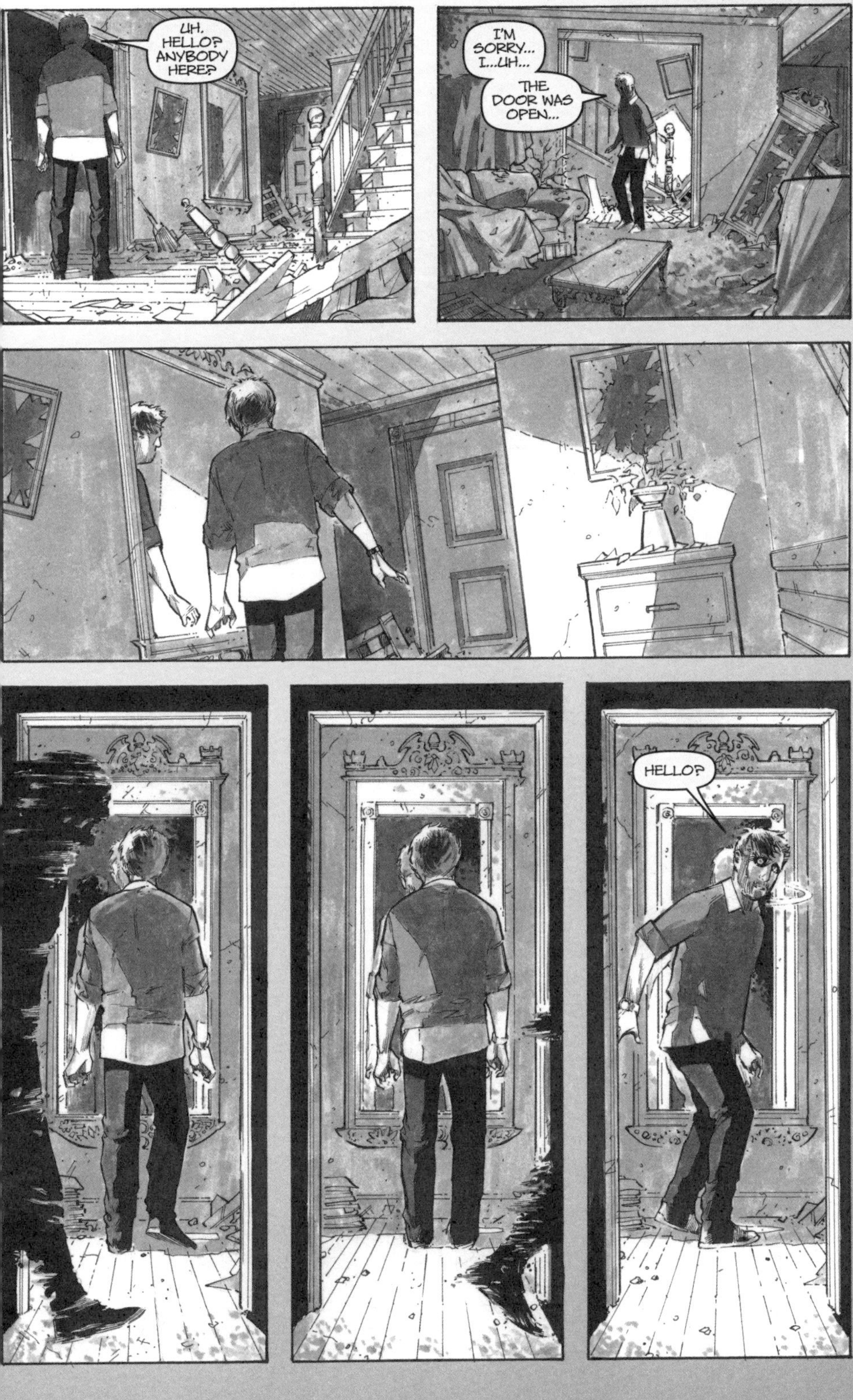
UH, HELLO? ANYBODY HERE?
I'M SORRY... I...UH...
THE DOOR WAS OPEN...
HELLO?

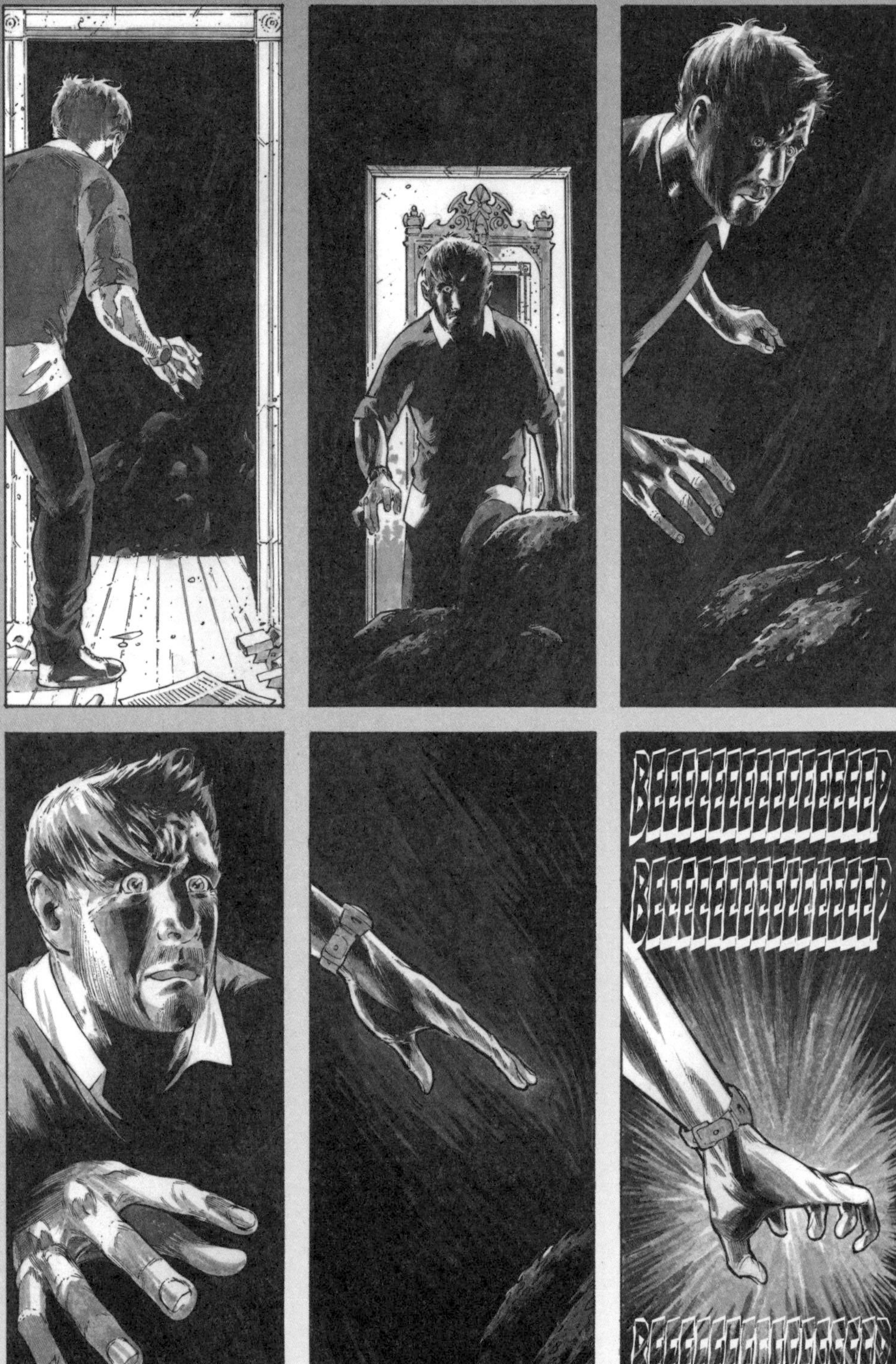
BEEEEEEEEEEEEEEEP
BEEEEEEEEEEEEEEEP
BEEEEEEEEEEEEEEEP

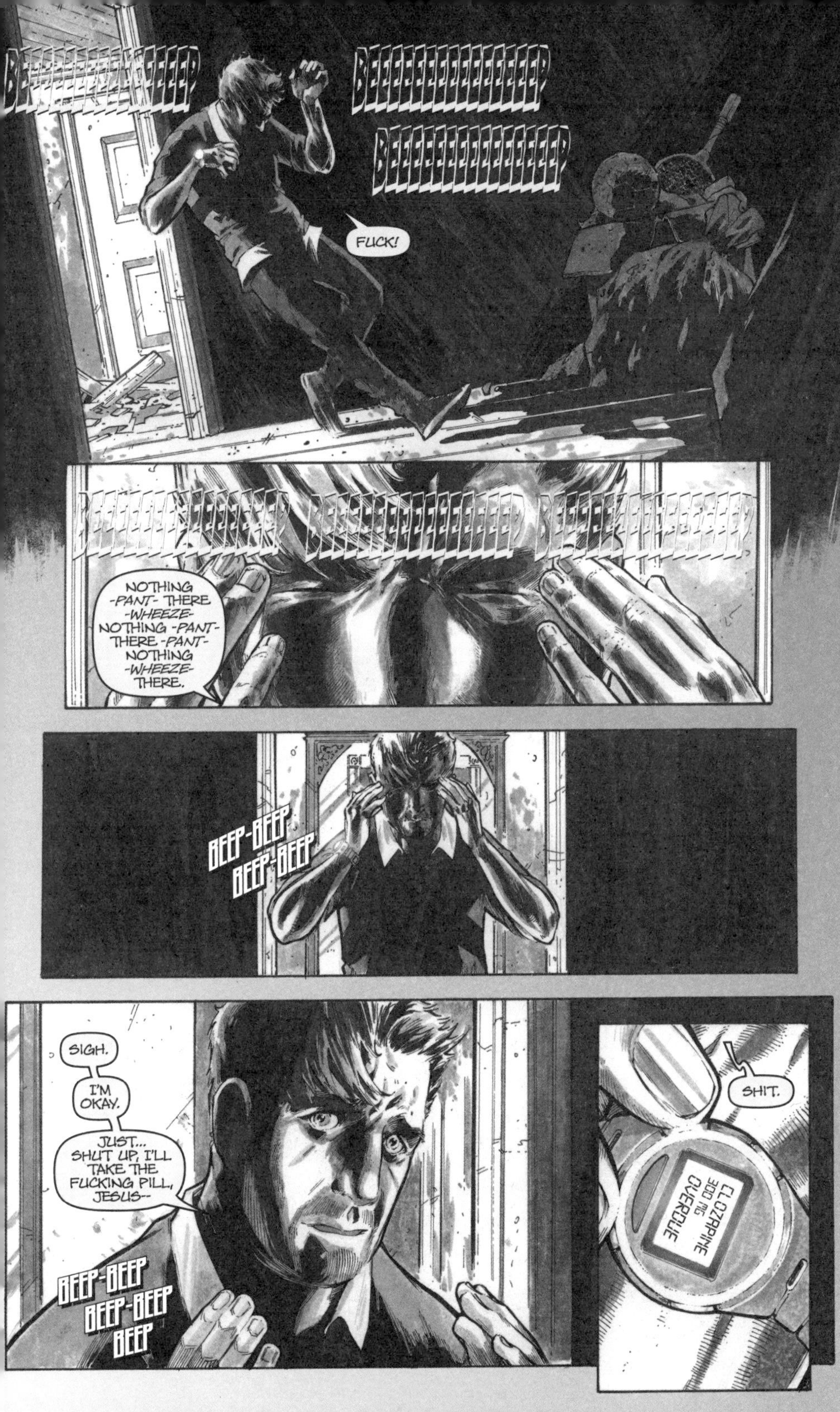
BEEEEEEEEEEEEEEP
BEEEEEEEEEEEEEEP
BEEEEEEEEEEEEEEP
FUCK!
BEEEEEEEEEEEEEEP BEEEEEEEEEEEEEEP BEEEEEEEEEEEEEEP
NOTHING -PANT- THERE -WHEEZE- NOTHING -PANT- THERE -PANT- NOTHING -WHEEZE- THERE.
BEEP-BEEP BEEP-BEEP
SIGH.
I'M OKAY.
JUST... SHUT UP, I'LL TAKE THE FUCKING PILL, JESUS--
BEEP-BEEP BEEP-BEEP BEEP
SHIT.
CLOZAPINE 300 MG OVERDUE

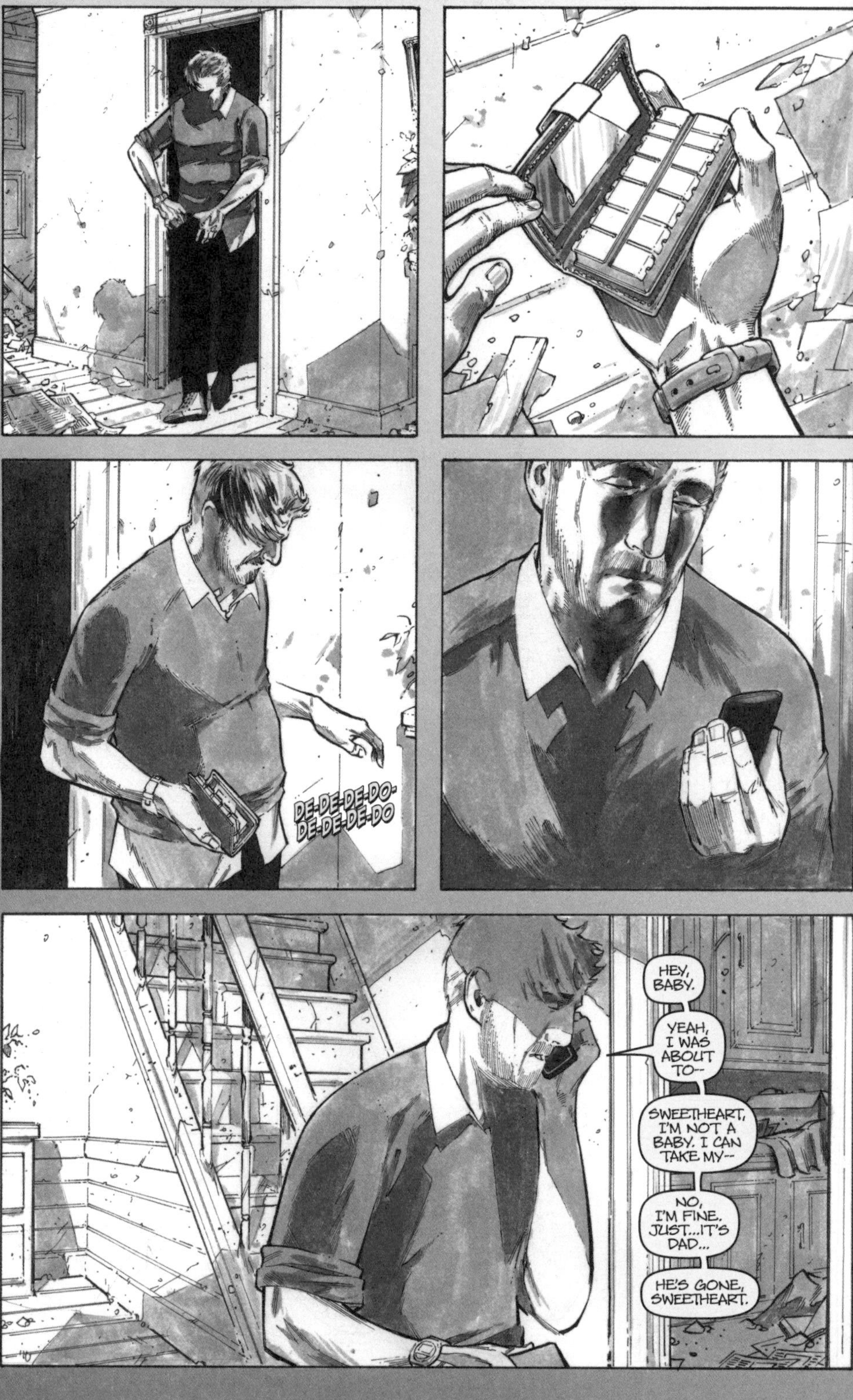
DE-DE-DE-DO-
DE-DE-DE-DO
HEY, BABY.
YEAH, I WAS ABOUT TO--
SWEETHEART, I'M NOT A BABY. I CAN TAKE MY--
NO, I'M FINE. JUST...IT'S DAD...
HE'S GONE, SWEETHEART.

I JUST NEEDED SOME TIME TO MYSELF.

NO. I'LL BE HOME, SOON. I'LL...

YEAH, I TOLD YOU I'M TAKING IT RIGHT NOW.

I'M UNDER ENOUGH PRESSURE WITHOUT YOU--

CH-CH-CH-CH-CH-CH

SHIT. I BETTER PAY ATTENTION. I LOVE YOU AND THE TURNIP VERY MUCH.

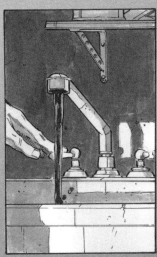

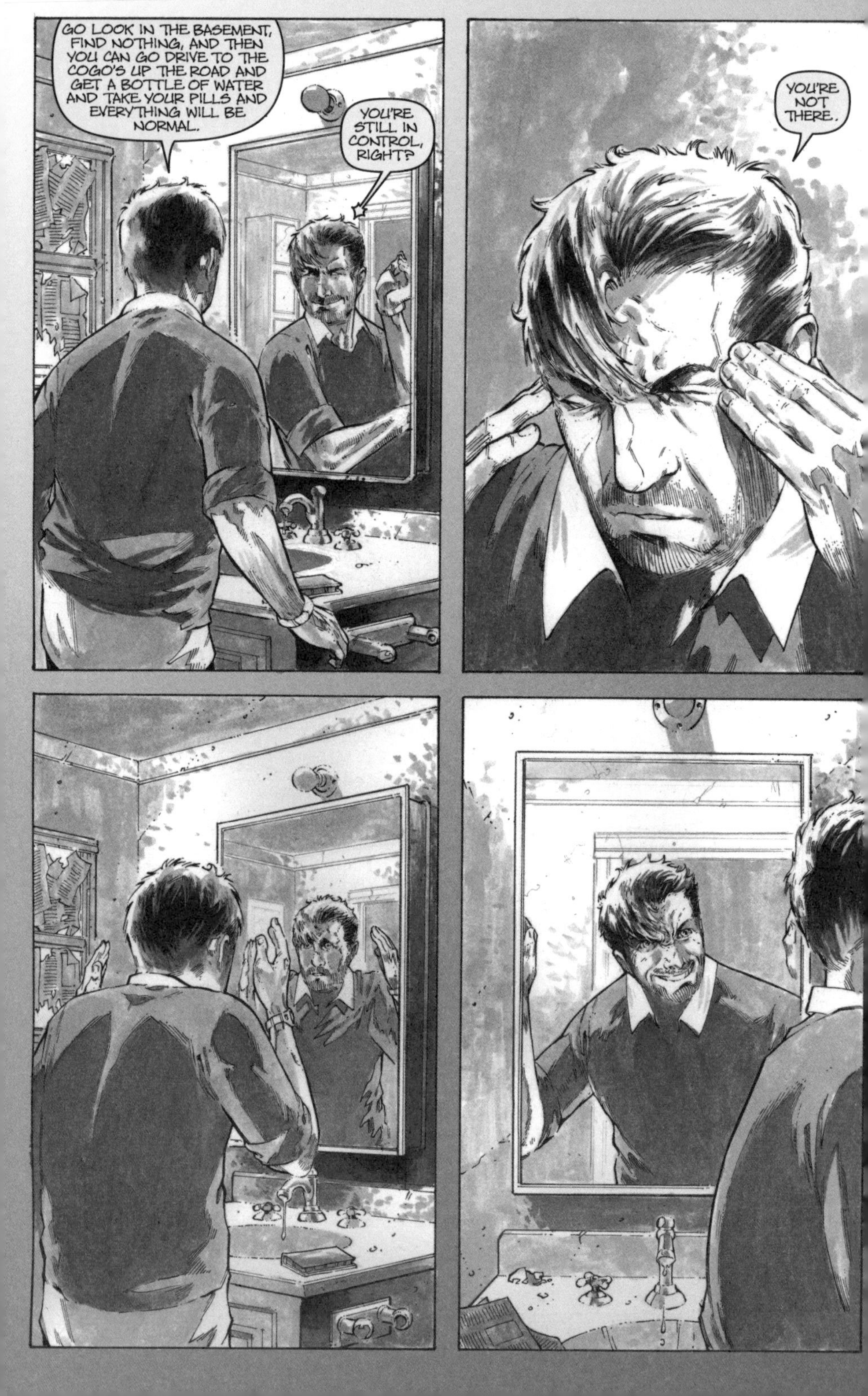
GO LOOK IN THE BASEMENT, FIND NOTHING, AND THEN YOU CAN GO DRIVE TO THE COGO'S UP THE ROAD AND GET A BOTTLE OF WATER AND TAKE YOUR PILLS AND EVERYTHING WILL BE NORMAL.
YOU'RE STILL IN CONTROL, RIGHT?
YOU'RE NOT THERE.

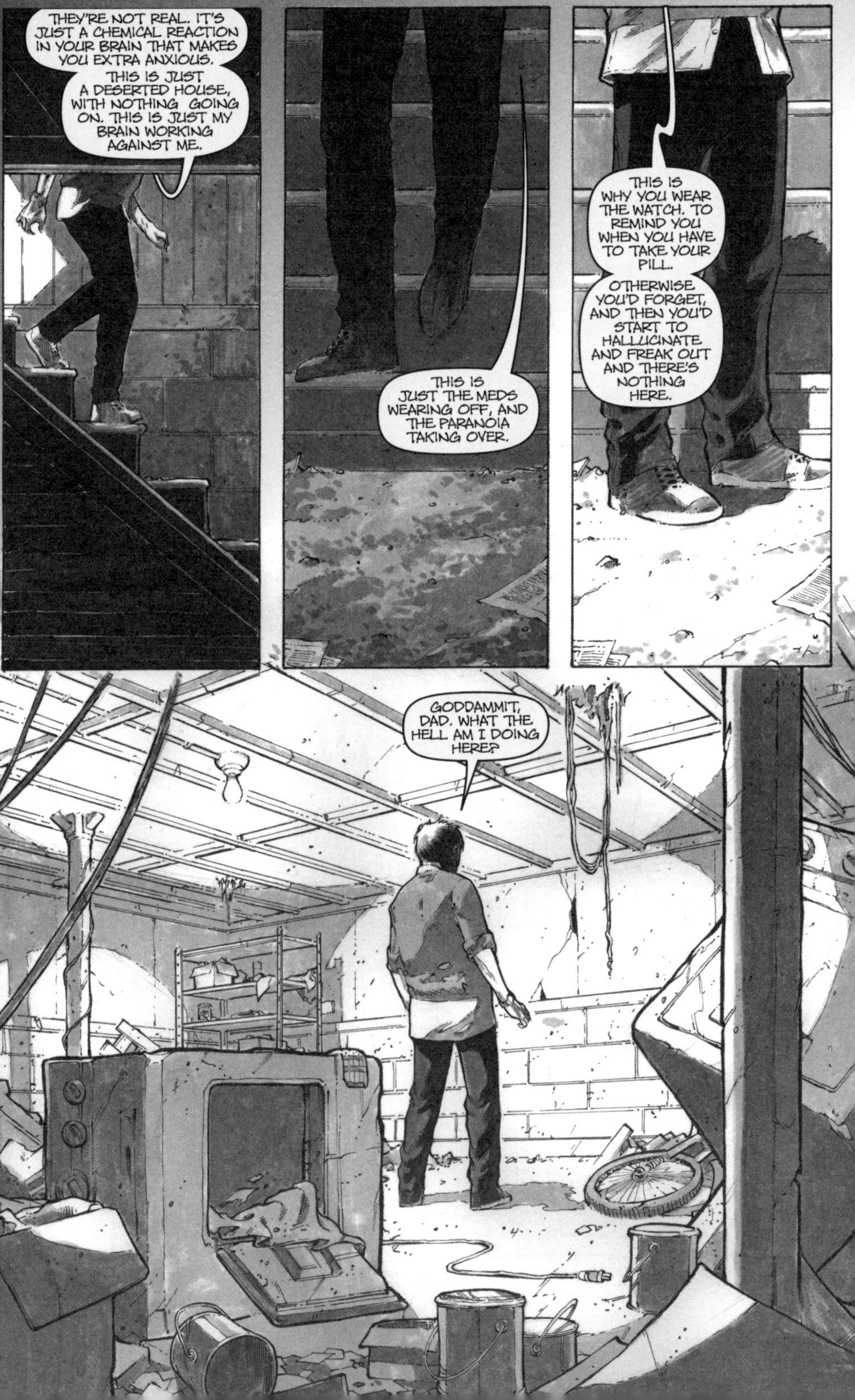
THEY'RE NOT REAL. IT'S JUST A CHEMICAL REACTION IN YOUR BRAIN THAT MAKES YOU EXTRA ANXIOUS.
THIS IS JUST A DESERTED HOUSE, WITH NOTHING GOING ON. THIS IS JUST MY BRAIN WORKING AGAINST ME.
THIS IS JUST THE MEDS WEARING OFF, AND THE PARANOIA TAKING OVER.
THIS IS WHY YOU WEAR THE WATCH. TO REMIND YOU WHEN YOU HAVE TO TAKE YOUR PILL.
OTHERWISE YOU'D FORGET, AND THEN YOU'D START TO HALLUCINATE AND FREAK OUT AND THERE'S NOTHING HERE.
GODDAMMIT, DAD. WHAT THE HELL AM I DOING HERE?

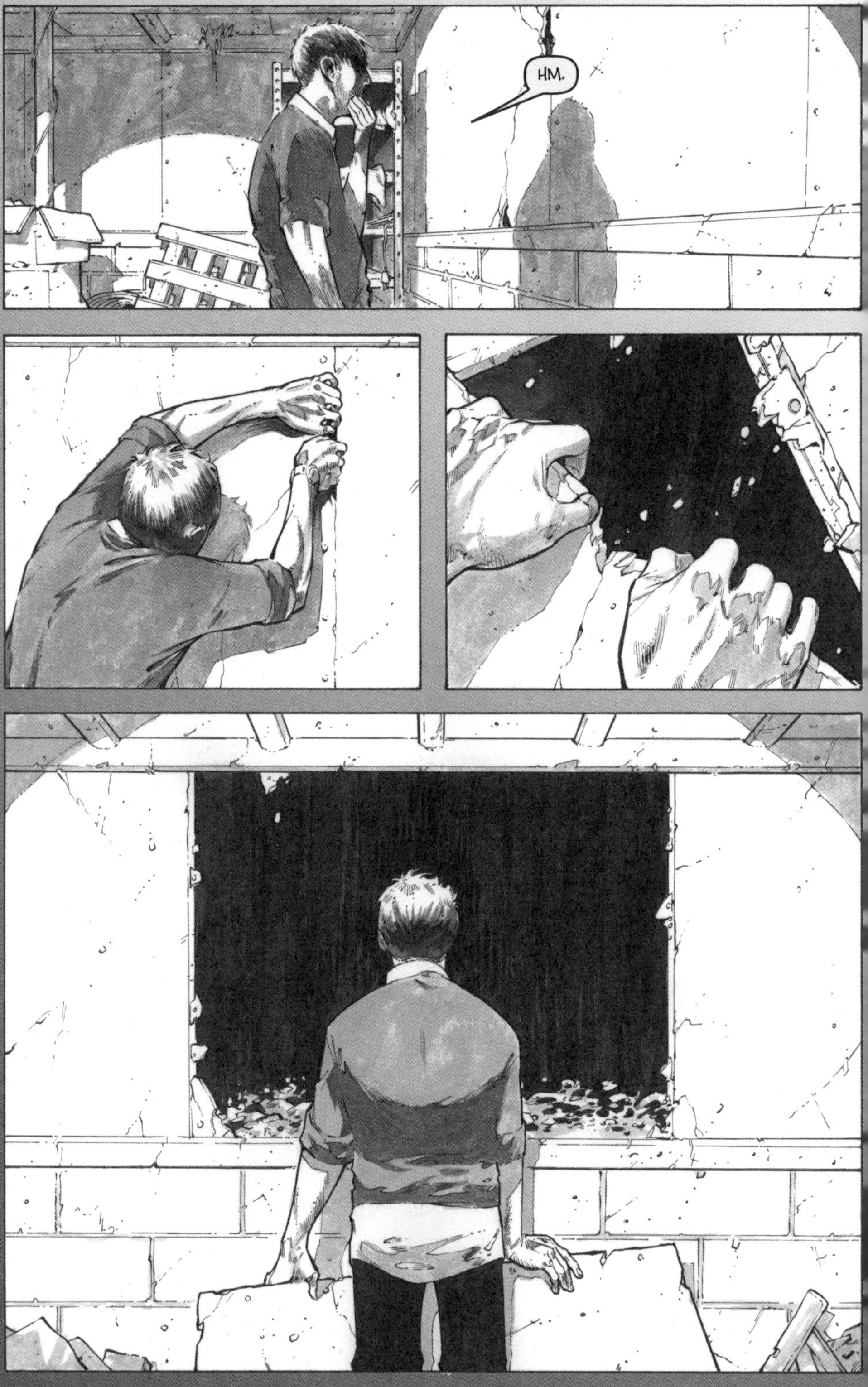
HM.

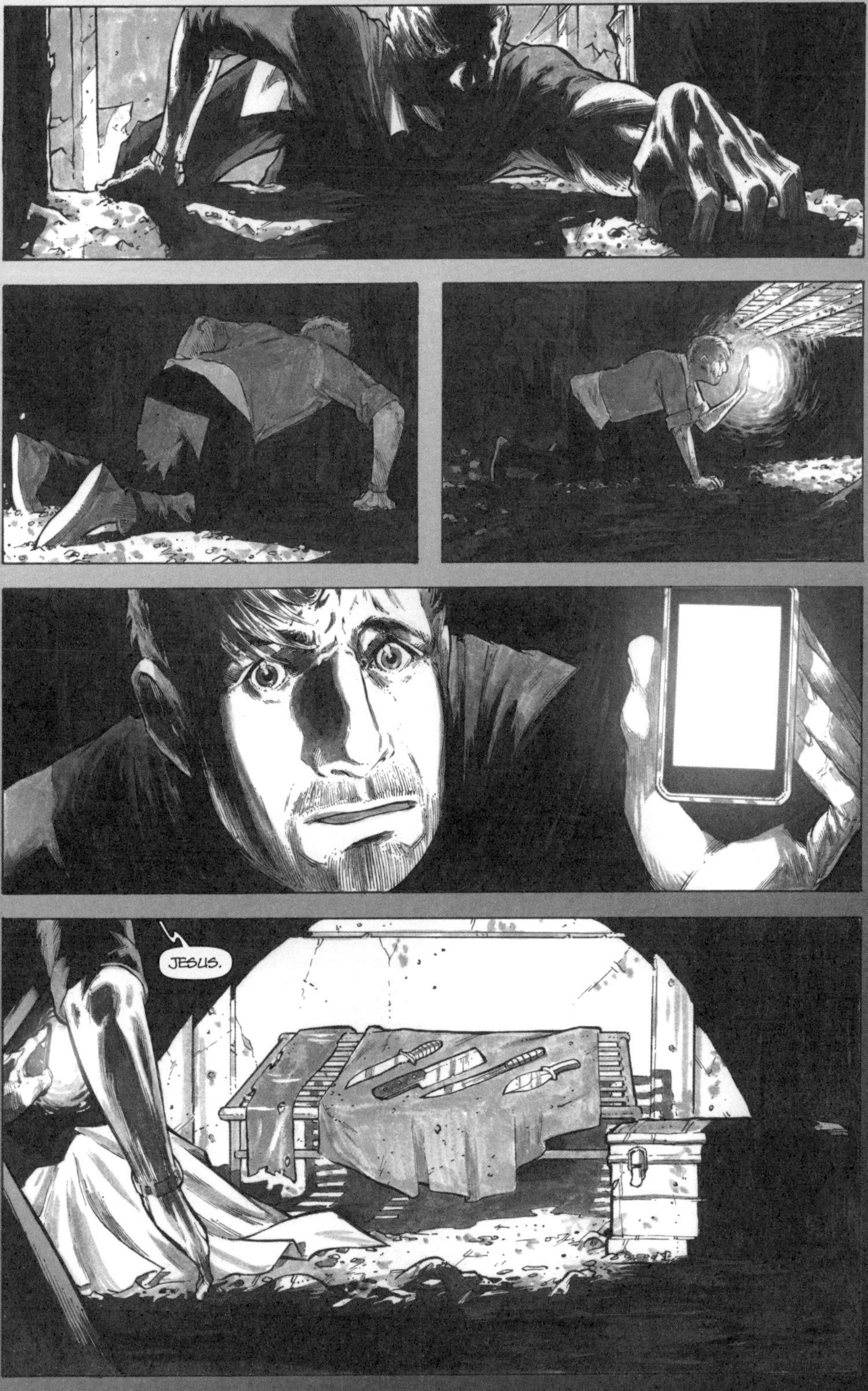
JESUS.

DAD...

YOU ARE IN CONTROL, BRIAN.

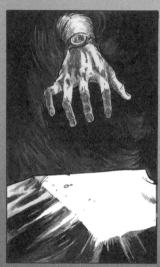

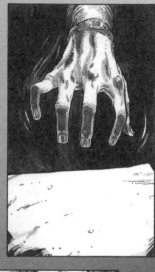

CREEEEEEEEEAK

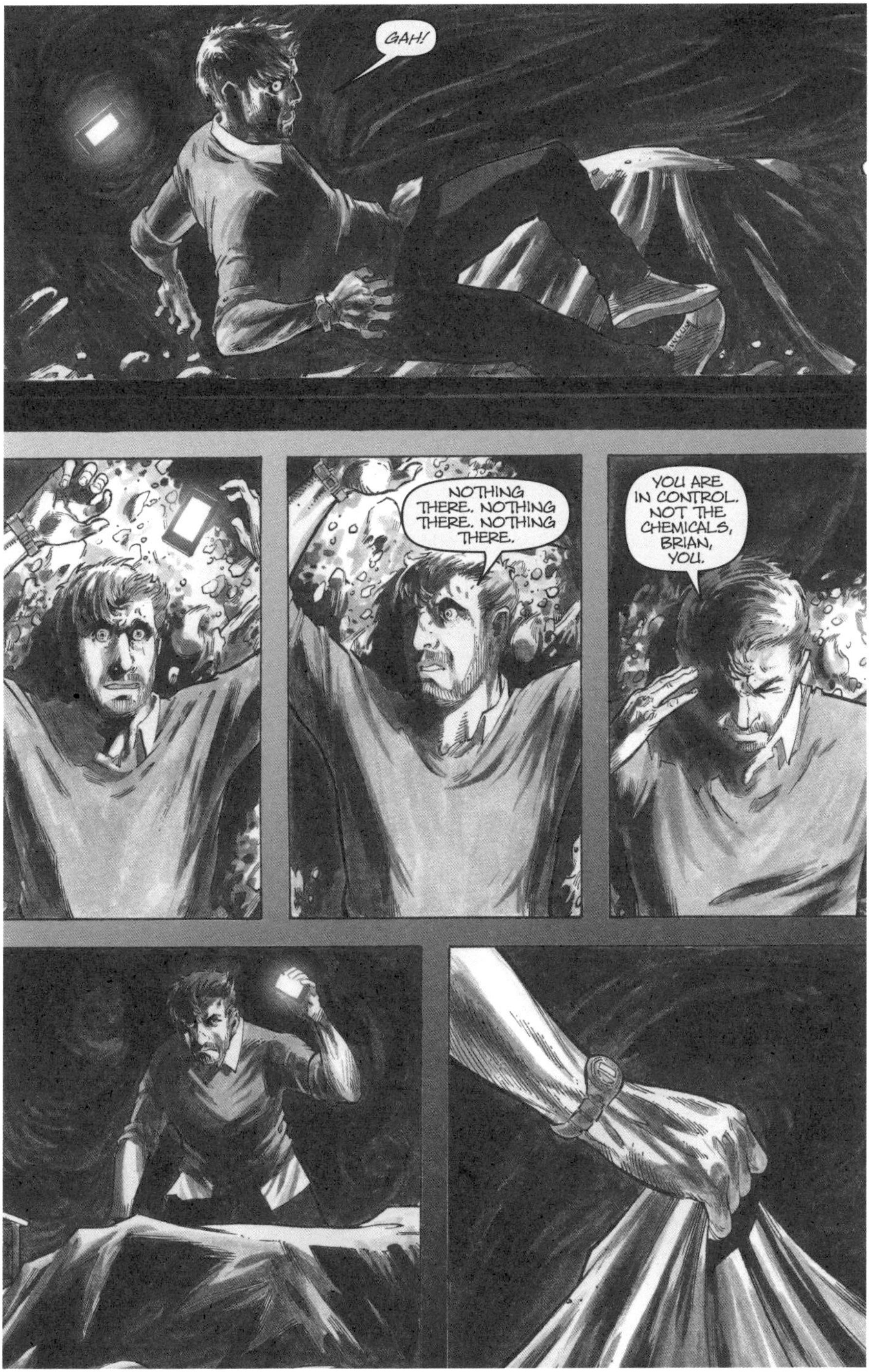
GAH!
NOTHING THERE. NOTHING THERE. NOTHING THERE.
YOU ARE IN CONTROL. NOT THE CHEMICALS, BRIAN, YOU.

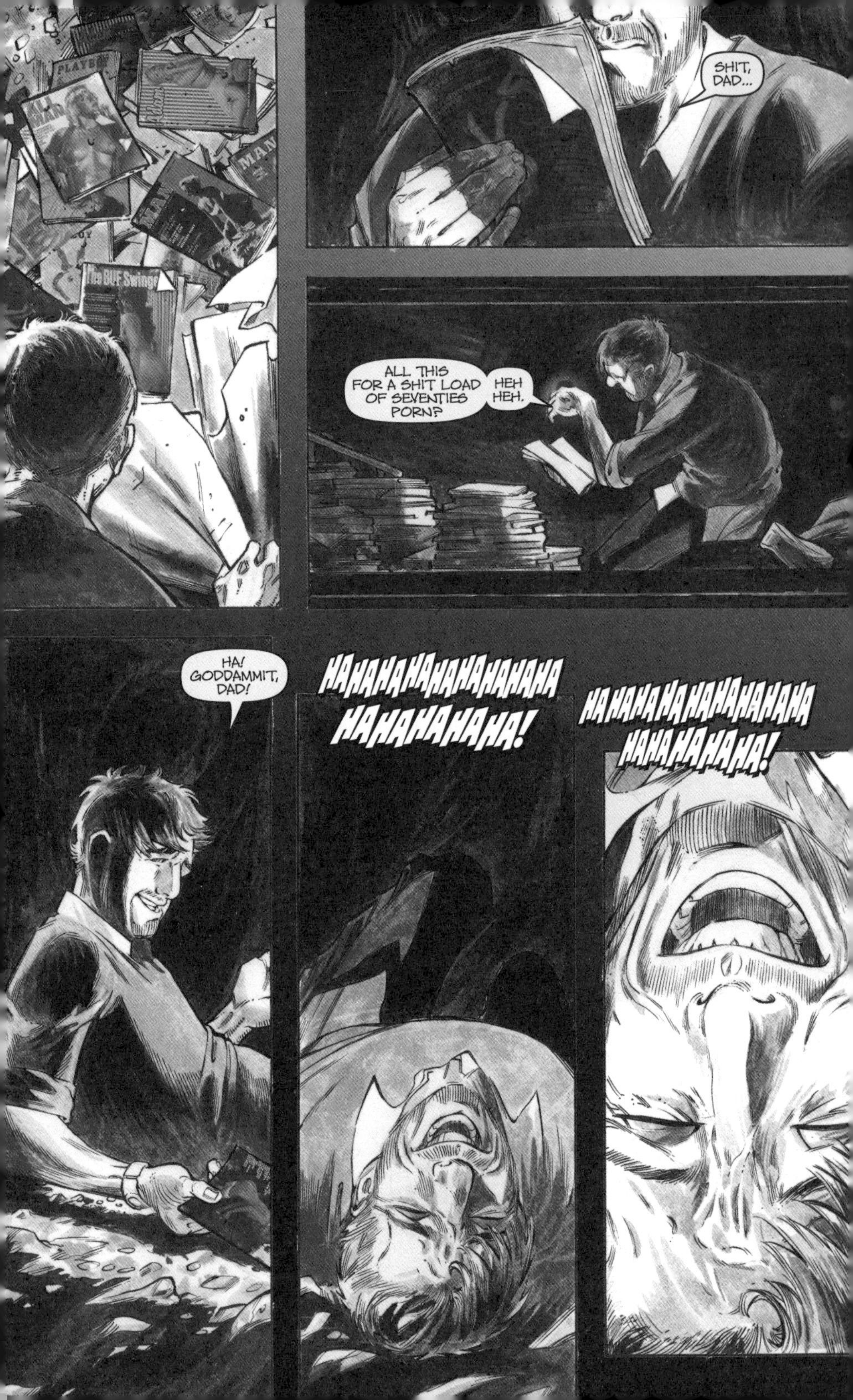
PLAYBOY
SHIT, DAD...
ALL THIS FOR A SHIT LOAD OF SEVENTIES PORN?
HEH HEH.
HA! GODDAMMIT, DAD!
HAHAHAHAHAHAHAHAHA HAHAHAHAHA!
HAHAHAHAHAHAHAHAHA HAHAHAHAHA!

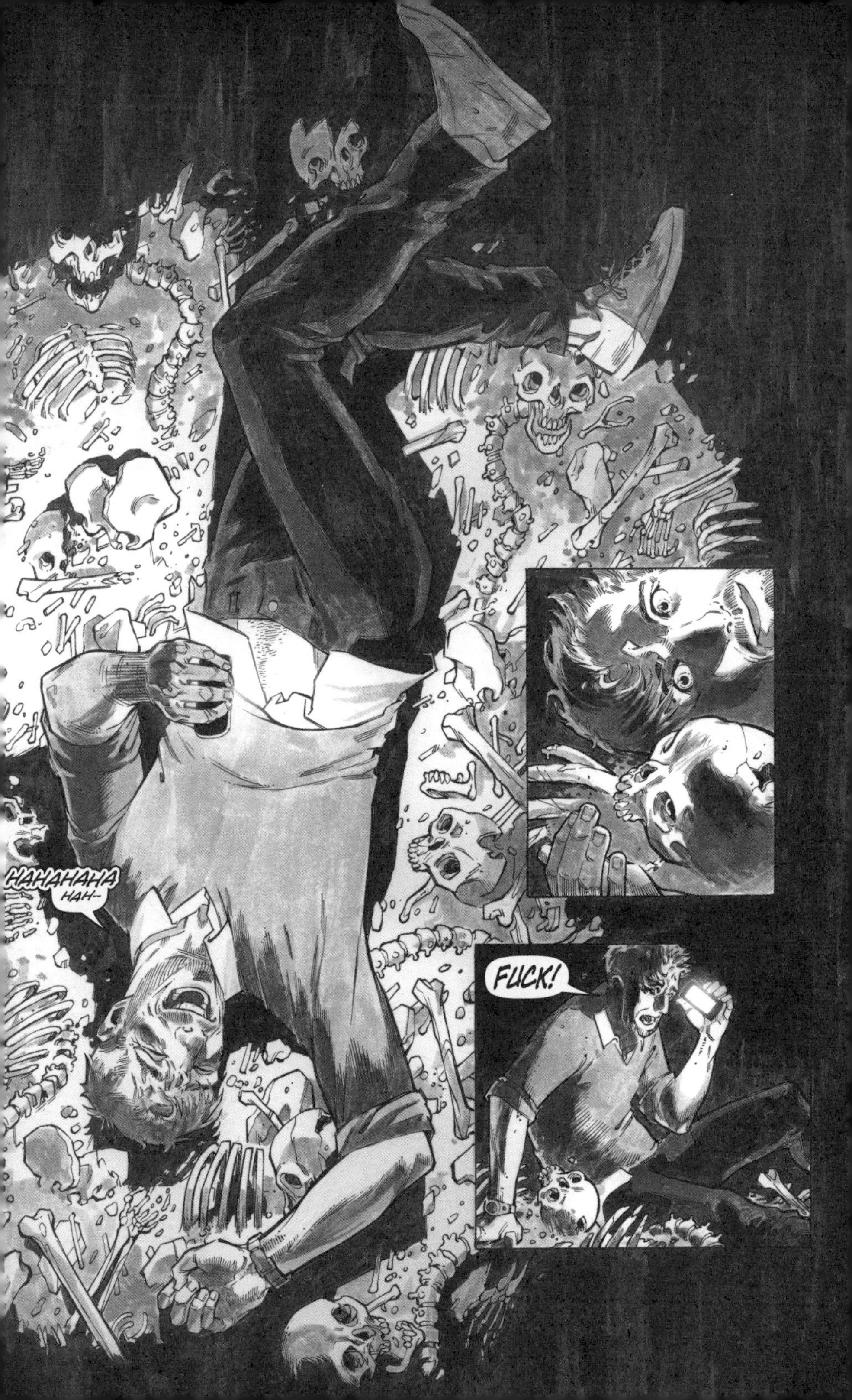
HAHAHAHA HAH-
FUCK!

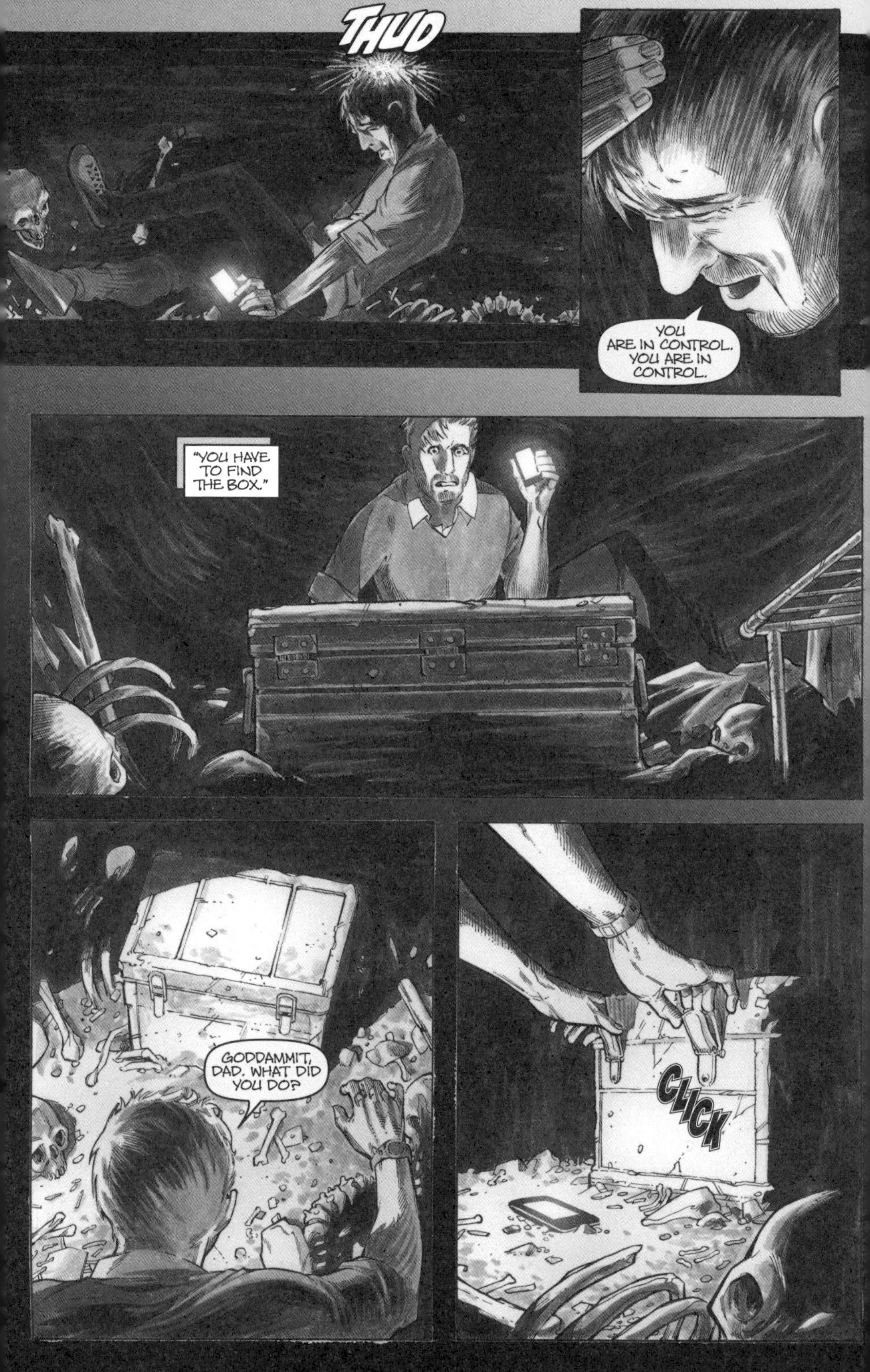
THUD
YOU ARE IN CONTROL. YOU ARE IN CONTROL.
"YOU HAVE TO FIND THE BOX."
GODDAMMIT, DAD. WHAT DID YOU DO?
CLICK

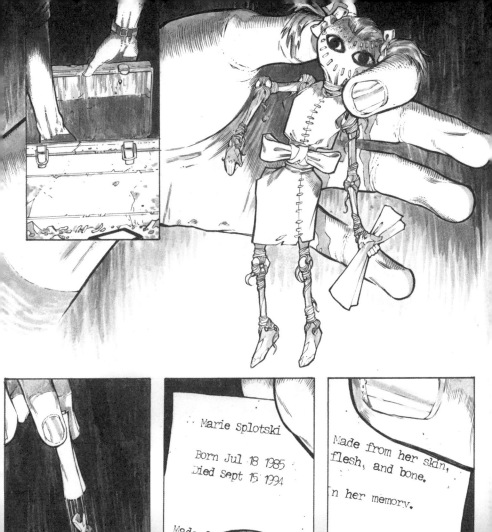

Marie Splotski

Born Jul 18 1985
Died Sept 15 1994

Made from her skin,
flesh, and bone.

n her memory.

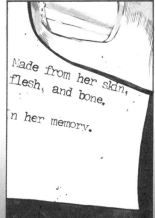

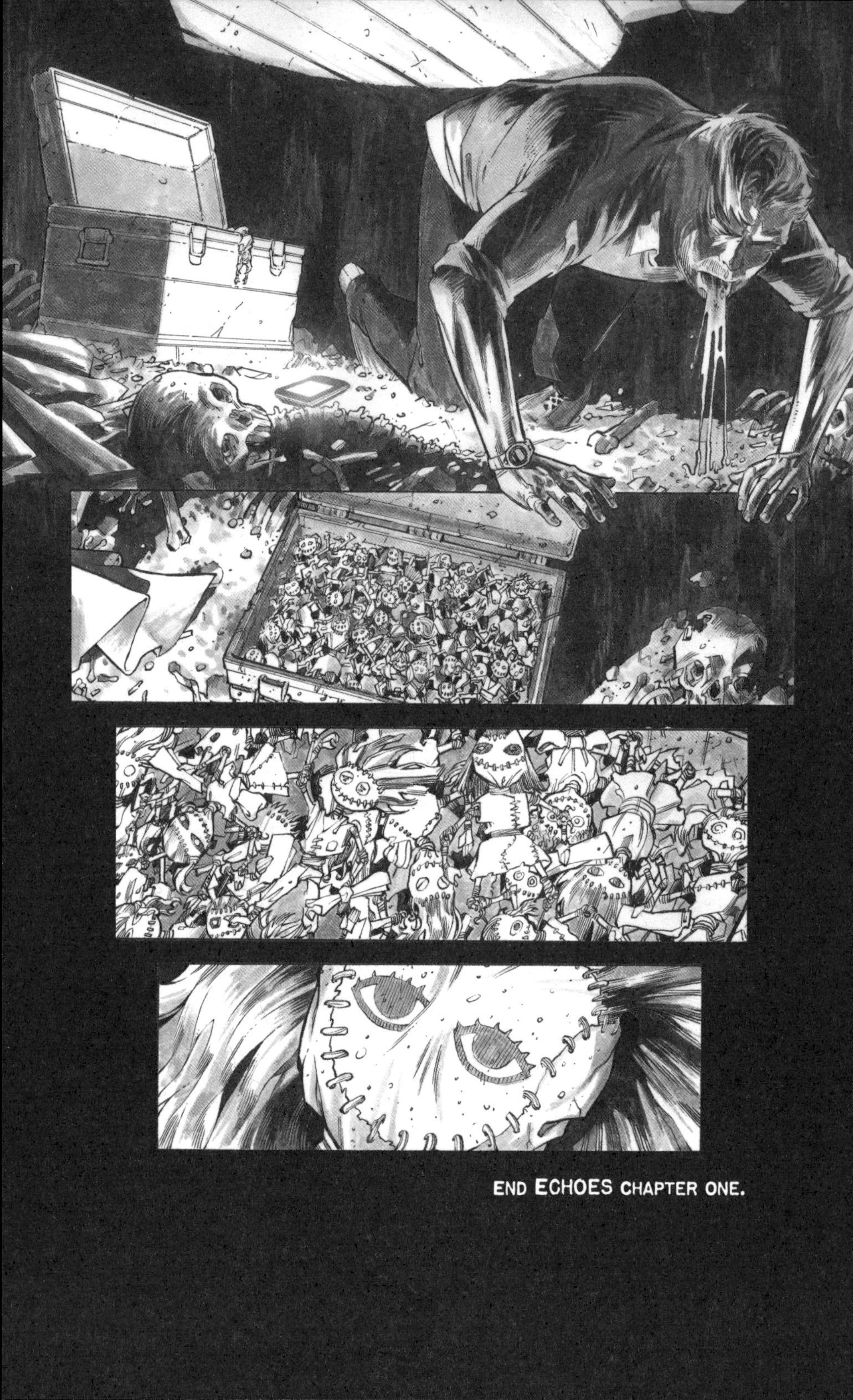

END ECHOES CHAPTER ONE.

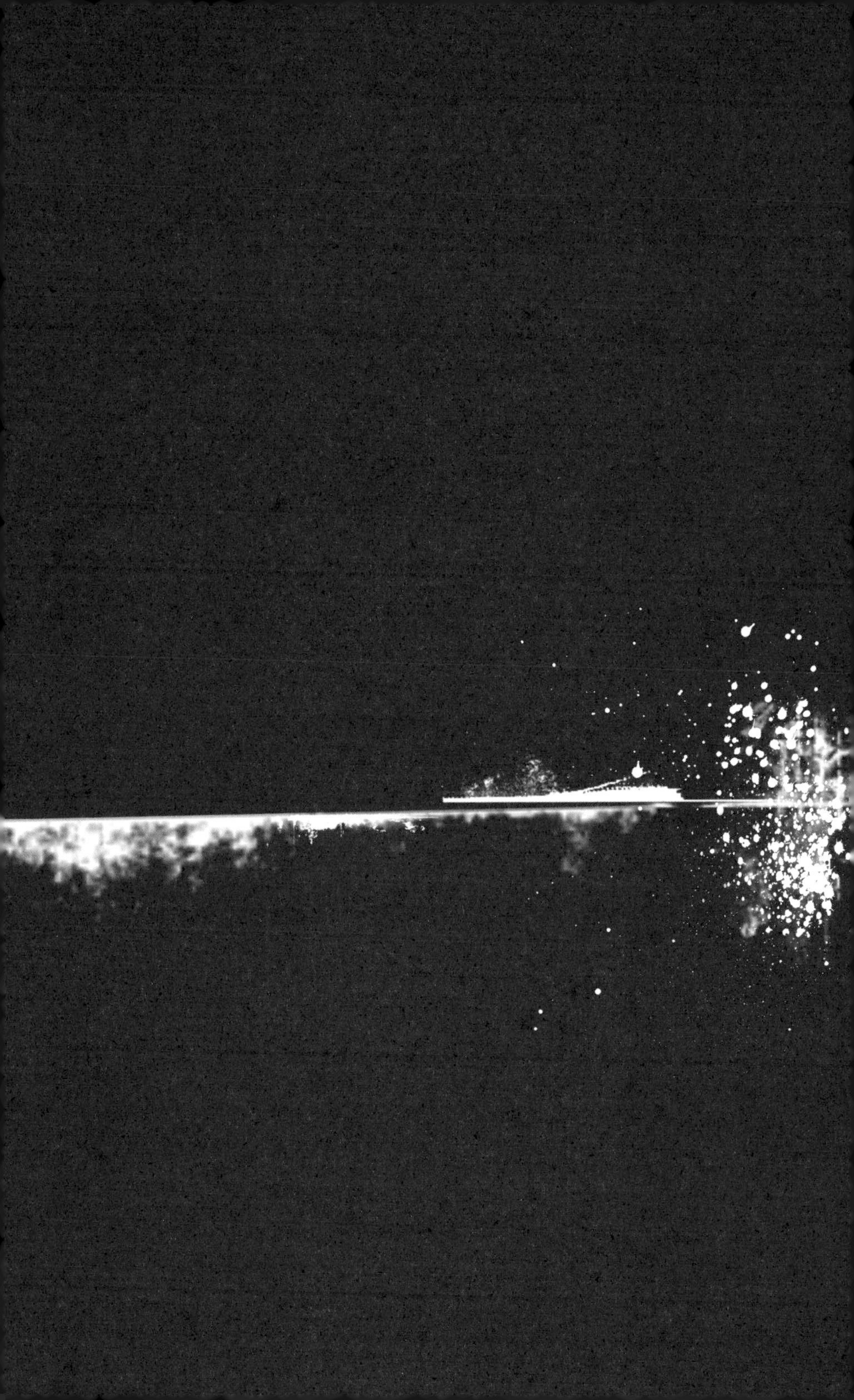

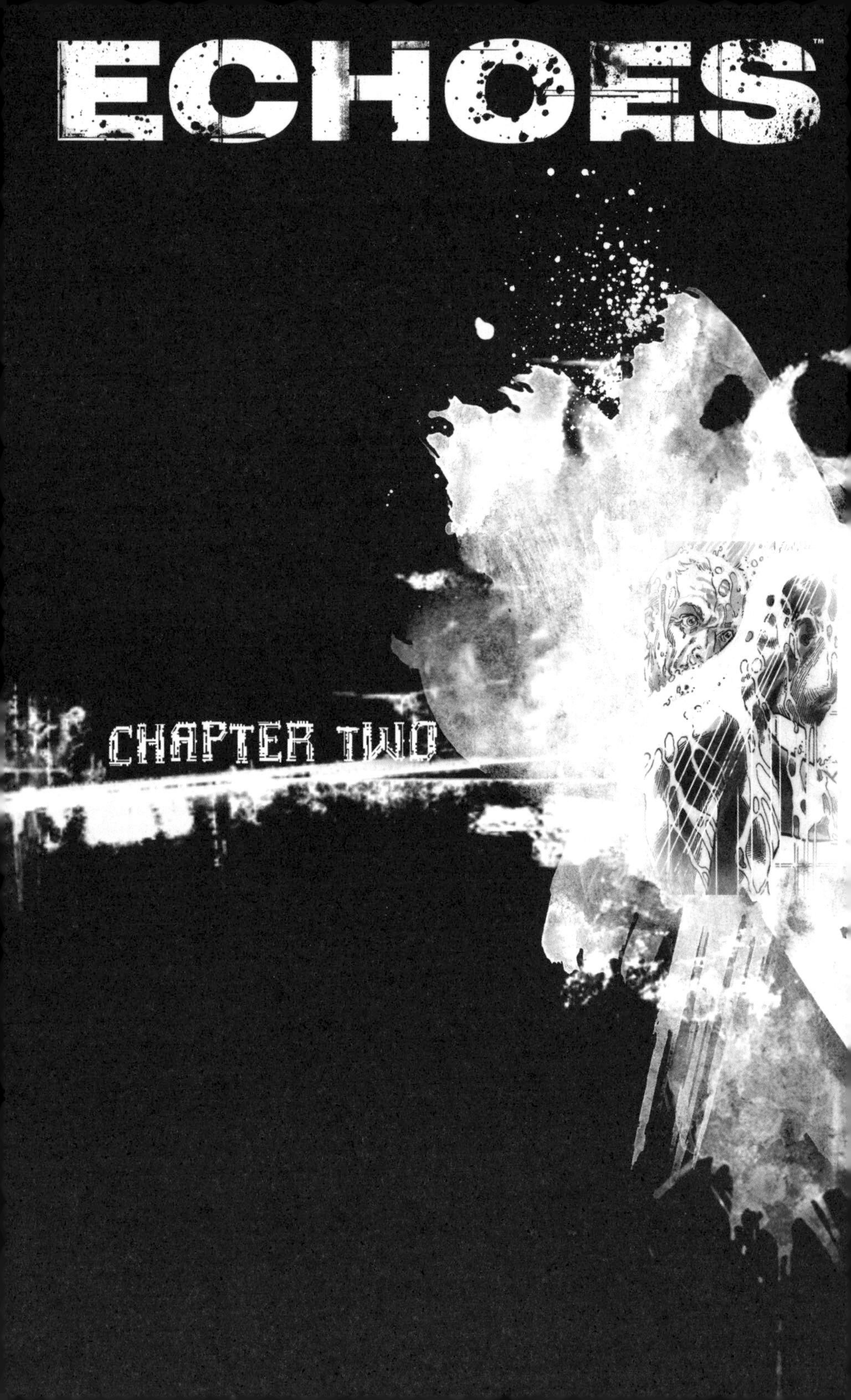
ECHOES™
CHAPTER TWO

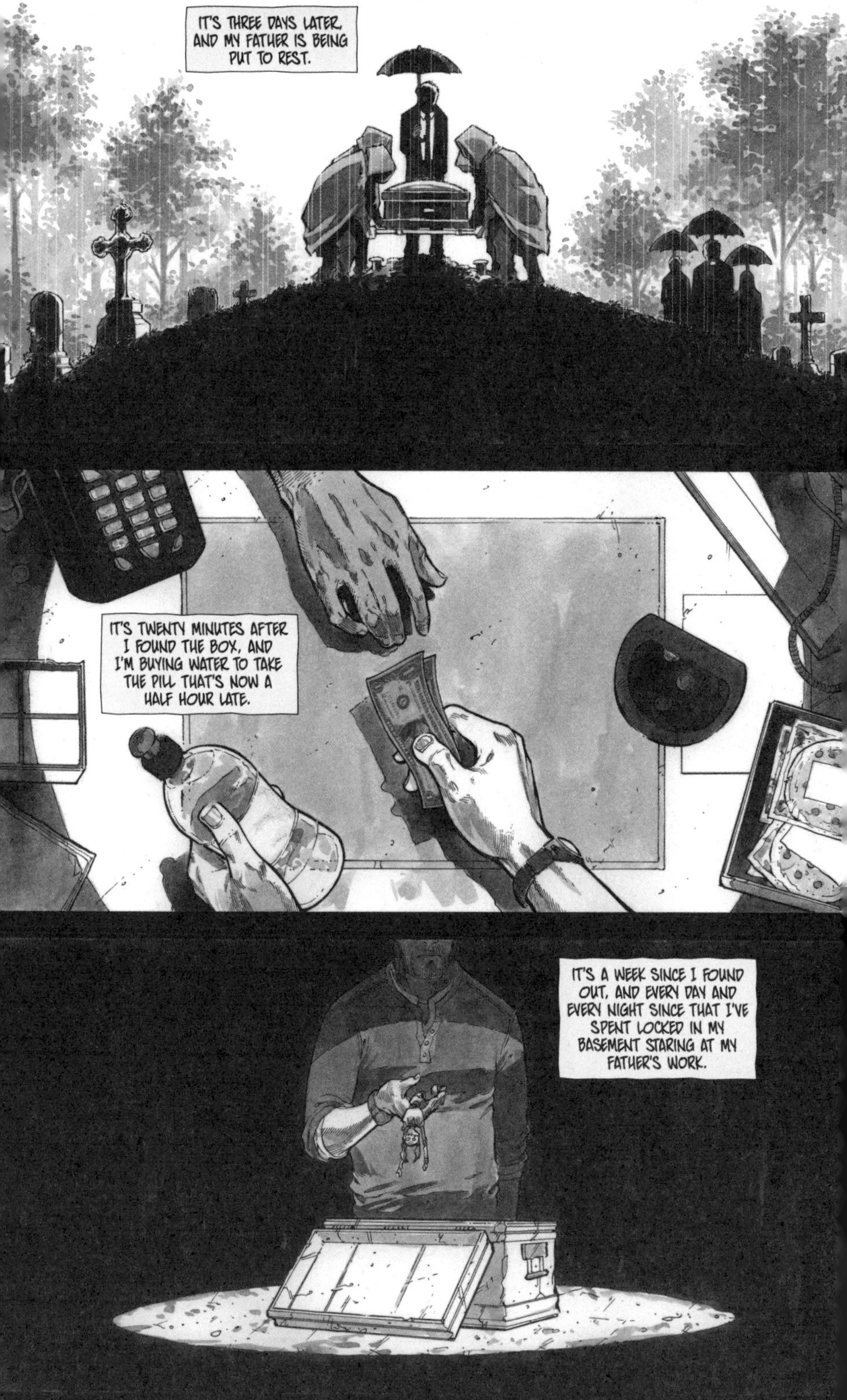
IT'S THREE DAYS LATER, AND MY FATHER IS BEING PUT TO REST.
IT'S TWENTY MINUTES AFTER I FOUND THE BOX, AND I'M BUYING WATER TO TAKE THE PILL THAT'S NOW A HALF HOUR LATE.
IT'S A WEEK SINCE I FOUND OUT, AND EVERY DAY AND EVERY NIGHT SINCE THAT I'VE SPENT LOCKED IN MY BASEMENT STARING AT MY FATHER'S WORK.

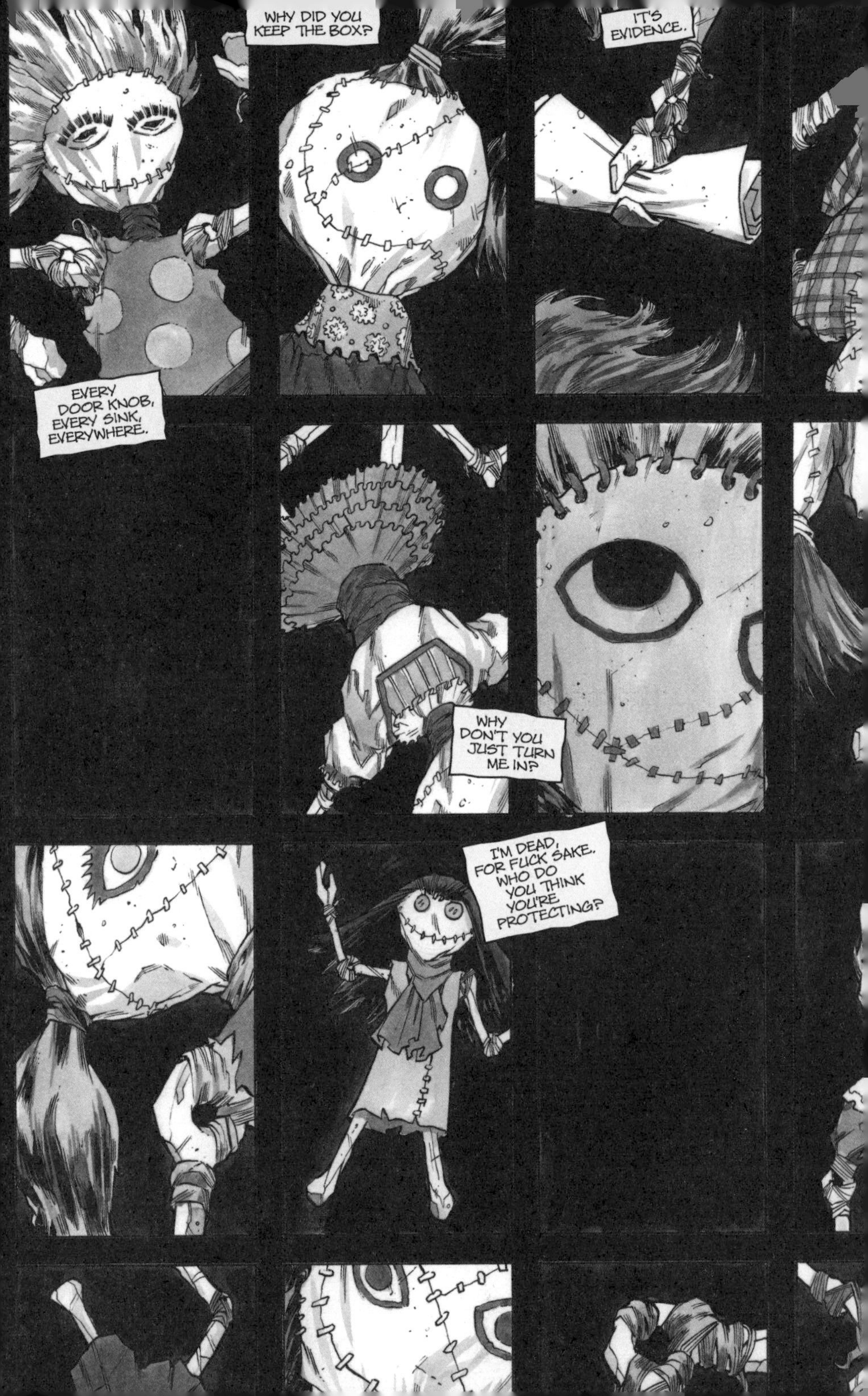
EVERY DOOR KNOB, EVERY SINK, EVERYWHERE.
WHY DID YOU KEEP THE BOX?
IT'S EVIDENCE.
WHY DON'T YOU JUST TURN ME IN?
I'M DEAD, FOR FUCK SAKE. WHO DO YOU THINK YOU'RE PROTECTING?

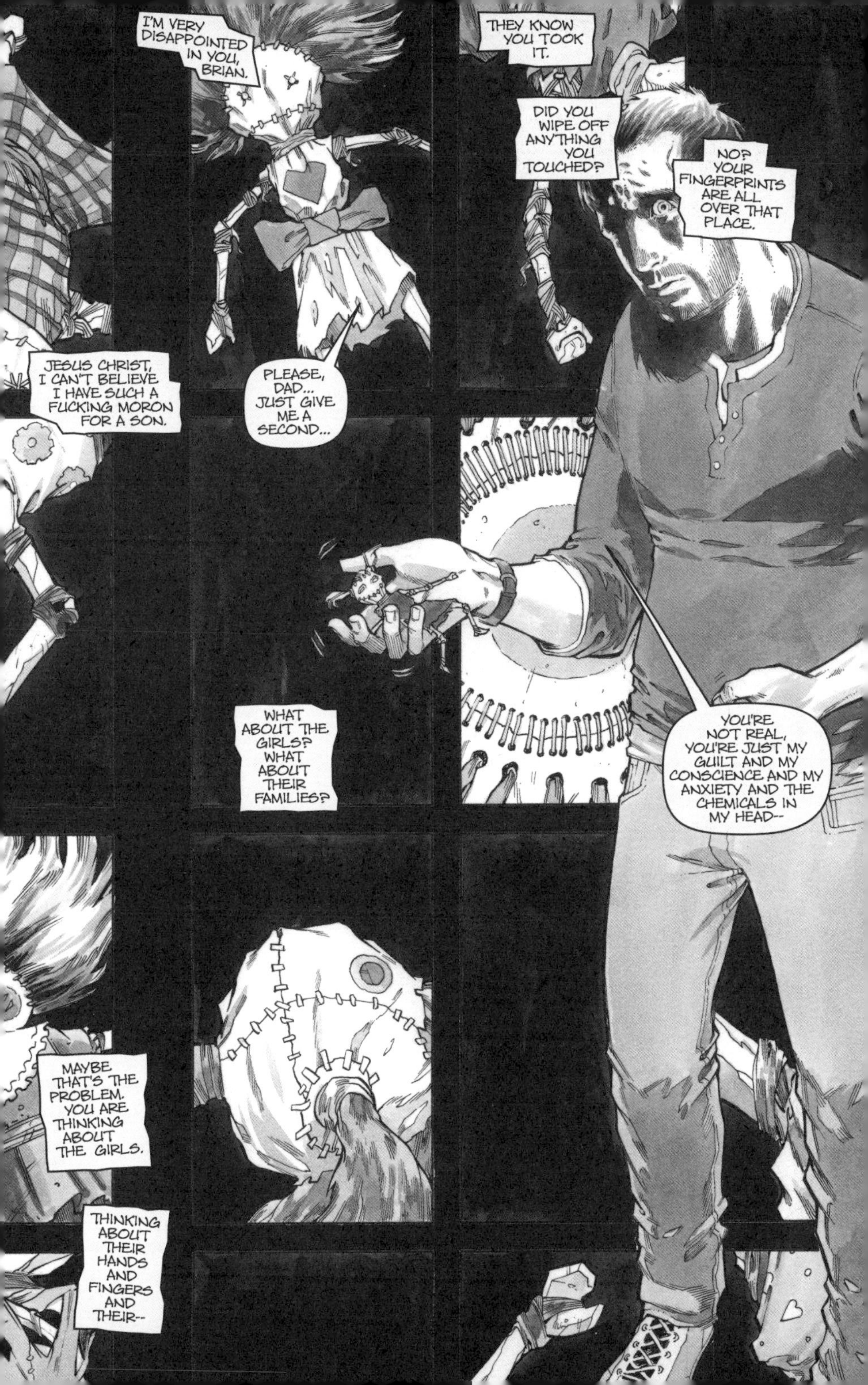
I'M VERY DISAPPOINTED IN YOU, BRIAN.
THEY KNOW YOU TOOK IT.
DID YOU WIPE OFF ANYTHING YOU TOUCHED?
NO? YOUR FINGERPRINTS ARE ALL OVER THAT PLACE.
JESUS CHRIST, I CAN'T BELIEVE I HAVE SUCH A FUCKING MORON FOR A SON.
PLEASE, DAD... JUST GIVE ME A SECOND...
WHAT ABOUT THE GIRLS? WHAT ABOUT THEIR FAMILIES?
YOU'RE NOT REAL, YOU'RE JUST MY GUILT AND MY CONSCIENCE AND MY ANXIETY AND THE CHEMICALS IN MY HEAD--
MAYBE THAT'S THE PROBLEM. YOU ARE THINKING ABOUT THE GIRLS.
THINKING ABOUT THEIR HANDS AND FINGERS AND THEIR--

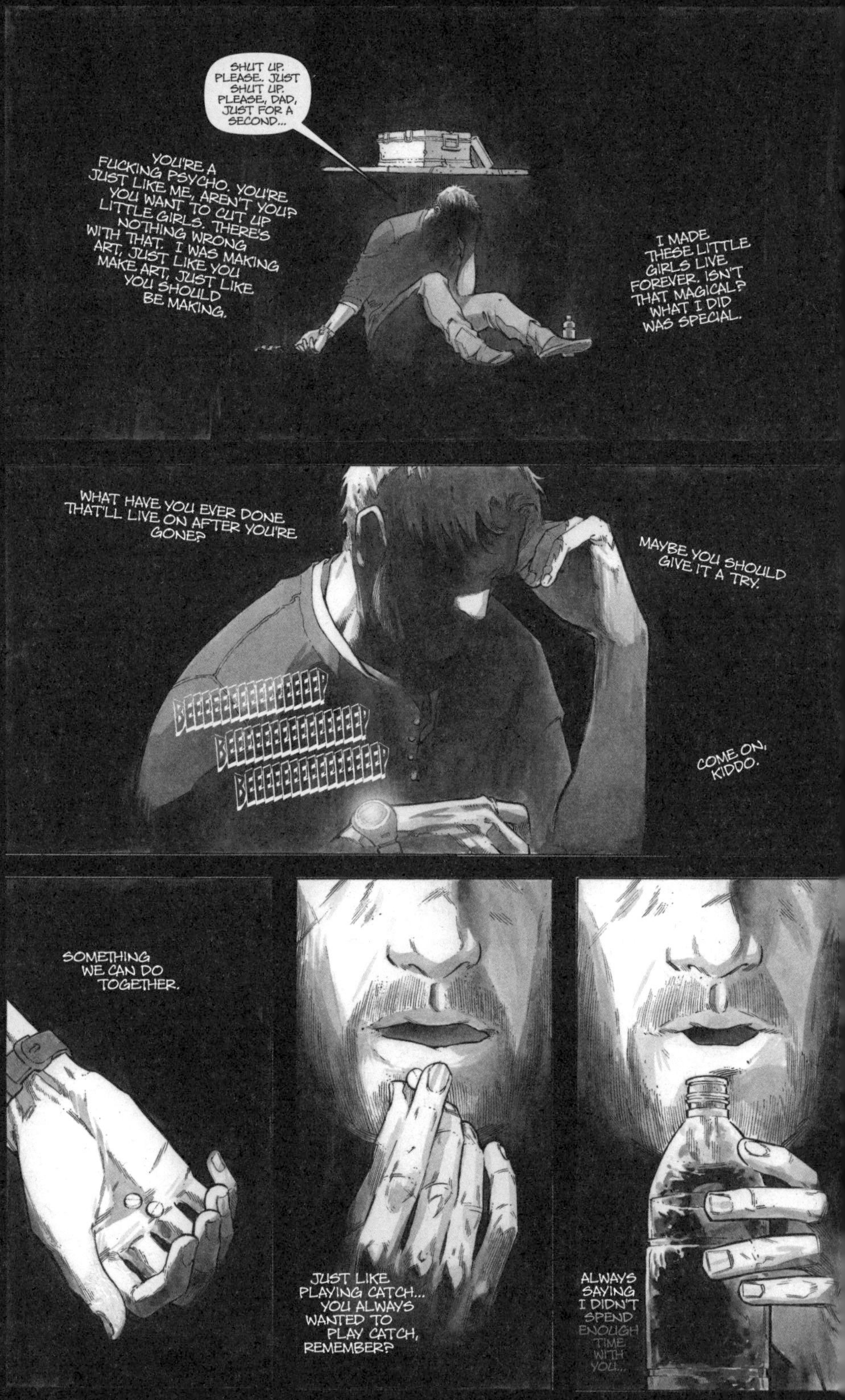
SHUT UP. PLEASE. JUST SHUT UP. PLEASE, DAD, JUST FOR A SECOND...
YOU'RE A FUCKING PSYCHO. YOU'RE JUST LIKE ME, AREN'T YOU? YOU WANT TO CUT UP LITTLE GIRLS. THERE'S NOTHING WRONG WITH THAT. I WAS MAKING ART, JUST LIKE YOU MAKE ART, JUST LIKE YOU SHOULD BE MAKING.
I MADE THESE LITTLE GIRLS LIVE FOREVER. ISN'T THAT MAGICAL? WHAT I DID WAS SPECIAL.
WHAT HAVE YOU EVER DONE THAT'LL LIVE ON AFTER YOU'RE GONE?
MAYBE YOU SHOULD GIVE IT A TRY.
BEEEEEEEEEEEEEEEEP
BEEEEEEEEEEEEEEEEP
BEEEEEEEEEEEEEEEEP
COME ON, KIDDO.
SOMETHING WE CAN DO TOGETHER.
JUST LIKE PLAYING CATCH... YOU ALWAYS WANTED TO PLAY CATCH, REMEMBER?
ALWAYS SAYING I DIDN'T SPEND ENOUGH TIME WITH YOU...

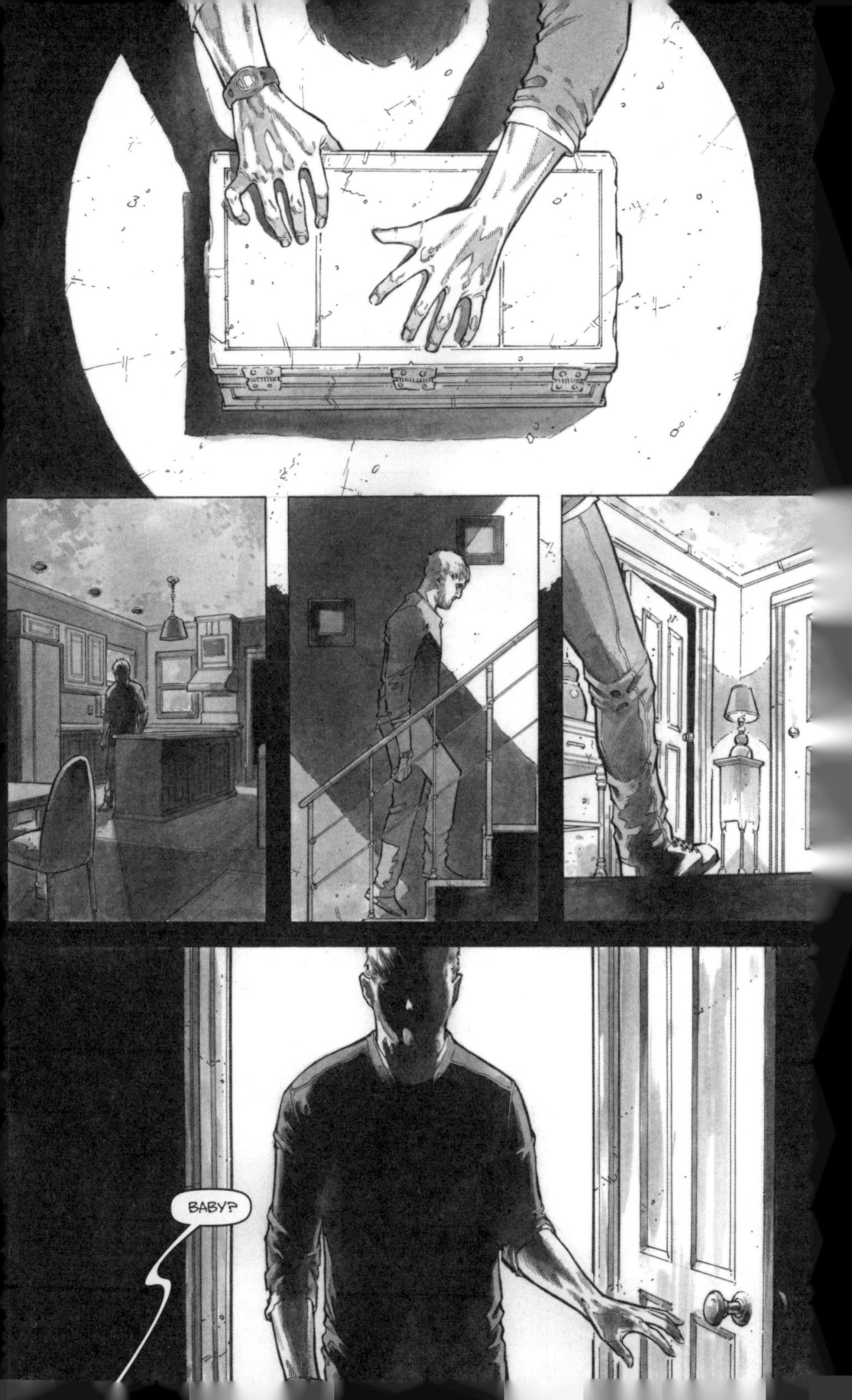
BABY?

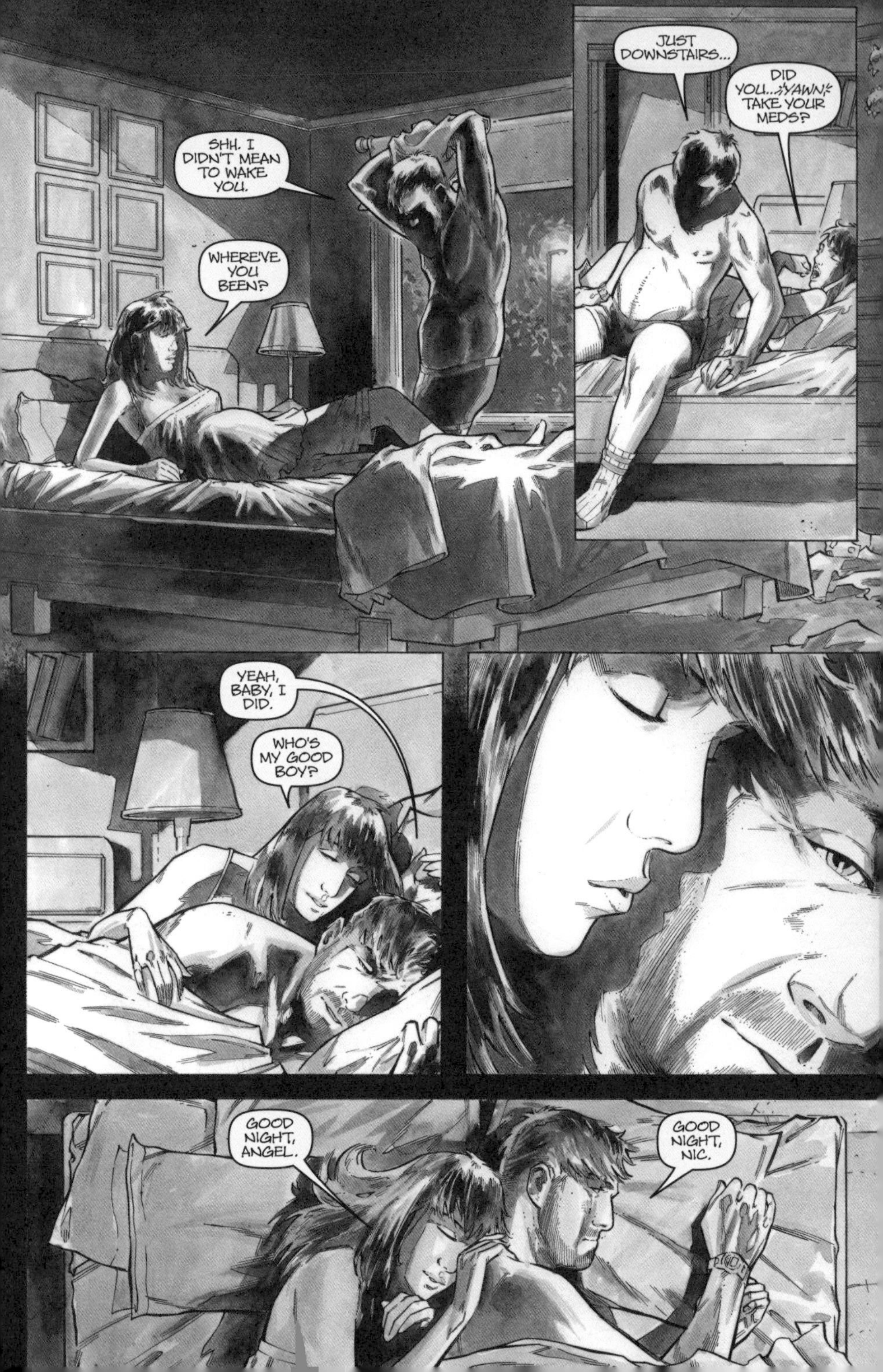
SHH. I DIDN'T MEAN TO WAKE YOU.
WHERE'VE YOU BEEN?
JUST DOWNSTAIRS...
DID YOU... *YAWN* TAKE YOUR MEDS?
YEAH, BABY, I DID.
WHO'S MY GOOD BOY?
GOOD NIGHT, ANGEL.
GOOD NIGHT, NIC.

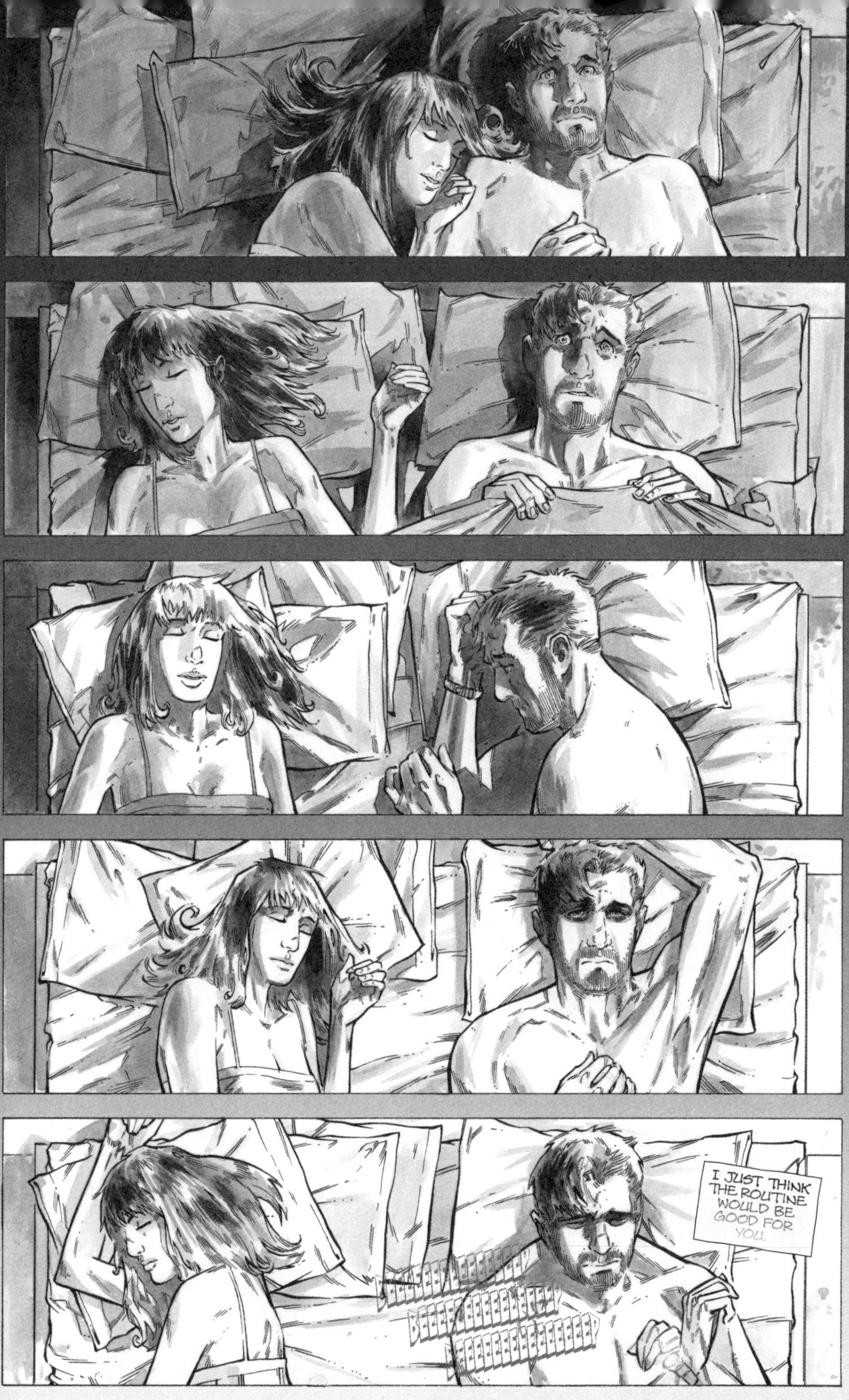
I JUST THINK THE ROUTINE WOULD BE GOOD FOR YOU.

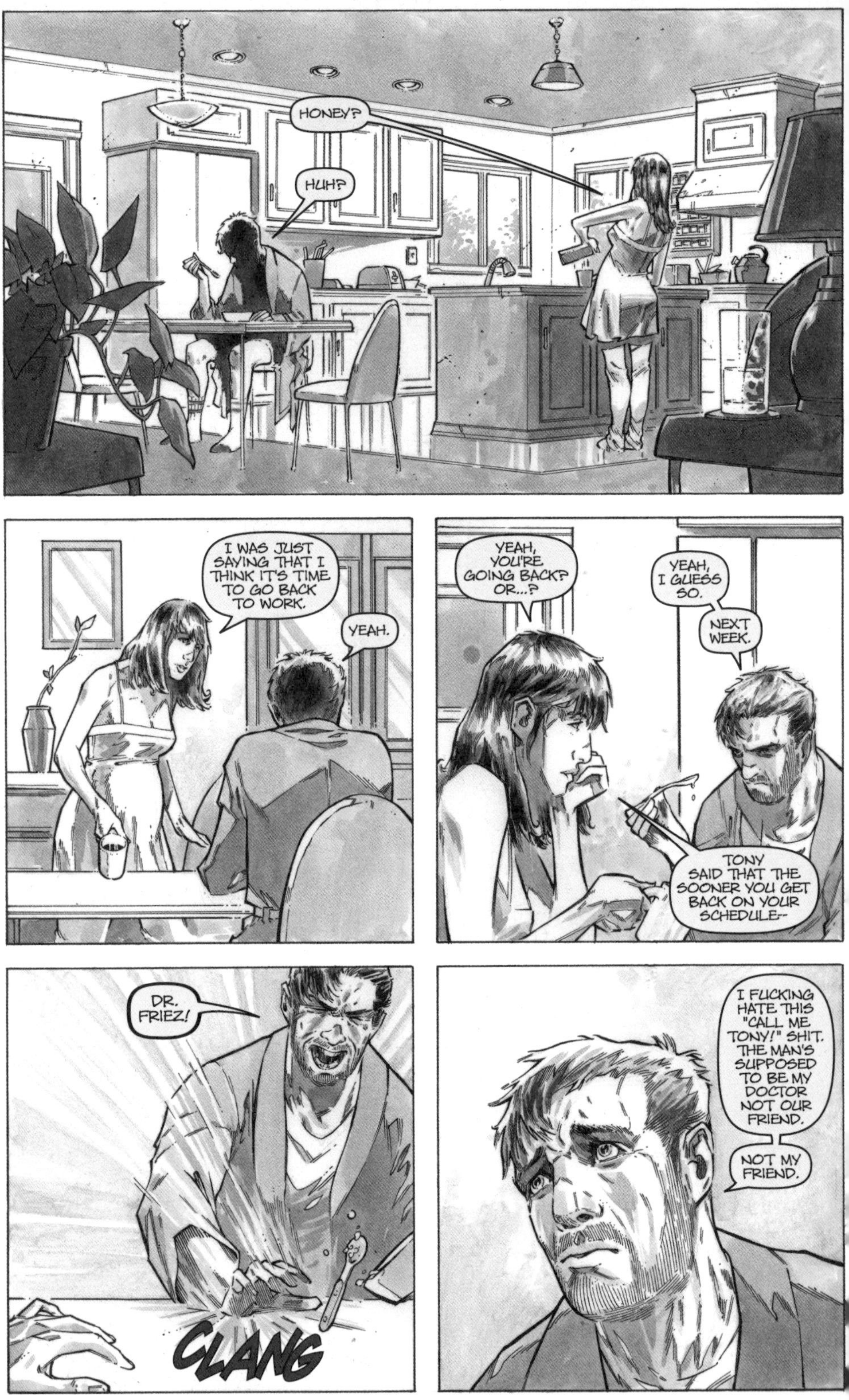
HONEY?
HUH?
I WAS JUST SAYING THAT I THINK IT'S TIME TO GO BACK TO WORK.
YEAH.
YEAH, YOU'RE GOING BACK? OR...?
YEAH, I GUESS SO.
NEXT WEEK.
TONY SAID THAT THE SOONER YOU GET BACK ON YOUR SCHEDULE--
DR. FRIEZ!
CLANG
I FUCKING HATE THIS "CALL ME TONY!" SHIT. THE MAN'S SUPPOSED TO BE MY DOCTOR NOT OUR FRIEND.
NOT MY FRIEND.

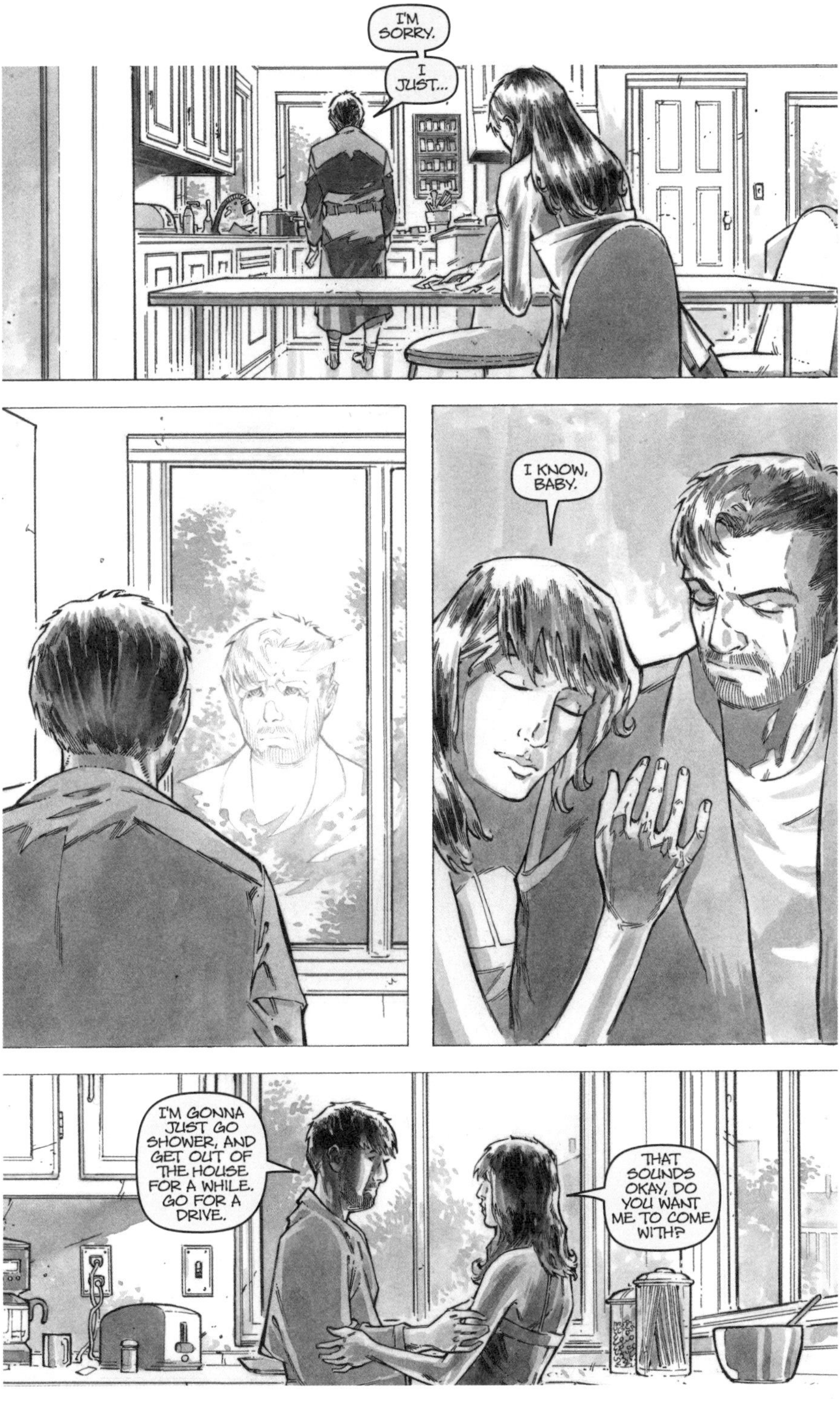
I'M SORRY.
I JUST...
I KNOW, BABY.
I'M GONNA JUST GO SHOWER, AND GET OUT OF THE HOUSE FOR A WHILE. GO FOR A DRIVE.
THAT SOUNDS OKAY, DO YOU WANT ME TO COME WITH?

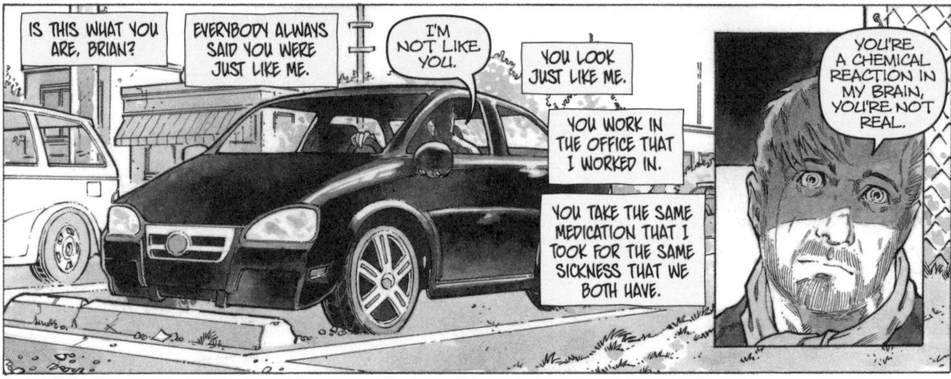
IS THIS WHAT YOU ARE, BRIAN?
EVERYBODY ALWAYS SAID YOU WERE JUST LIKE ME.
I'M NOT LIKE YOU.
YOU LOOK JUST LIKE ME.
YOU WORK IN THE OFFICE THAT I WORKED IN.
YOU TAKE THE SAME MEDICATION THAT I TOOK FOR THE SAME SICKNESS THAT WE BOTH HAVE.
YOU'RE A CHEMICAL REACTION IN MY BRAIN, YOU'RE NOT REAL.

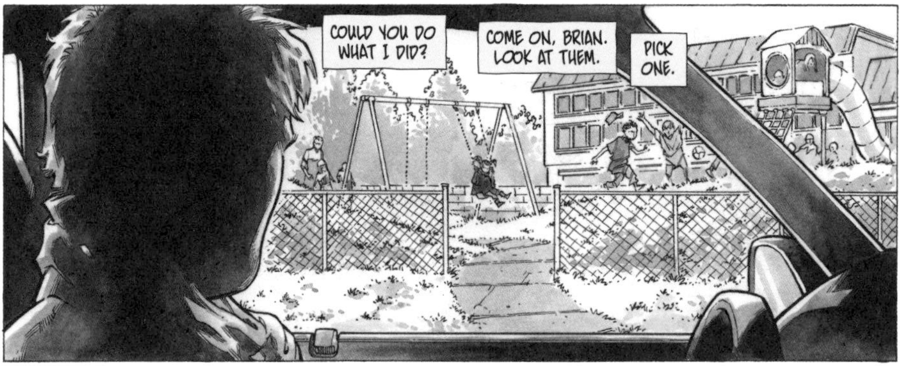
COULD YOU DO WHAT I DID?
COME ON, BRIAN. LOOK AT THEM.
PICK ONE.

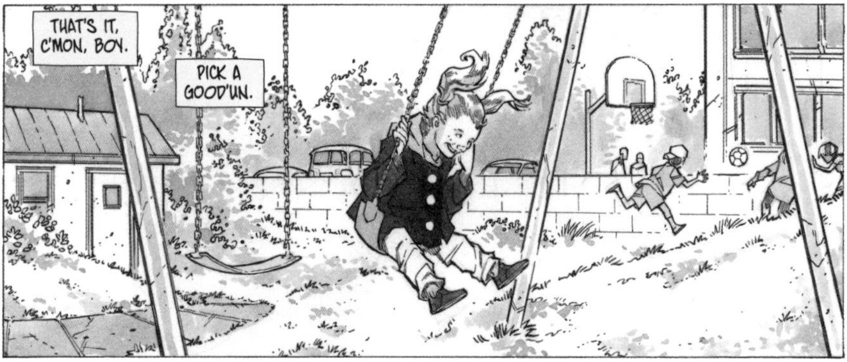
THAT'S IT, C'MON, BOY.
PICK A GOOD'UN.

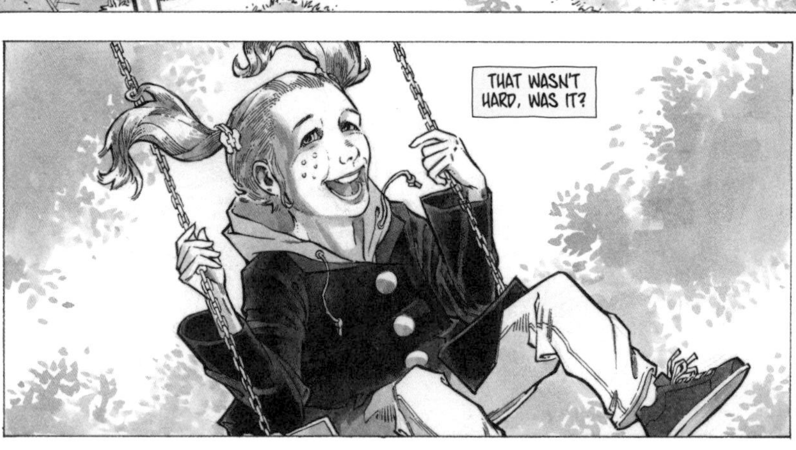
THAT WASN'T HARD, WAS IT?

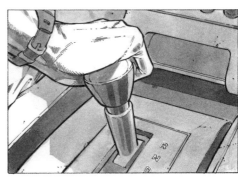

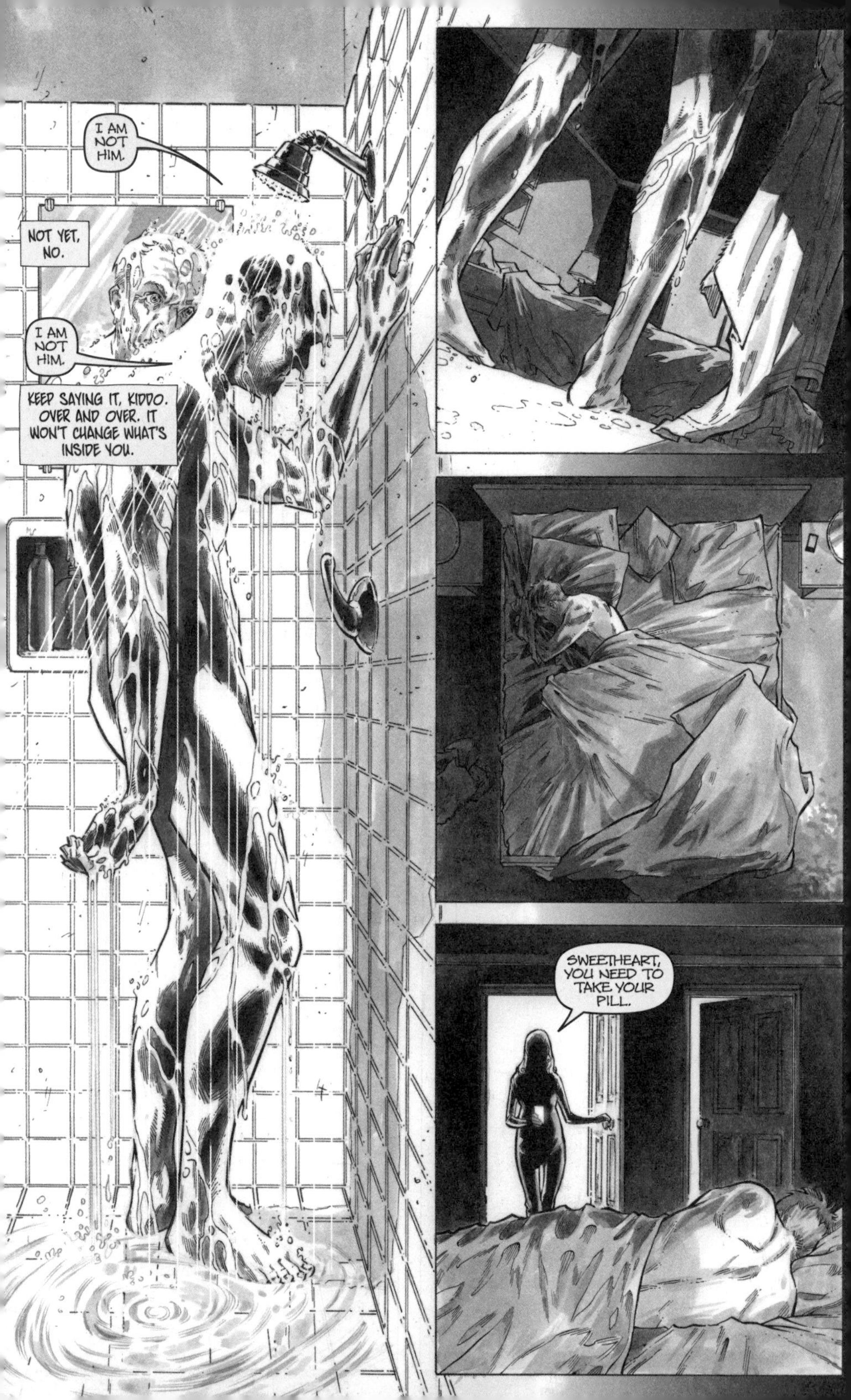
I AM NOT HIM.
NOT YET, NO.
I AM NOT HIM.
KEEP SAYING IT, KIDDO. OVER AND OVER. IT WON'T CHANGE WHAT'S INSIDE YOU.
SWEETHEART, YOU NEED TO TAKE YOUR PILL.

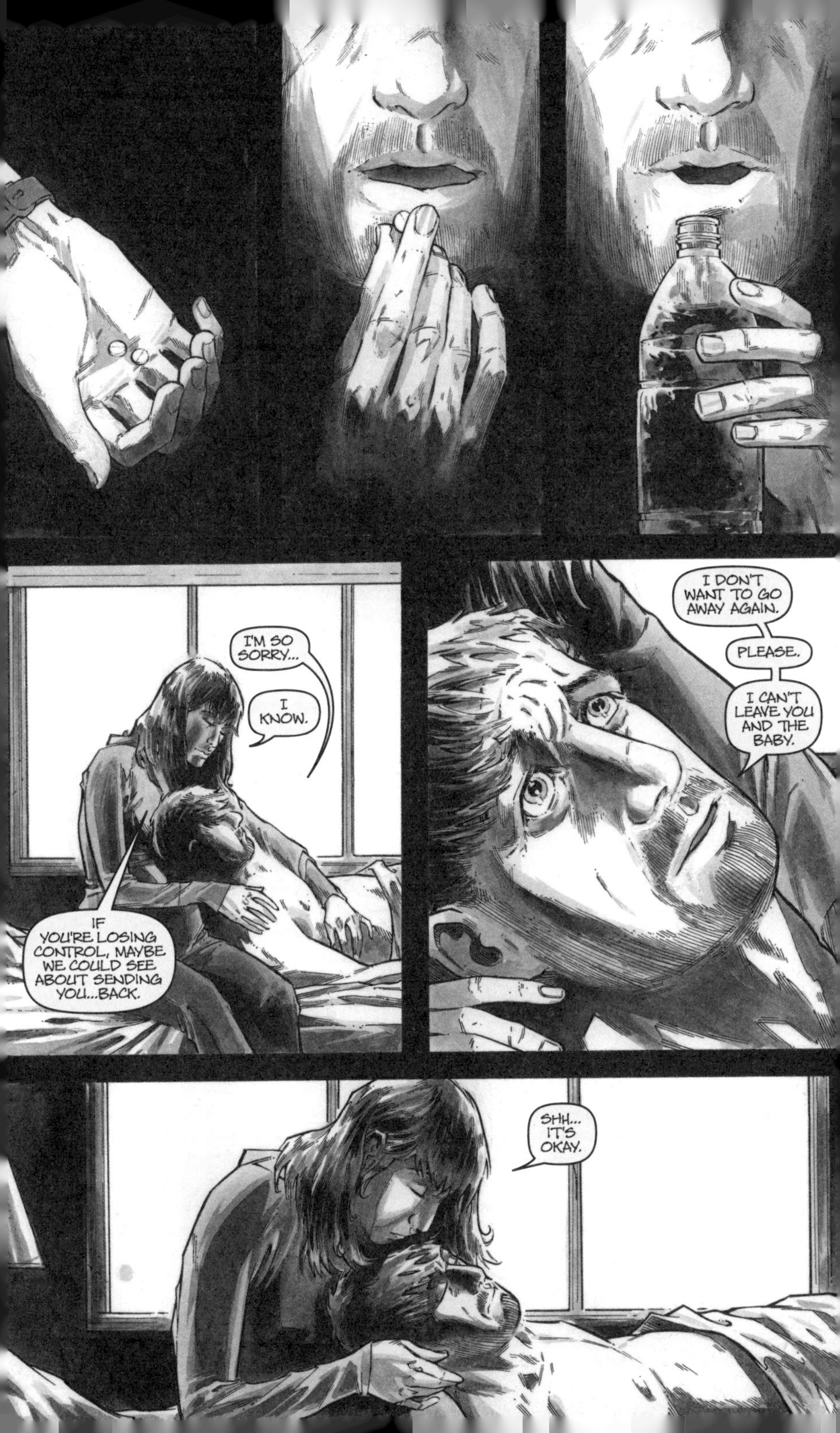
I'M SO SORRY...
I KNOW.
IF YOU'RE LOSING CONTROL, MAYBE WE COULD SEE ABOUT SENDING YOU...BACK.
I DON'T WANT TO GO AWAY AGAIN.
PLEASE.
I CAN'T LEAVE YOU AND THE BABY.
SHH... IT'S OKAY.

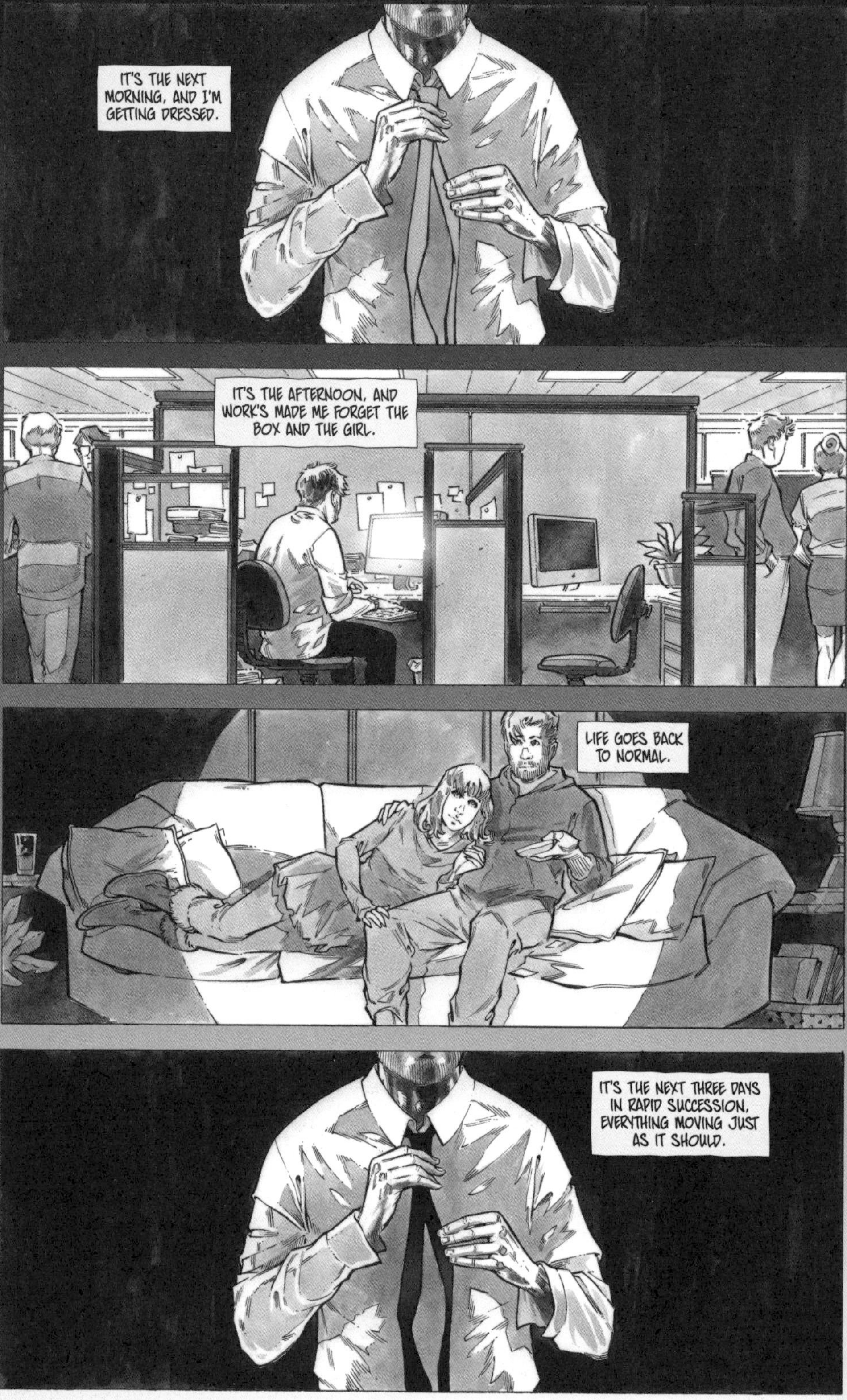
IT'S THE NEXT MORNING, AND I'M GETTING DRESSED.
IT'S THE AFTERNOON, AND WORK'S MADE ME FORGET THE BOX AND THE GIRL.
LIFE GOES BACK TO NORMAL.
IT'S THE NEXT THREE DAYS IN RAPID SUCCESSION, EVERYTHING MOVING JUST AS IT SHOULD.

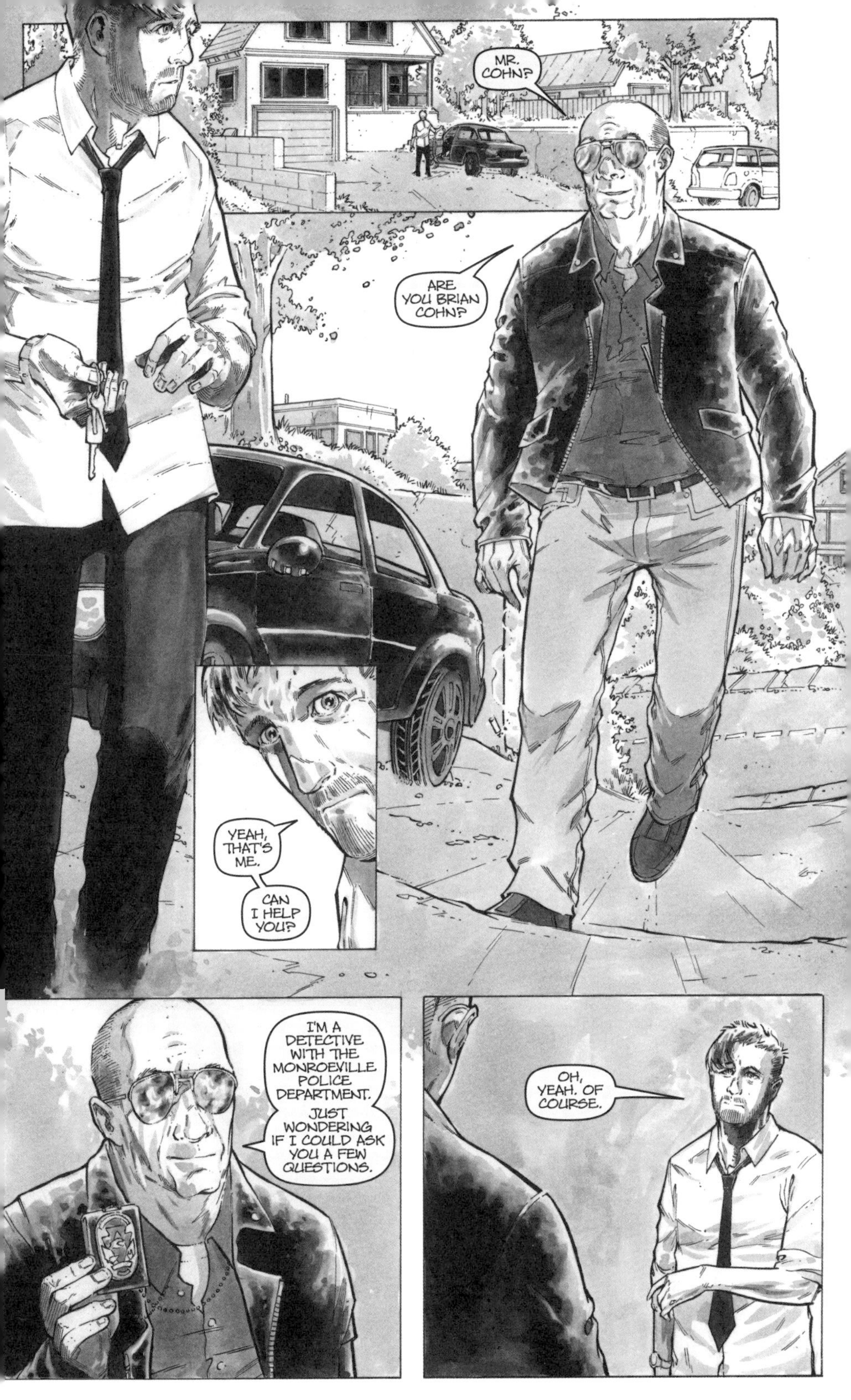
MR. COHN?
ARE YOU BRIAN COHN?
YEAH, THAT'S ME.
CAN I HELP YOU?
I'M A DETECTIVE WITH THE MONROEVILLE POLICE DEPARTMENT.
JUST WONDERING IF I COULD ASK YOU A FEW QUESTIONS.
OH, YEAH. OF COURSE.

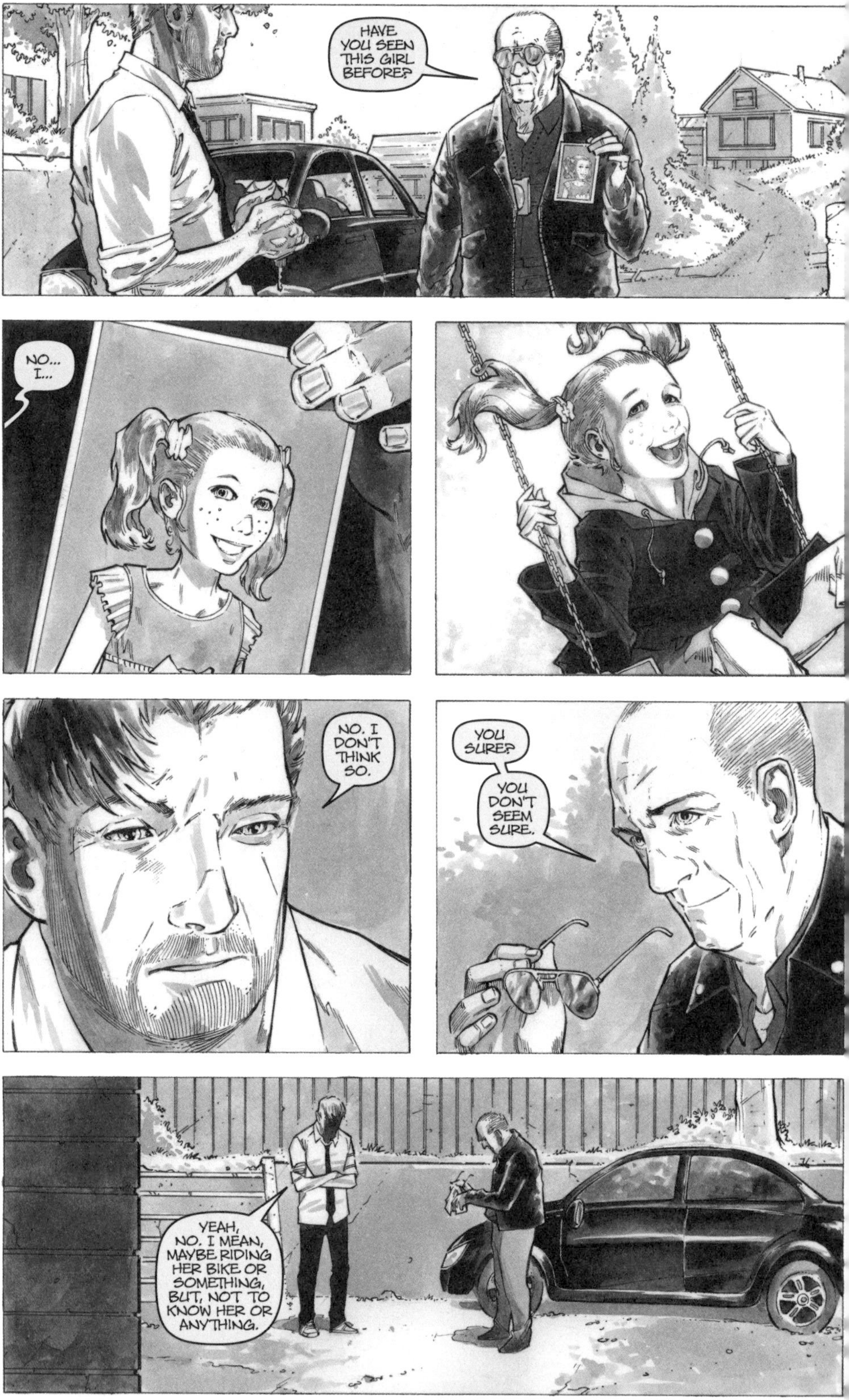
HAVE YOU SEEN THIS GIRL BEFORE?
NO... I...
NO. I DON'T THINK SO.
YOU SURE?
YOU DON'T SEEM SURE.
YEAH, NO. I MEAN, MAYBE RIDING HER BIKE OR SOMETHING, BUT, NOT TO KNOW HER OR ANYTHING.

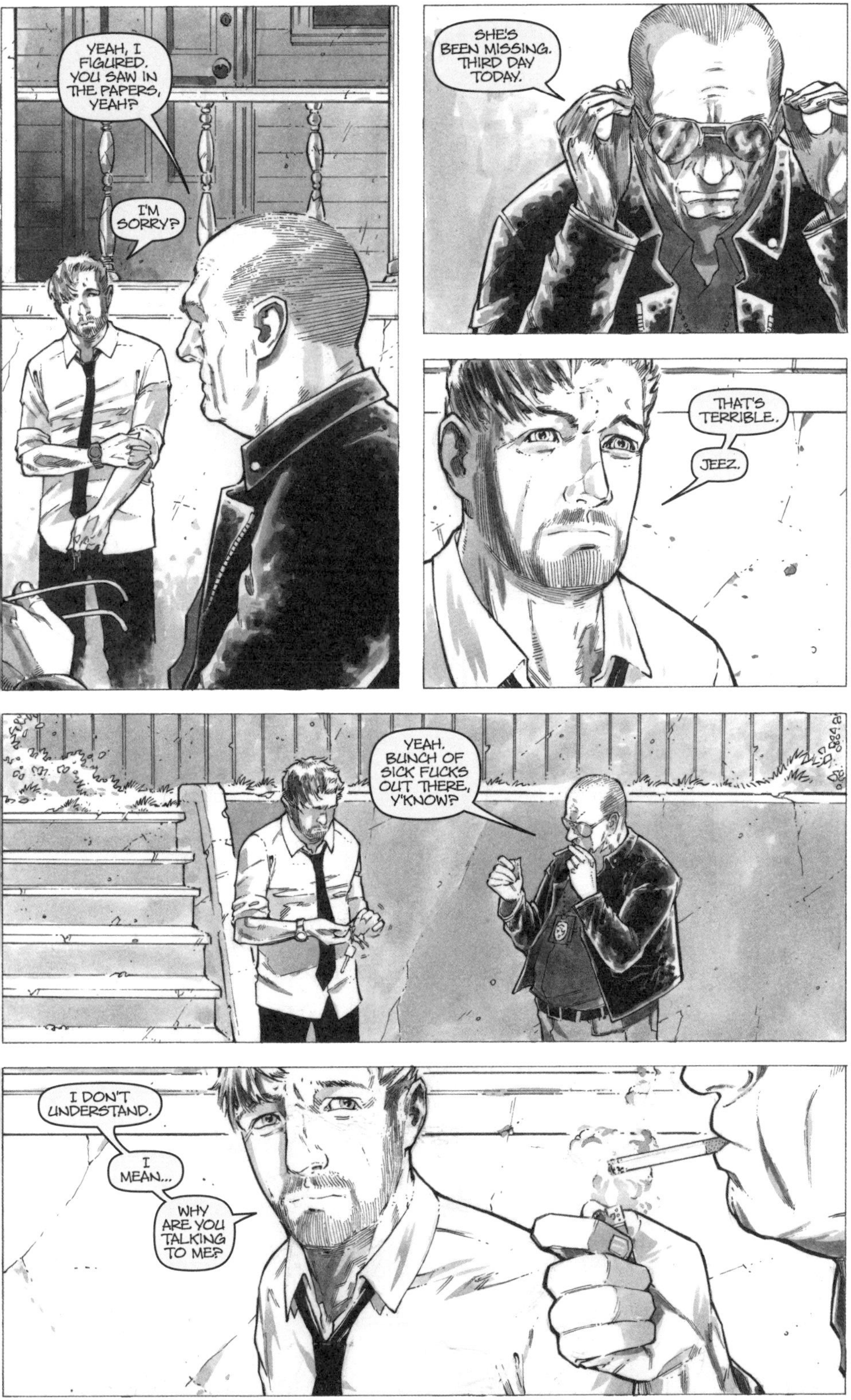
YEAH, I FIGURED. YOU SAW IN THE PAPERS, YEAH?
I'M SORRY?
SHE'S BEEN MISSING. THIRD DAY TODAY.
THAT'S TERRIBLE.
JEEZ.
YEAH. BUNCH OF SICK FUCKS OUT THERE, Y'KNOW?
I DON'T UNDERSTAND.
I MEAN...
WHY ARE YOU TALKING TO ME?

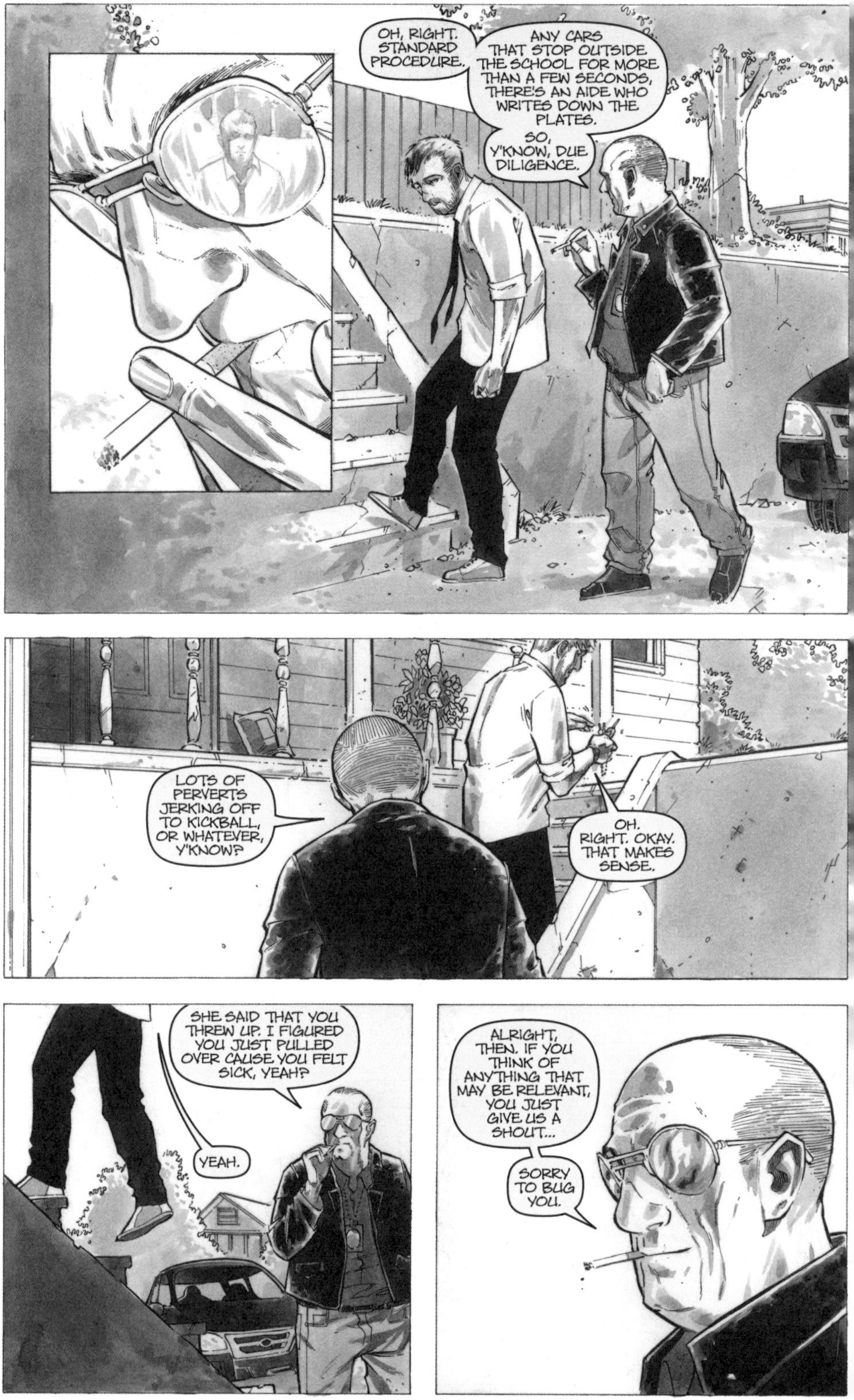
OH, RIGHT. STANDARD PROCEDURE.
ANY CARS THAT STOP OUTSIDE THE SCHOOL FOR MORE THAN A FEW SECONDS, THERE'S AN AIDE WHO WRITES DOWN THE PLATES.
SO, Y'KNOW, DUE DILIGENCE.
LOTS OF PERVERTS JERKING OFF TO KICKBALL, OR WHATEVER, Y'KNOW?
OH. RIGHT. OKAY. THAT MAKES SENSE.
SHE SAID THAT YOU THREW UP. I FIGURED YOU JUST PULLED OVER CAUSE YOU FELT SICK, YEAH?
YEAH.
ALRIGHT, THEN. IF YOU THINK OF ANYTHING THAT MAY BE RELEVANT, YOU JUST GIVE US A SHOUT...
SORRY TO BUG YOU.

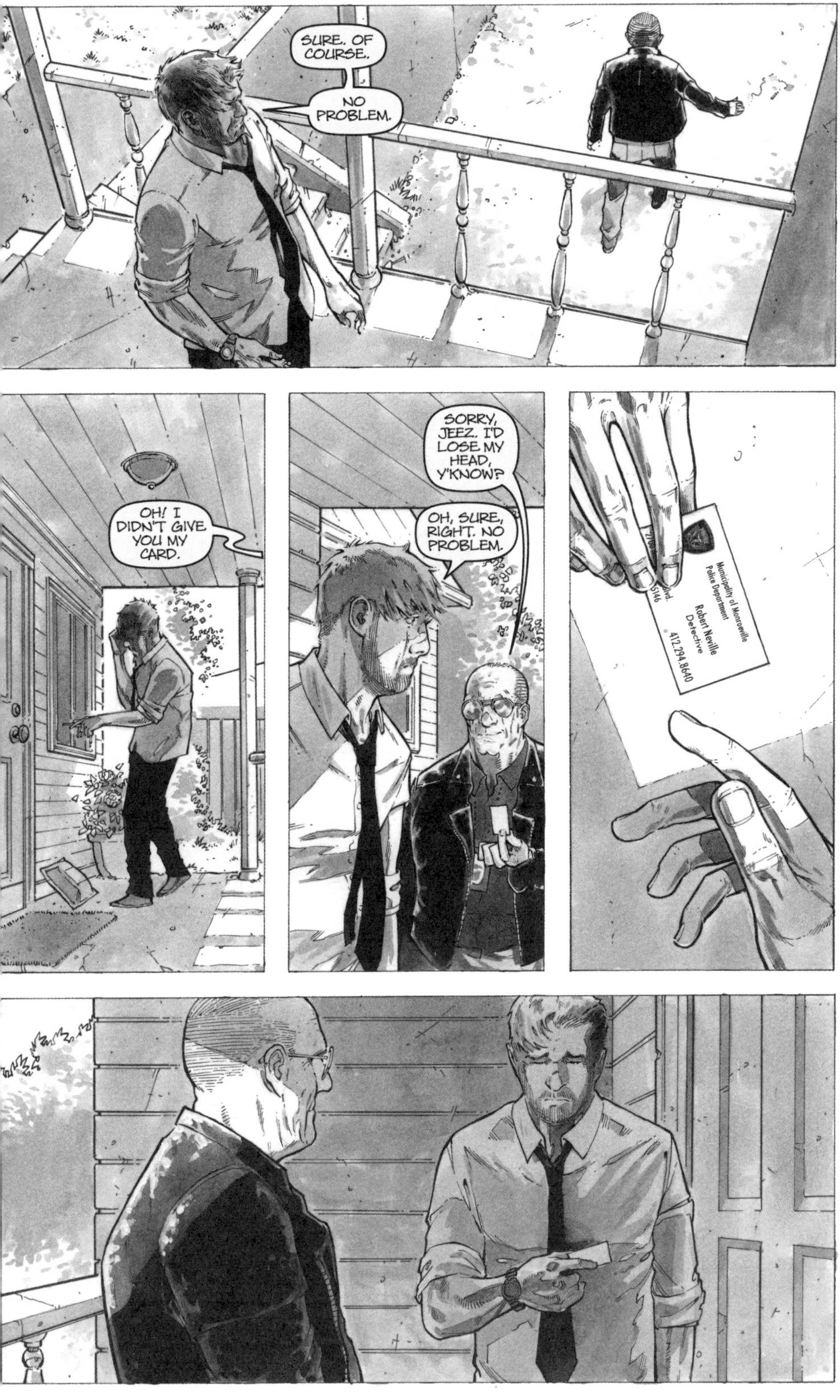
SURE. OF COURSE.
NO PROBLEM.
OH! I DIDN'T GIVE YOU MY CARD.
SORRY, JEEZ. I'D LOSE MY HEAD, Y'KNOW?
OH, SURE, RIGHT. NO PROBLEM.
Municipality of Monroeville
Police Department
Robert Neville
Detective
412.294.8640

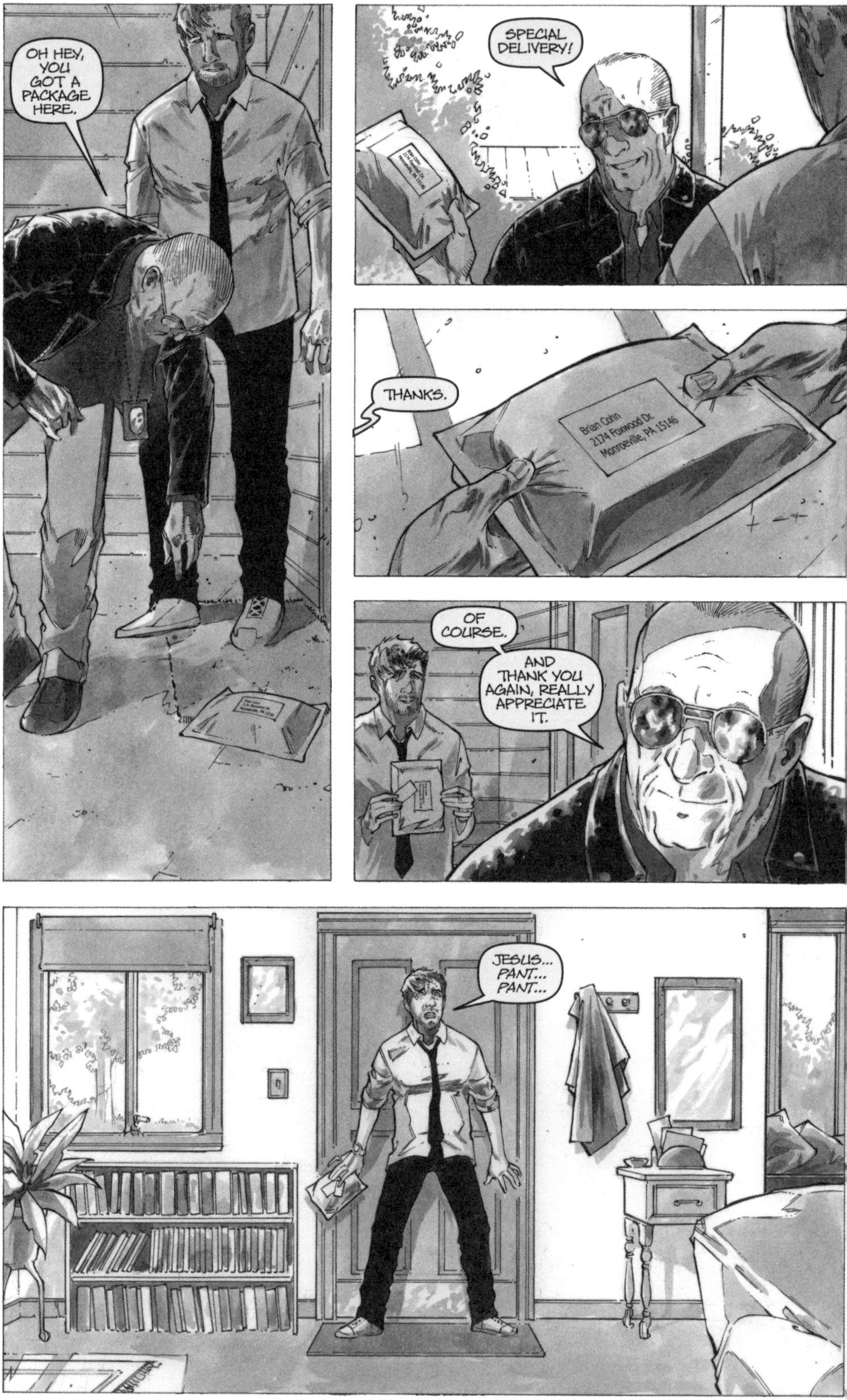
OH HEY, YOU GOT A PACKAGE HERE.
SPECIAL DELIVERY!
THANKS.
Brian Cohn
2174 Foxwood Dr.
Monroeville, PA 15146
OF COURSE.
AND THANK YOU AGAIN, REALLY APPRECIATE IT.
JESUS... PANT... PANT...

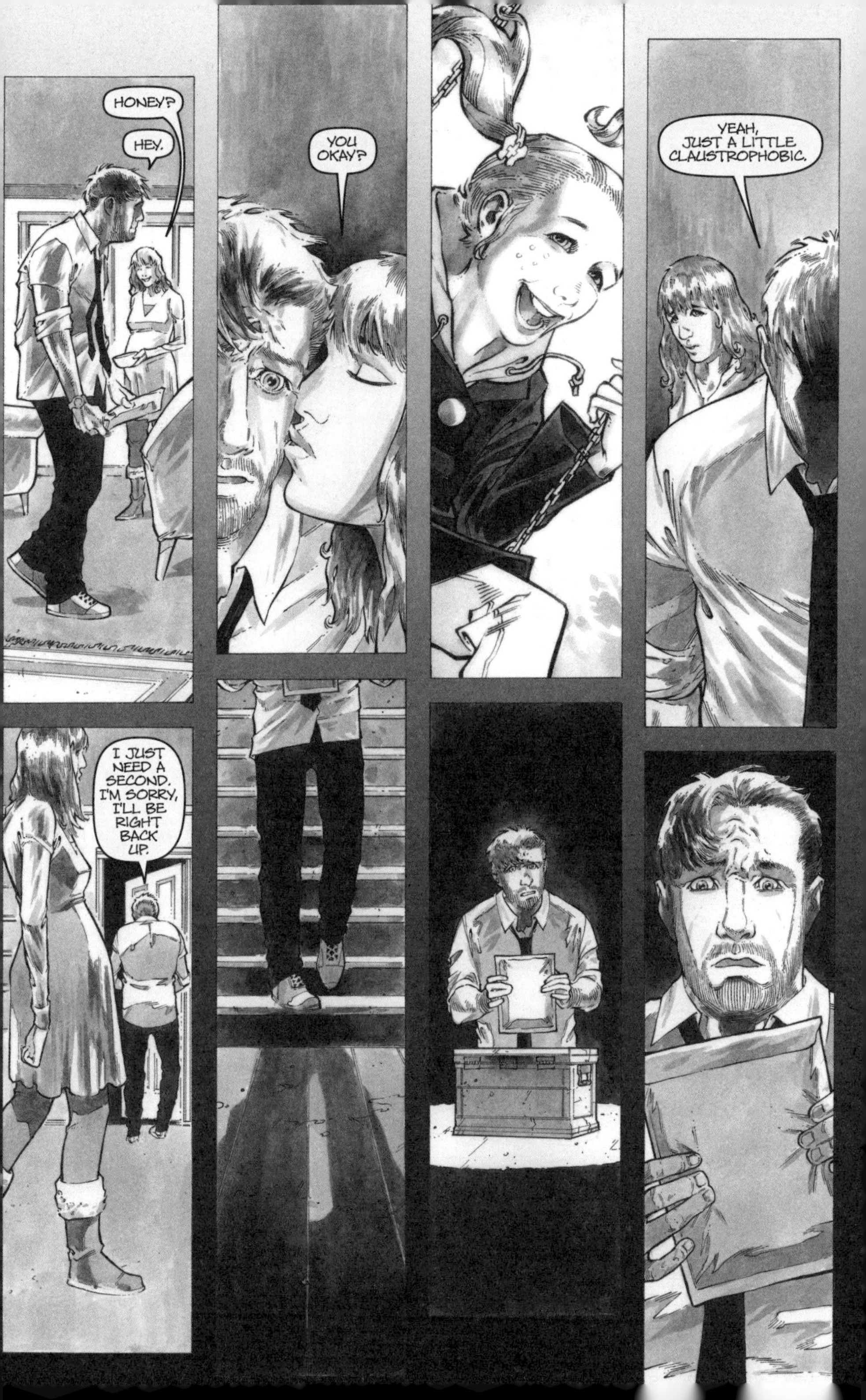
HONEY?
HEY.
YOU OKAY?
YEAH, JUST A LITTLE CLAUSTROPHOBIC.
I JUST NEED A SECOND. I'M SORRY, I'LL BE RIGHT BACK UP.

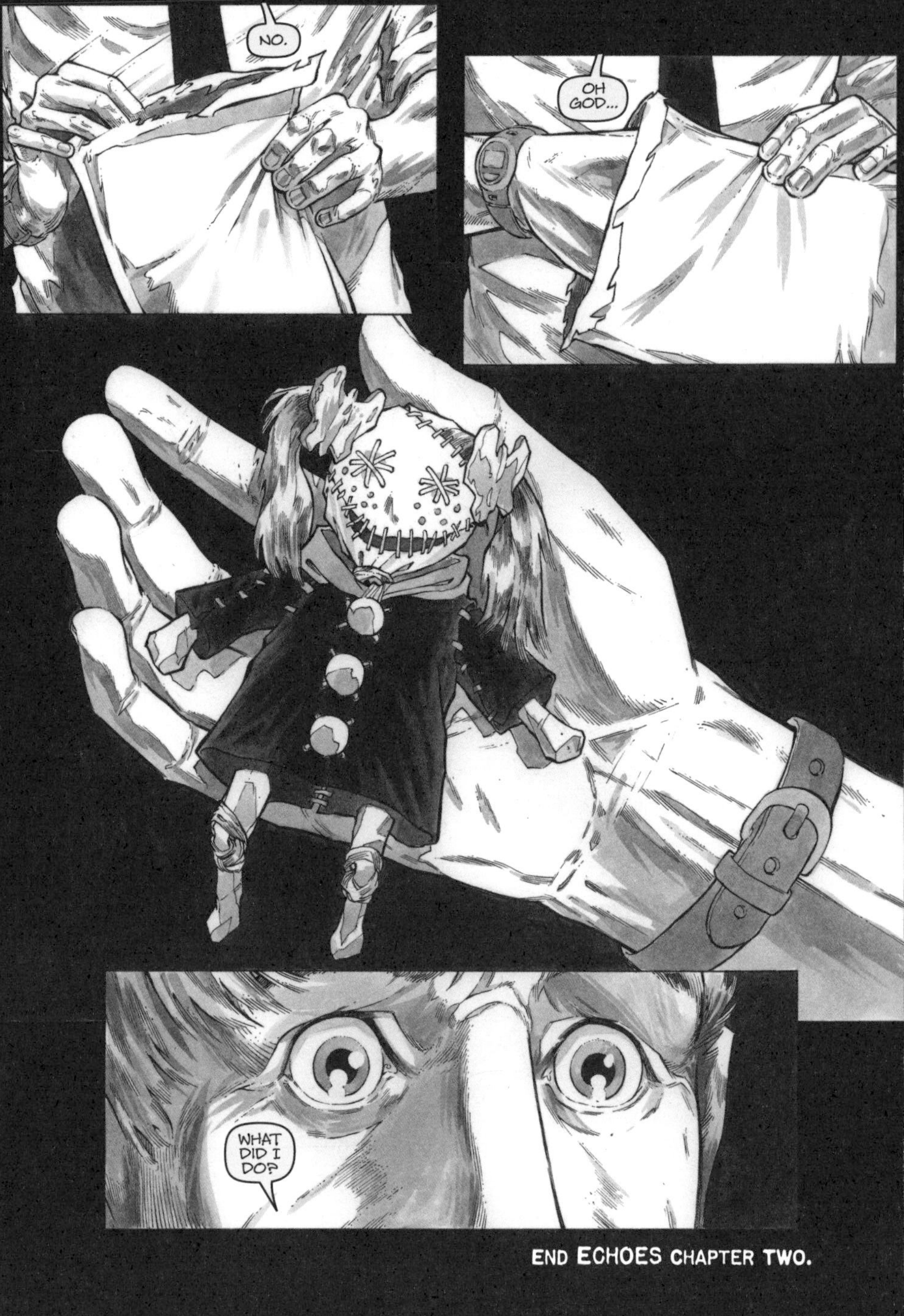
NO.
OH GOD...
WHAT DID I DO?

END ECHOES CHAPTER TWO.

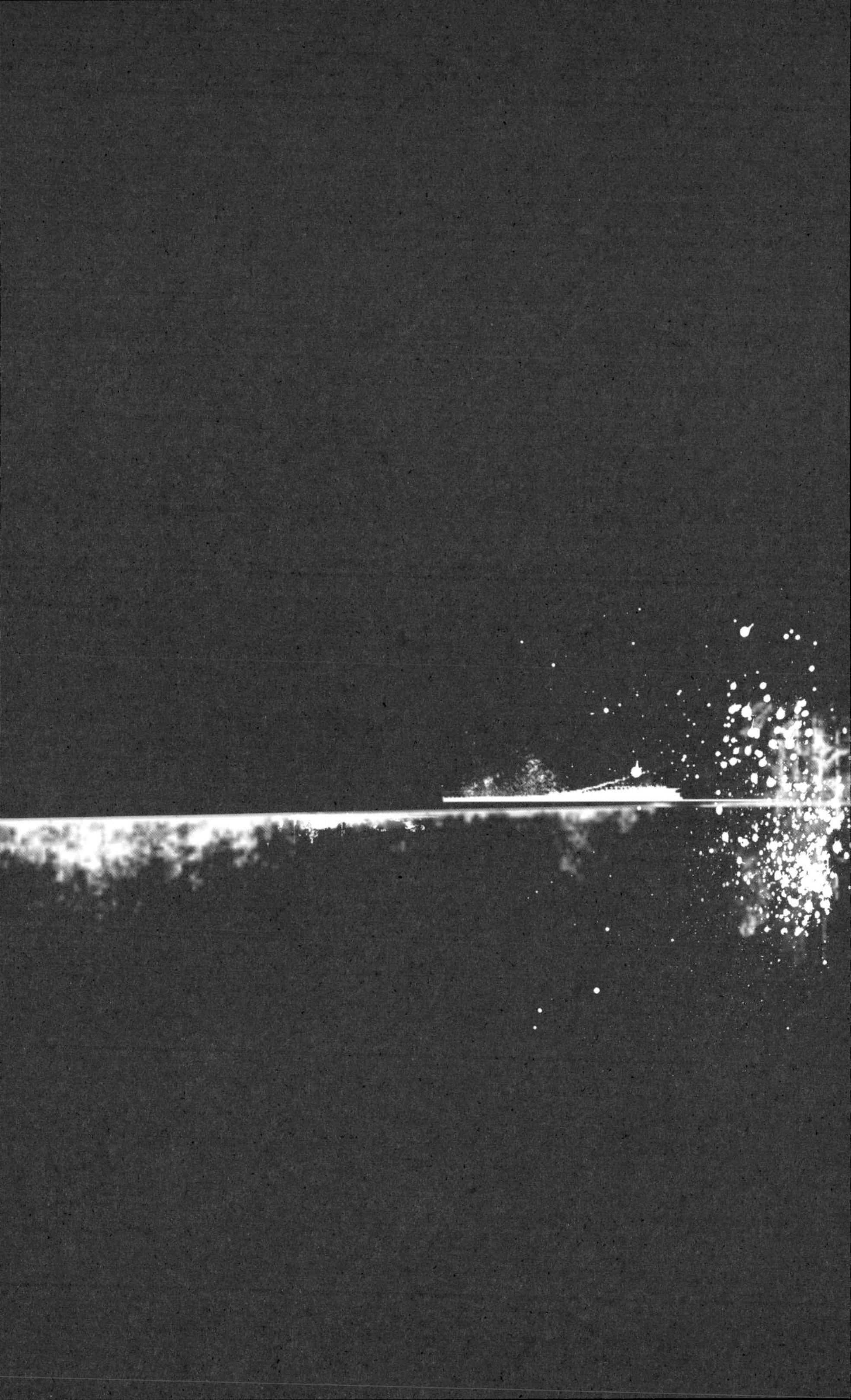

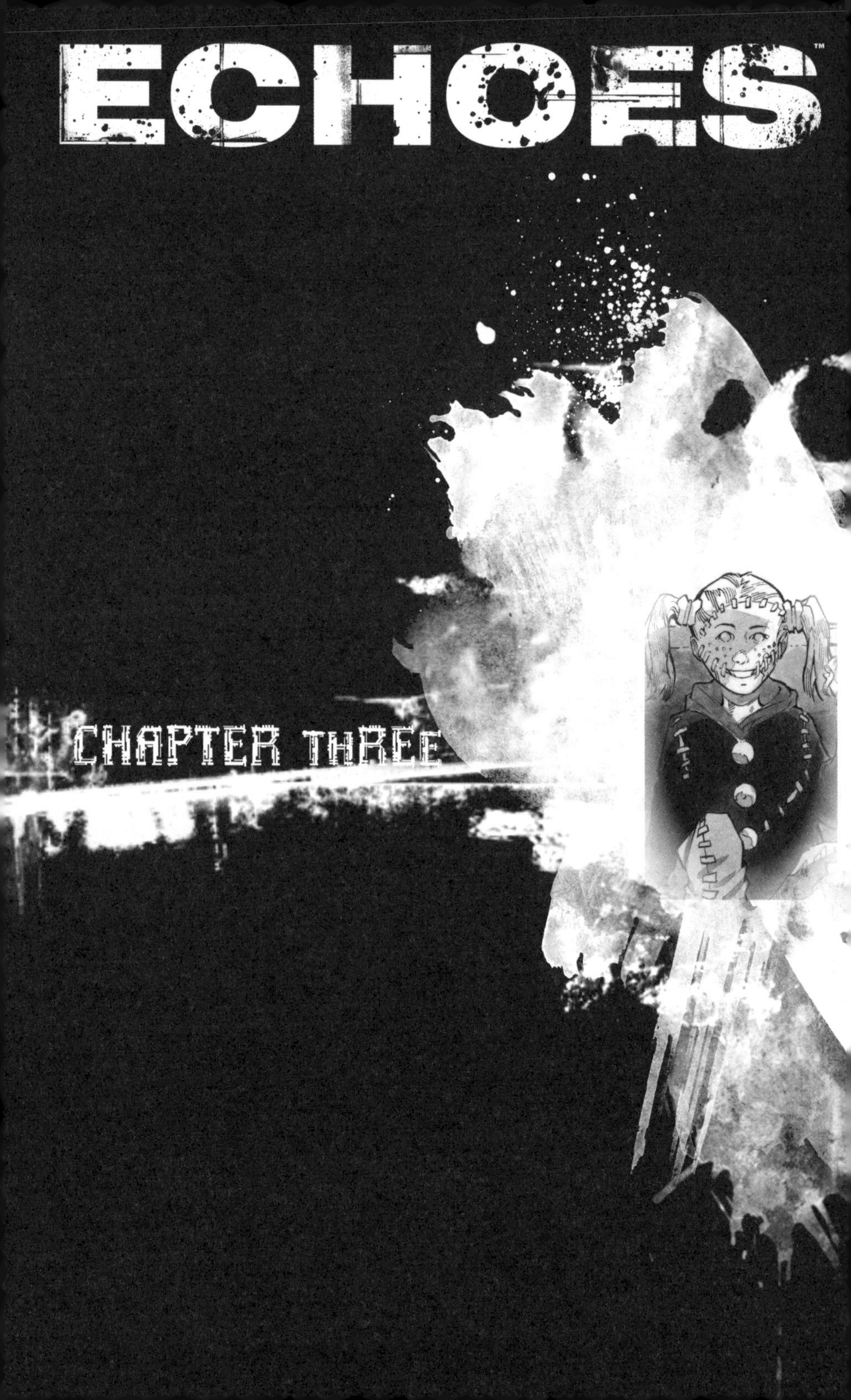
ECHOES™
CHAPTER THREE

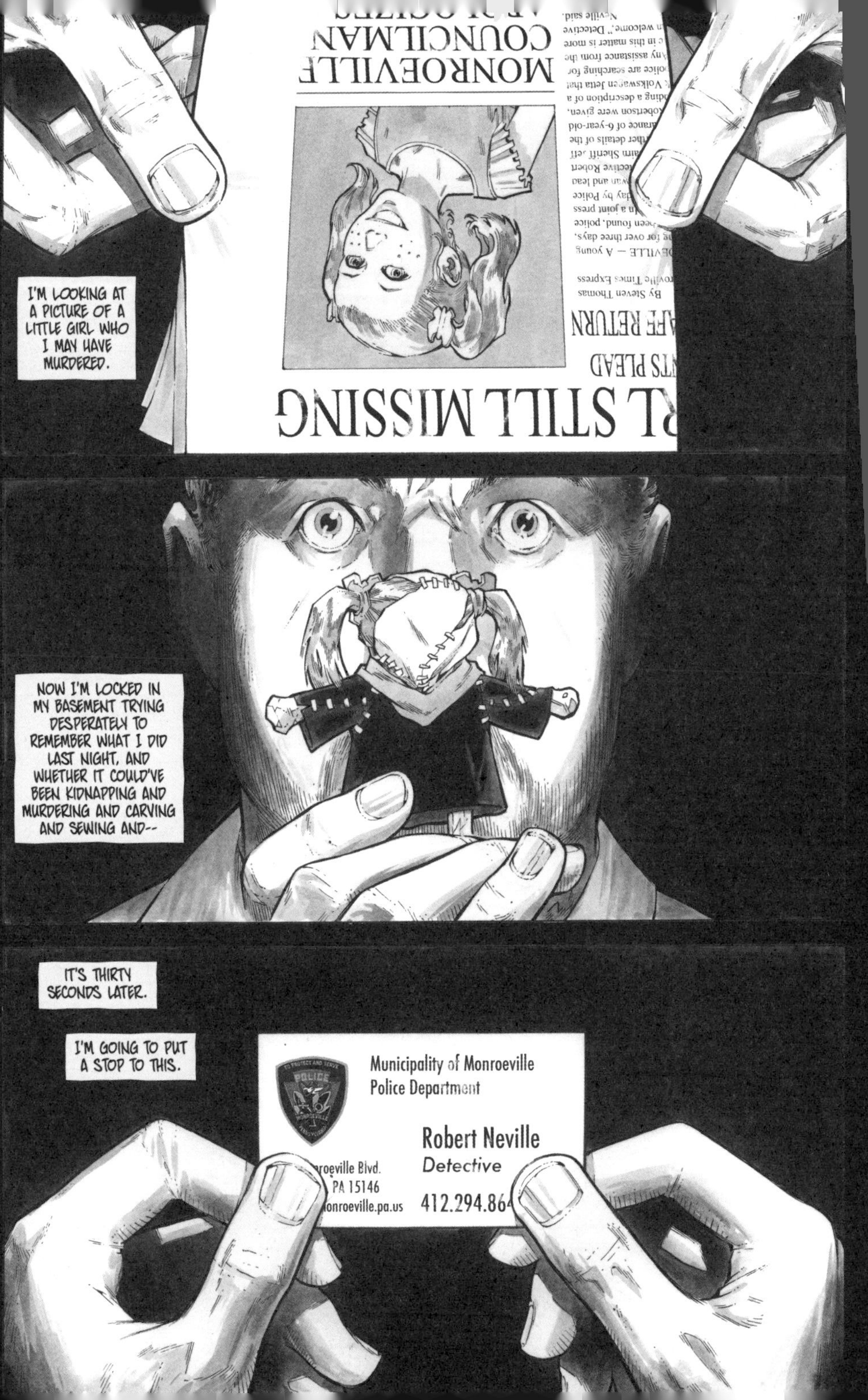

I'M LOOKING AT A PICTURE OF A LITTLE GIRL WHO I MAY HAVE MURDERED.

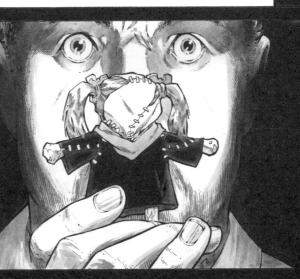

NOW I'M LOCKED IN MY BASEMENT TRYING DESPERATELY TO REMEMBER WHAT I DID LAST NIGHT, AND WHETHER IT COULD'VE BEEN KIDNAPPING AND MURDERING AND CARVING AND SEWING AND--

IT'S THIRTY SECONDS LATER.

I'M GOING TO PUT A STOP TO THIS.

Municipality of Monroeville Police Department

Robert Neville
Detective

roeville Blvd.
PA 15146
monroeville.pa.us

412.294.86

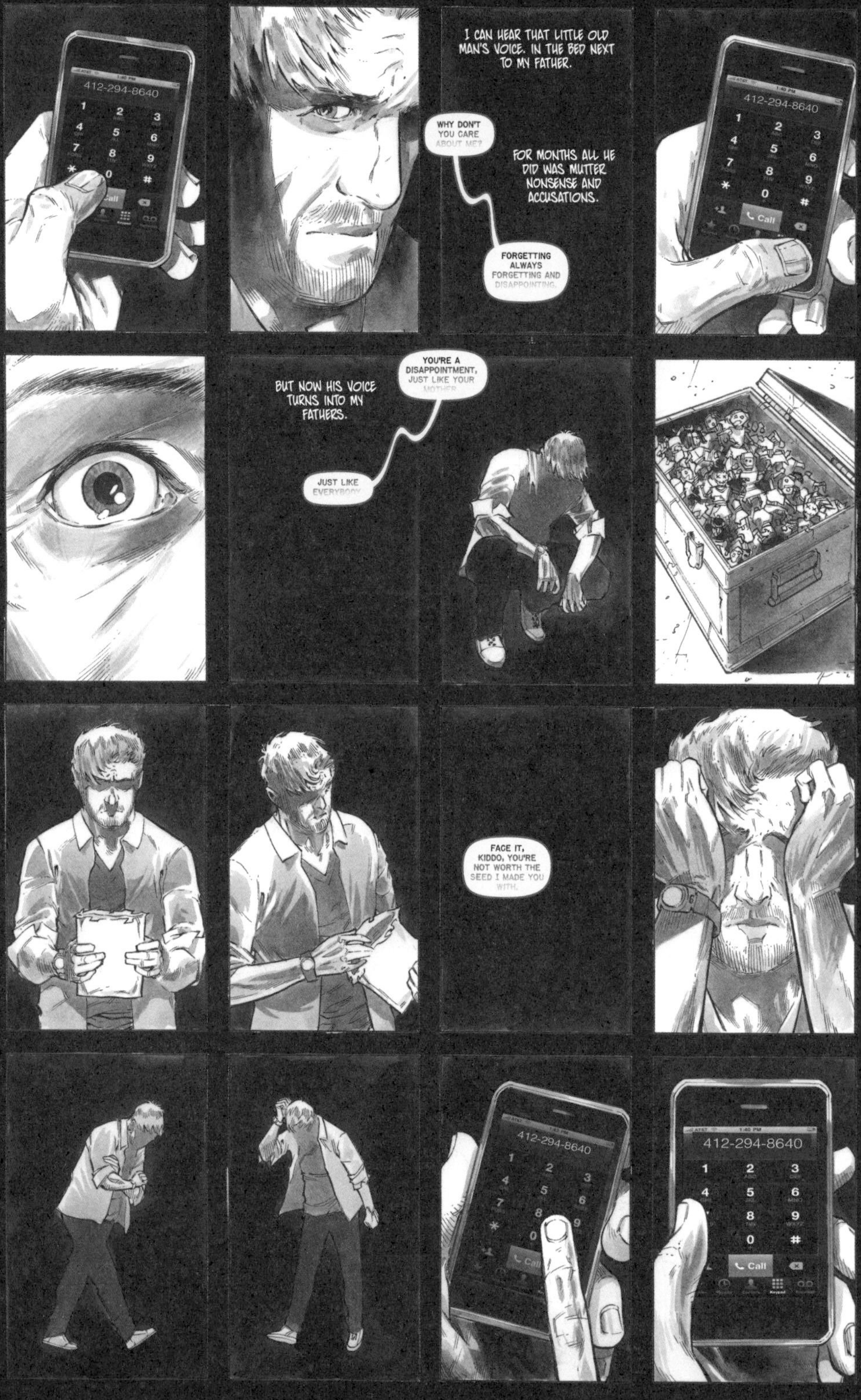
412-294-8640
I CAN HEAR THAT LITTLE OLD MAN'S VOICE. IN THE BED NEXT TO MY FATHER.
WHY DON'T YOU CARE ABOUT ME?
FOR MONTHS ALL HE DID WAS MUTTER NONSENSE AND ACCUSATIONS.
FORGETTING ALWAYS FORGETTING AND DISAPPOINTING.
412-294-8640
BUT NOW HIS VOICE TURNS INTO MY FATHERS.
YOU'RE A DISAPPOINTMENT, JUST LIKE YOUR MOTHER
JUST LIKE EVERYBODY
FACE IT, KIDDO, YOU'RE NOT WORTH THE SEED I MADE YOU WITH.
412-294-8640
412-294-8640

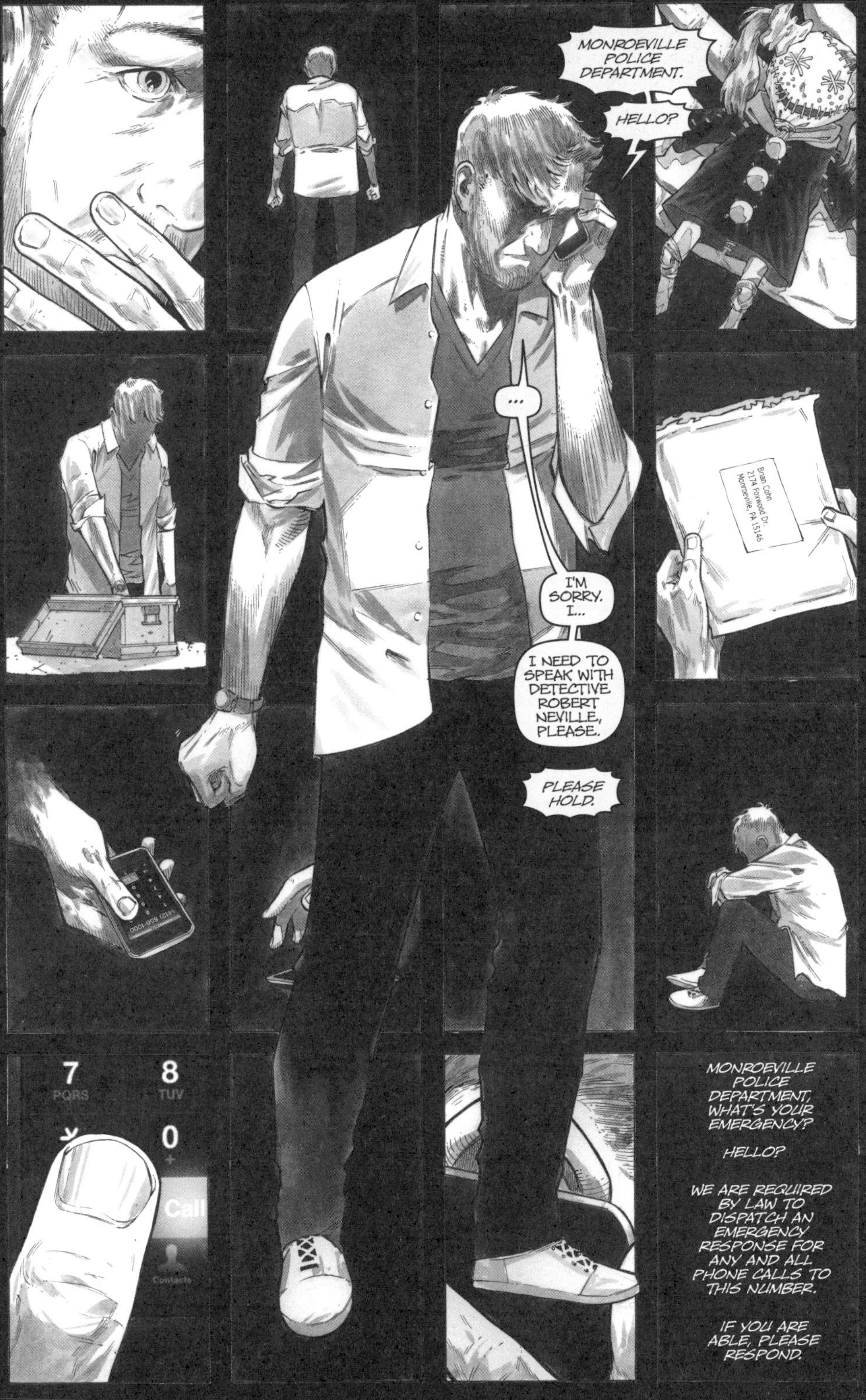
MONROEVILLE POLICE DEPARTMENT.
HELLO?
...
Brian Cohn
2174 Foxwood Dr.
Monroeville, PA 15146
I'M SORRY. I...
I NEED TO SPEAK WITH DETECTIVE ROBERT NEVILLE, PLEASE.
PLEASE HOLD.
7 PQRS
8 TUV
0 +
Call
Contacts
MONROEVILLE POLICE DEPARTMENT, WHAT'S YOUR EMERGENCY?
HELLO?
WE ARE REQUIRED BY LAW TO DISPATCH AN EMERGENCY RESPONSE FOR ANY AND ALL PHONE CALLS TO THIS NUMBER.
IF YOU ARE ABLE, PLEASE RESPOND.

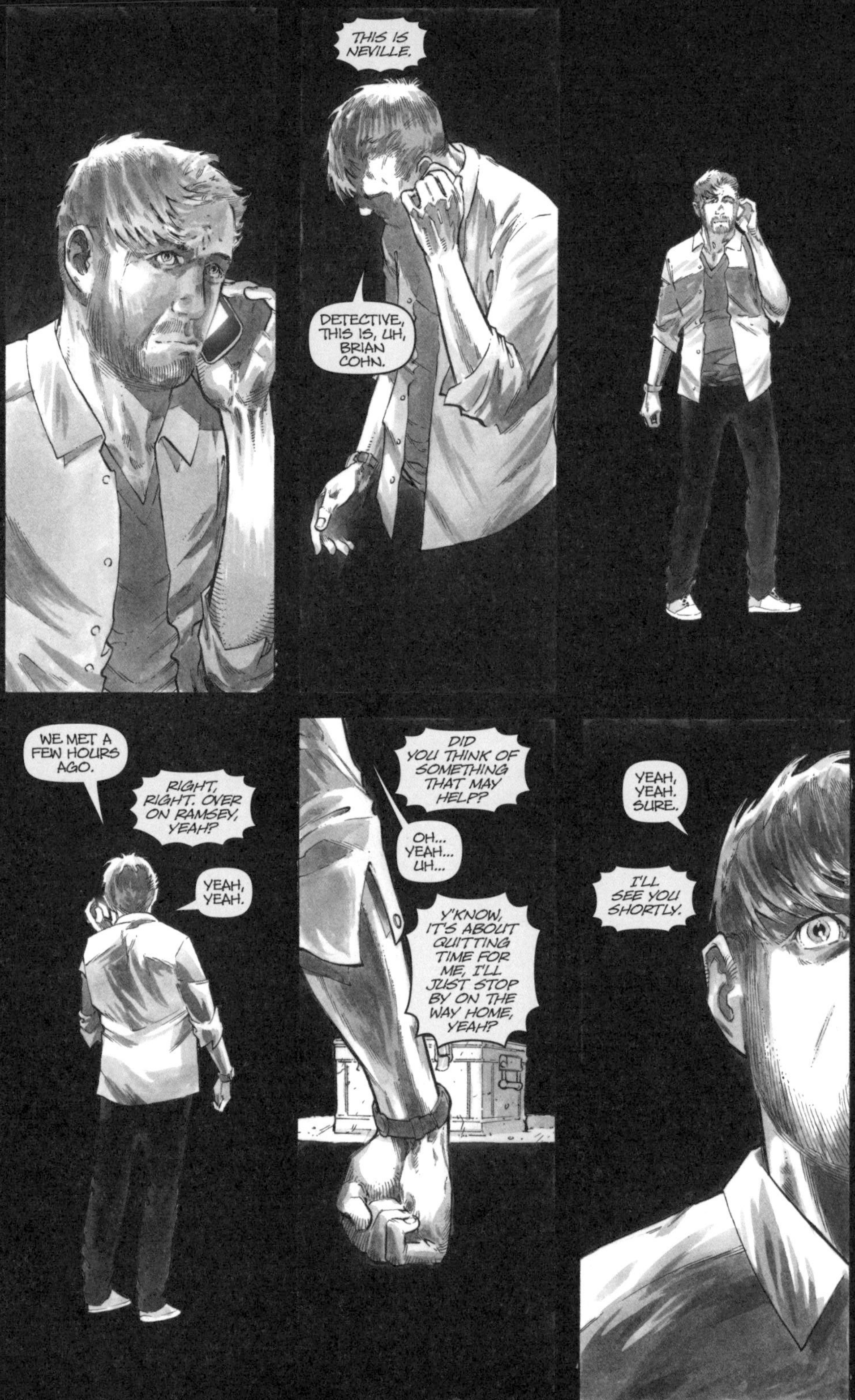
THIS IS NEVILLE.
DETECTIVE, THIS IS, UH, BRIAN COHN.
WE MET A FEW HOURS AGO.
RIGHT, RIGHT. OVER ON RAMSEY, YEAH?
YEAH, YEAH.
DID YOU THINK OF SOMETHING THAT MAY HELP?
OH... YEAH... UH...
Y'KNOW, IT'S ABOUT QUITTING TIME FOR ME, I'LL JUST STOP BY ON THE WAY HOME, YEAH?
YEAH, YEAH. SURE.
I'LL SEE YOU SHORTLY.

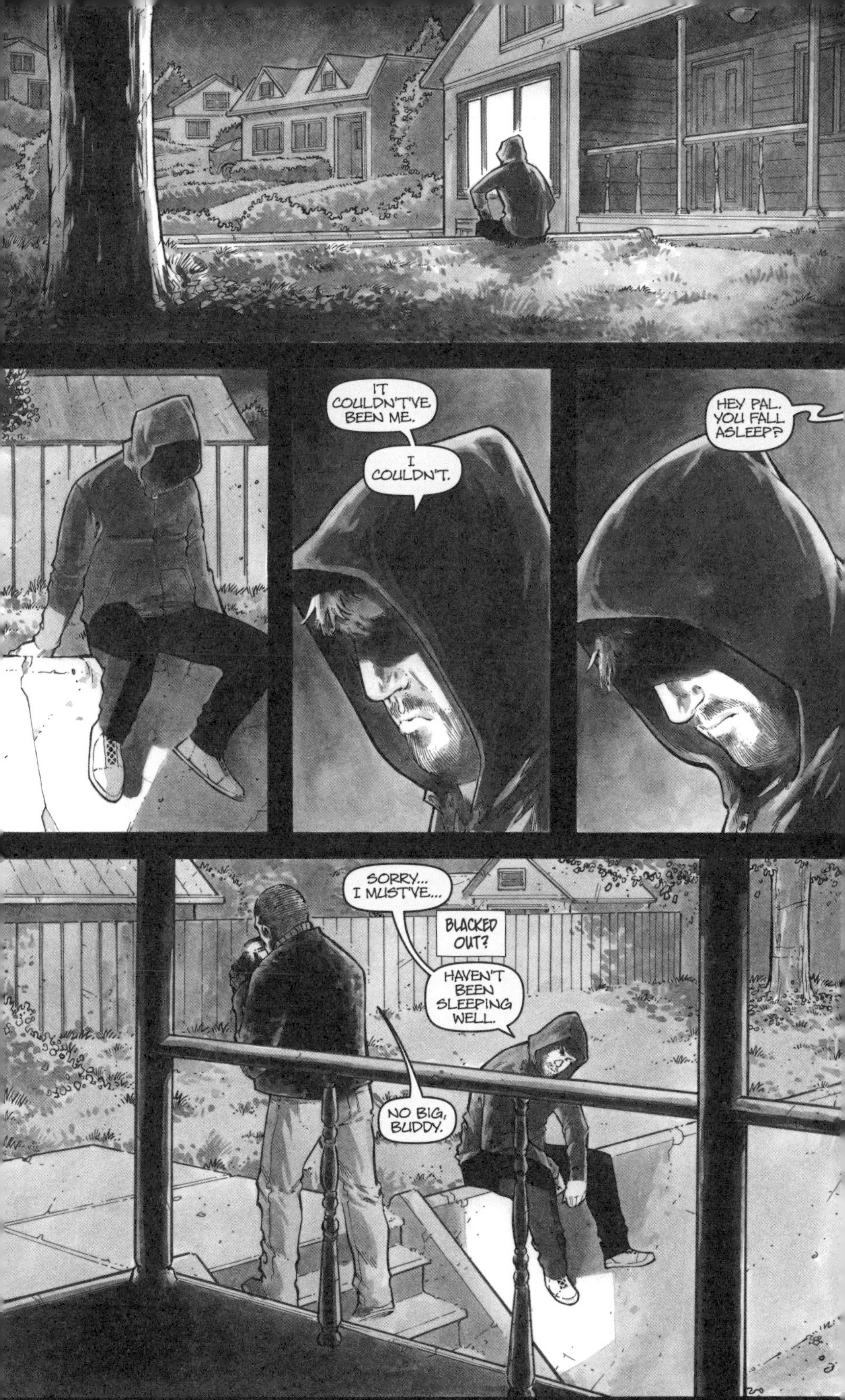
IT COULDN'T'VE BEEN ME.
I COULDN'T.
HEY PAL. YOU FALL ASLEEP?
SORRY... I MUST'VE...
BLACKED OUT?
HAVEN'T BEEN SLEEPING WELL.
NO BIG, BUDDY.

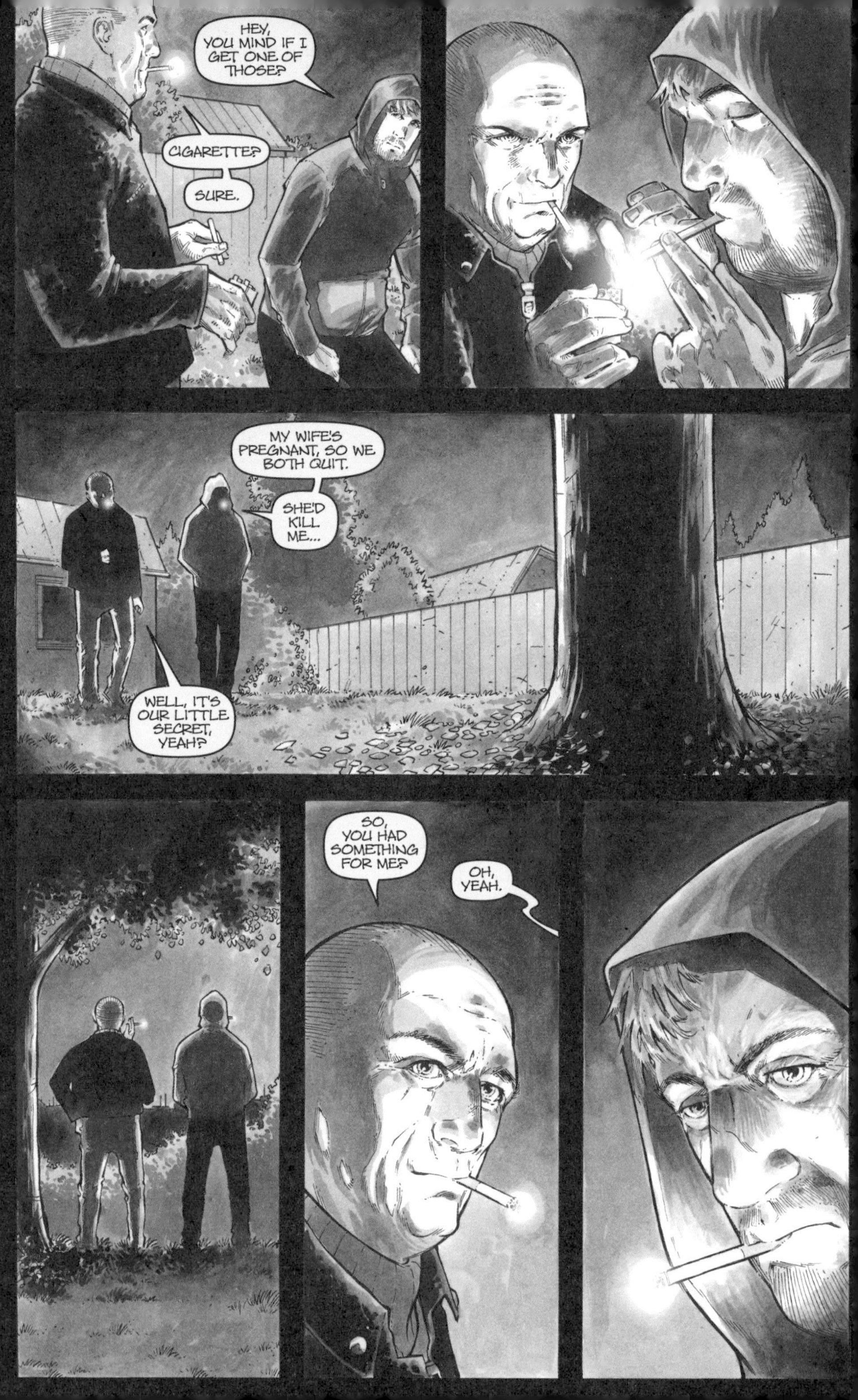
HEY, YOU MIND IF I GET ONE OF THOSE?
CIGARETTE?
SURE.
MY WIFE'S PREGNANT, SO WE BOTH QUIT.
SHE'D KILL ME...
WELL, IT'S OUR LITTLE SECRET, YEAH?
SO, YOU HAD SOMETHING FOR ME?
OH, YEAH.

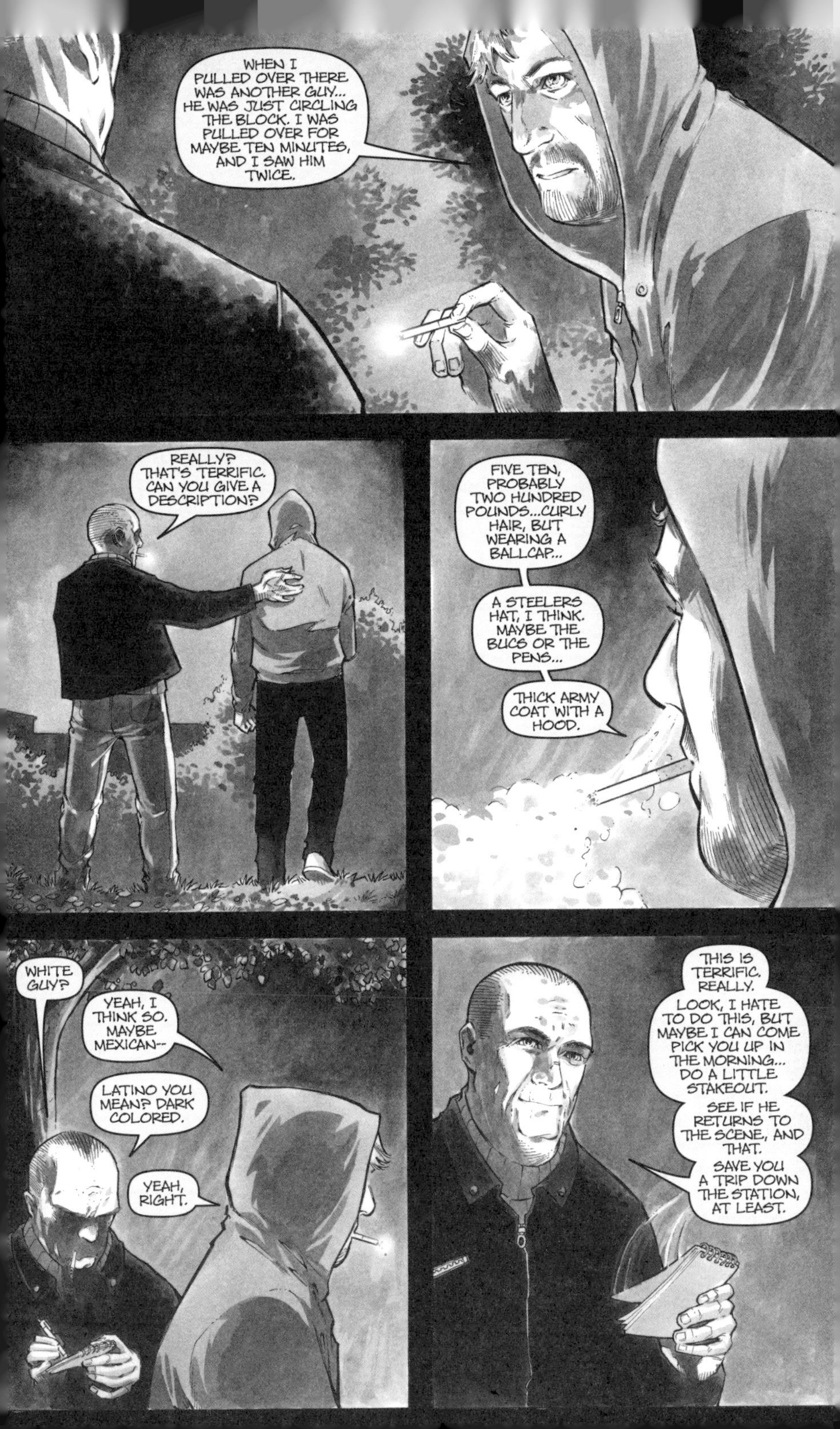
WHEN I PULLED OVER THERE WAS ANOTHER GUY... HE WAS JUST CIRCLING THE BLOCK. I WAS PULLED OVER FOR MAYBE TEN MINUTES, AND I SAW HIM TWICE.
REALLY? THAT'S TERRIFIC. CAN YOU GIVE A DESCRIPTION?
FIVE TEN, PROBABLY TWO HUNDRED POUNDS...CURLY HAIR, BUT WEARING A BALLCAP...
A STEELERS HAT, I THINK. MAYBE THE BUCS OR THE PENS...
THICK ARMY COAT WITH A HOOD.
WHITE GUY?
YEAH, I THINK SO. MAYBE MEXICAN--
LATINO YOU MEAN? DARK COLORED.
YEAH, RIGHT.
THIS IS TERRIFIC. REALLY.
LOOK, I HATE TO DO THIS, BUT MAYBE I CAN COME PICK YOU UP IN THE MORNING... DO A LITTLE STAKEOUT.
SEE IF HE RETURNS TO THE SCENE, AND THAT.
SAVE YOU A TRIP DOWN THE STATION, AT LEAST.

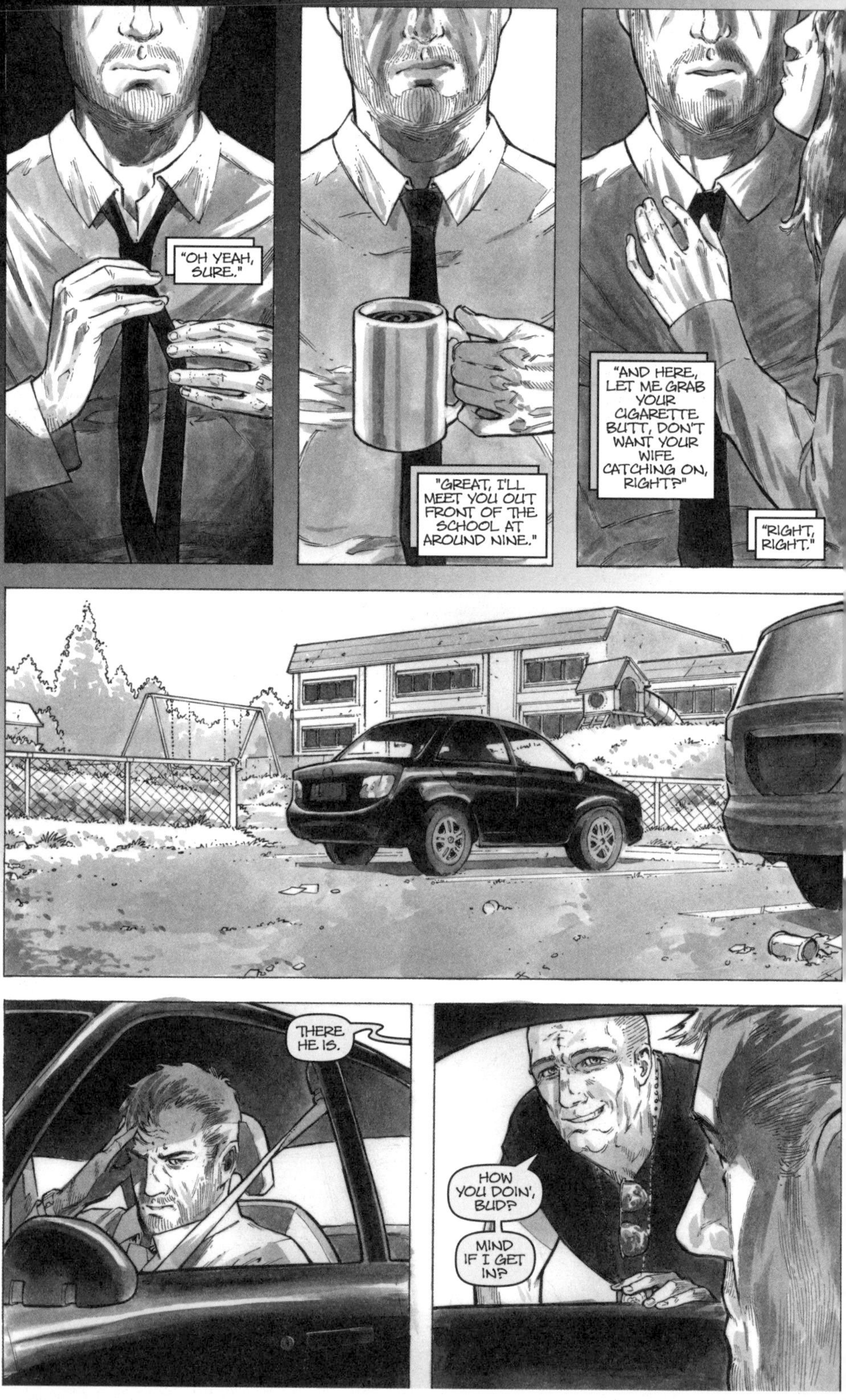
"OH YEAH, SURE."
"GREAT, I'LL MEET YOU OUT FRONT OF THE SCHOOL AT AROUND NINE."
"AND HERE, LET ME GRAB YOUR CIGARETTE BUTT, DON'T WANT YOUR WIFE CATCHING ON, RIGHT?"
"RIGHT, RIGHT."
THERE HE IS.
HOW YOU DOIN', BUD?
MIND IF I GET IN?

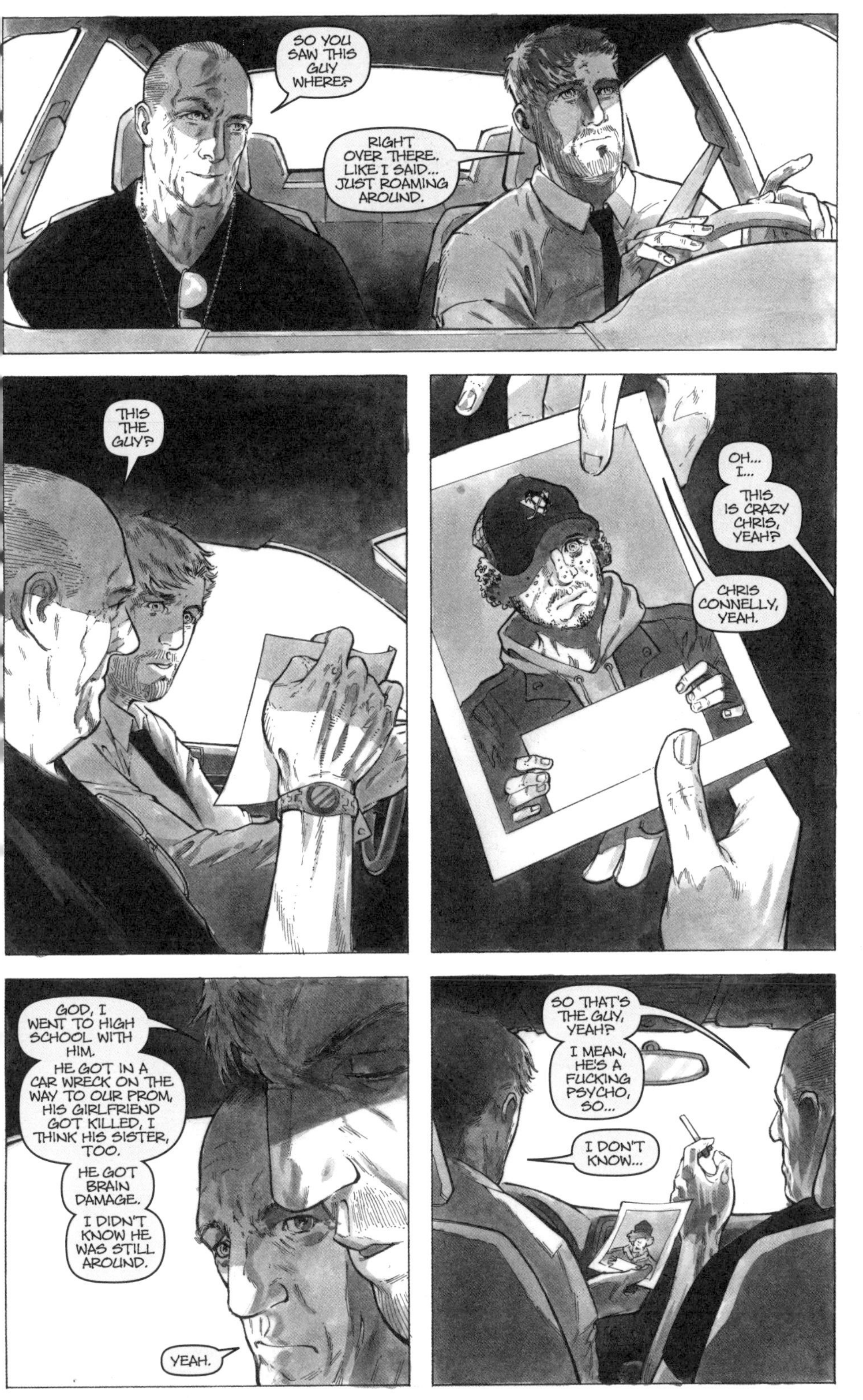
SO YOU SAW THIS GUY WHERE?
RIGHT OVER THERE. LIKE I SAID... JUST ROAMING AROUND.
THIS THE GUY?
OH... I...
THIS IS CRAZY CHRIS, YEAH?
CHRIS CONNELLY, YEAH.
GOD, I WENT TO HIGH SCHOOL WITH HIM.
HE GOT IN A CAR WRECK ON THE WAY TO OUR PROM, HIS GIRLFRIEND GOT KILLED, I THINK HIS SISTER, TOO.
HE GOT BRAIN DAMAGE.
I DIDN'T KNOW HE WAS STILL AROUND.
YEAH.
SO THAT'S THE GUY, YEAH?
I MEAN, HE'S A FUCKING PSYCHO, SO...
I DON'T KNOW...

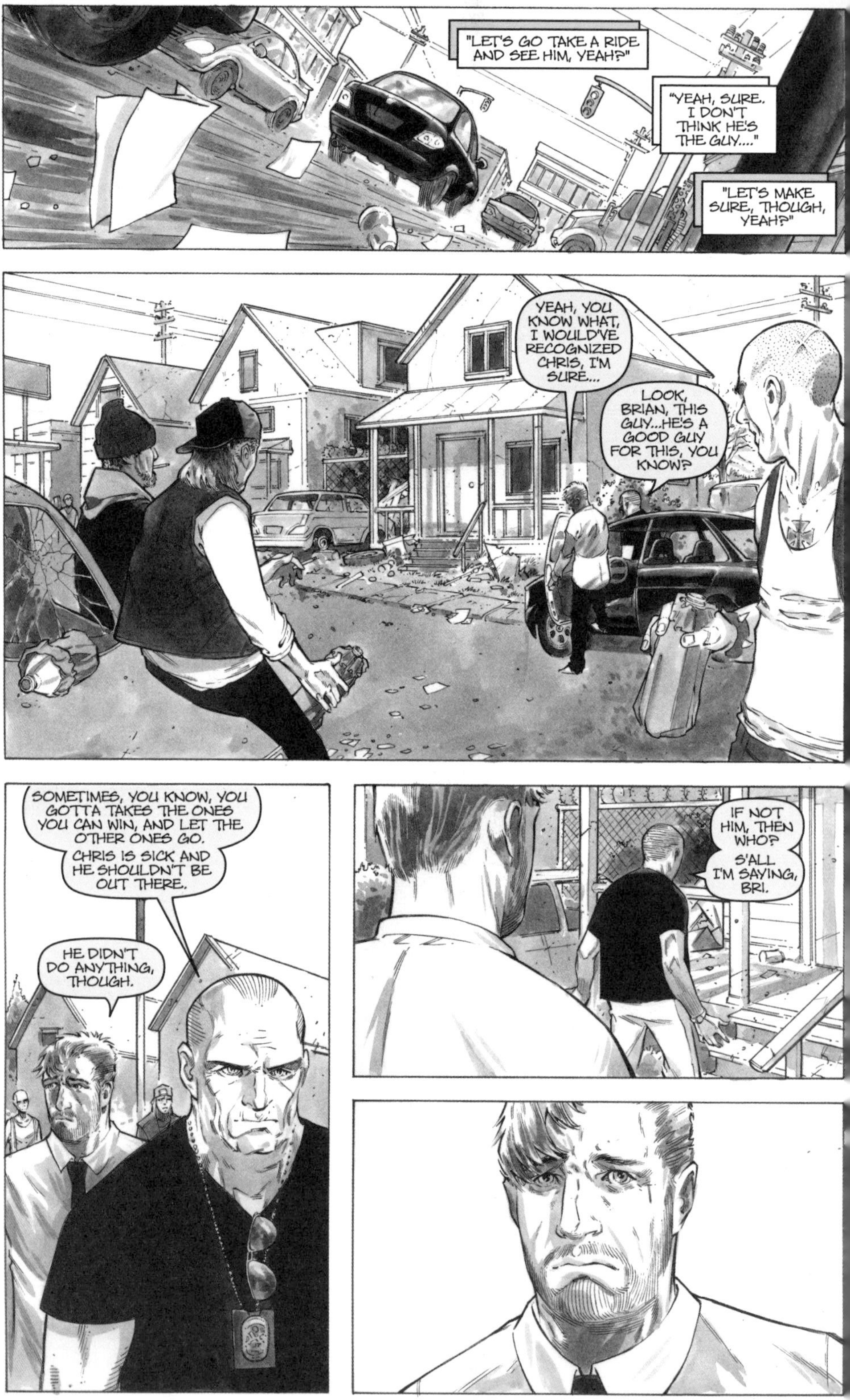
"LET'S GO TAKE A RIDE AND SEE HIM, YEAH?"
"YEAH, SURE. I DON'T THINK HE'S THE GUY...."
"LET'S MAKE SURE, THOUGH, YEAH?"
YEAH, YOU KNOW WHAT, I WOULD'VE RECOGNIZED CHRIS, I'M SURE...
LOOK, BRIAN, THIS GUY...HE'S A GOOD GUY FOR THIS, YOU KNOW?
SOMETIMES, YOU KNOW, YOU GOTTA TAKES THE ONES YOU CAN WIN, AND LET THE OTHER ONES GO.
CHRIS IS SICK AND HE SHOULDN'T BE OUT THERE.
HE DIDN'T DO ANYTHING, THOUGH.
IF NOT HIM, THEN WHO?
S'ALL I'M SAYING, BRI.

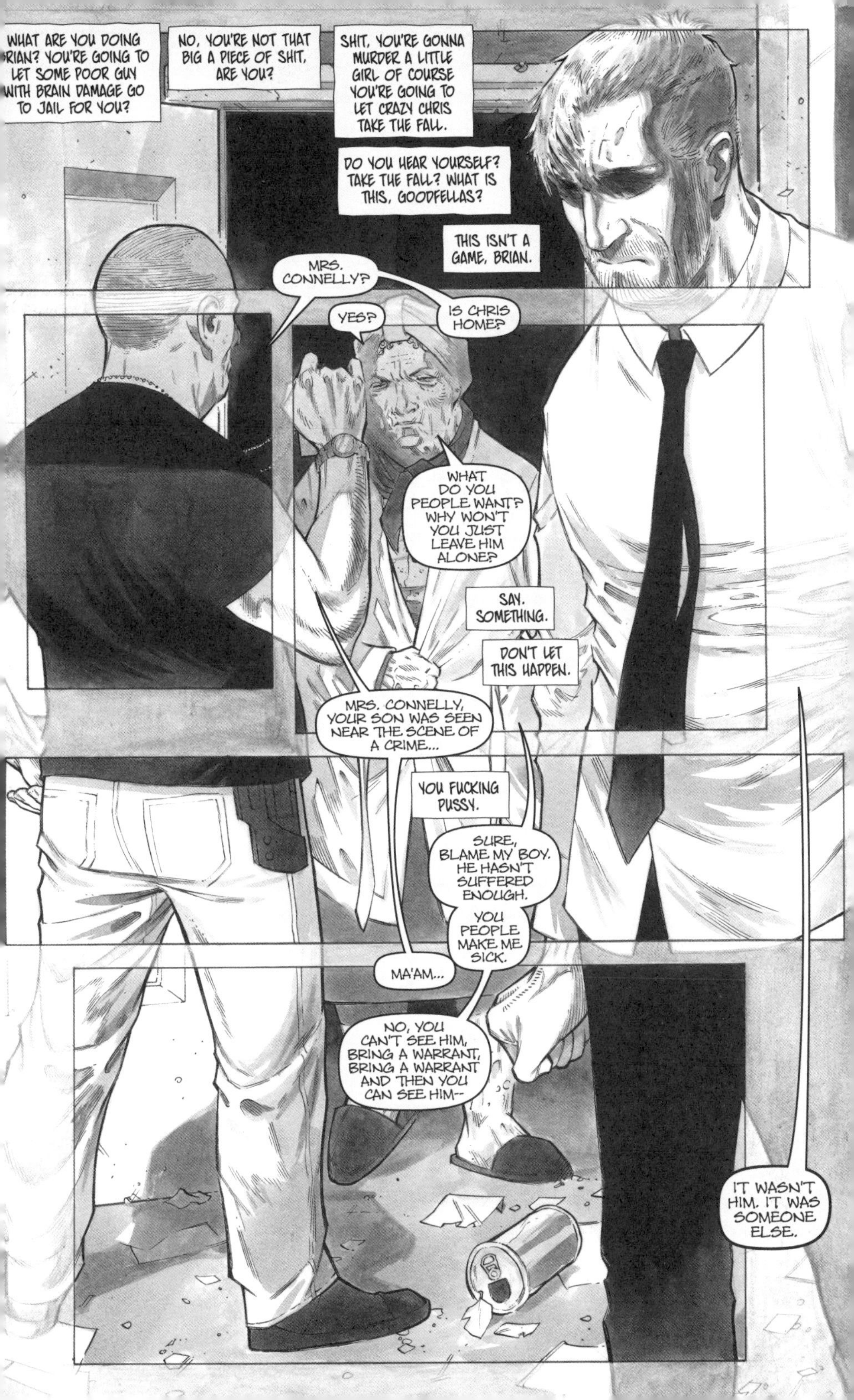
WHAT ARE YOU DOING BRIAN? YOU'RE GOING TO LET SOME POOR GUY WITH BRAIN DAMAGE GO TO JAIL FOR YOU?
NO, YOU'RE NOT THAT BIG A PIECE OF SHIT, ARE YOU?
SHIT, YOU'RE GONNA MURDER A LITTLE GIRL OF COURSE YOU'RE GOING TO LET CRAZY CHRIS TAKE THE FALL.
DO YOU HEAR YOURSELF? TAKE THE FALL? WHAT IS THIS, GOODFELLAS?
THIS ISN'T A GAME, BRIAN.
MRS. CONNELLY?
YES?
IS CHRIS HOME?
WHAT DO YOU PEOPLE WANT? WHY WON'T YOU JUST LEAVE HIM ALONE?
SAY. SOMETHING.
DON'T LET THIS HAPPEN.
MRS. CONNELLY, YOUR SON WAS SEEN NEAR THE SCENE OF A CRIME...
YOU FUCKING PUSSY.
SURE, BLAME MY BOY. HE HASN'T SUFFERED ENOUGH.
YOU PEOPLE MAKE ME SICK.
MA'AM...
NO, YOU CAN'T SEE HIM, BRING A WARRANT, BRING A WARRANT AND THEN YOU CAN SEE HIM--
IT WASN'T HIM. IT WAS SOMEONE ELSE.

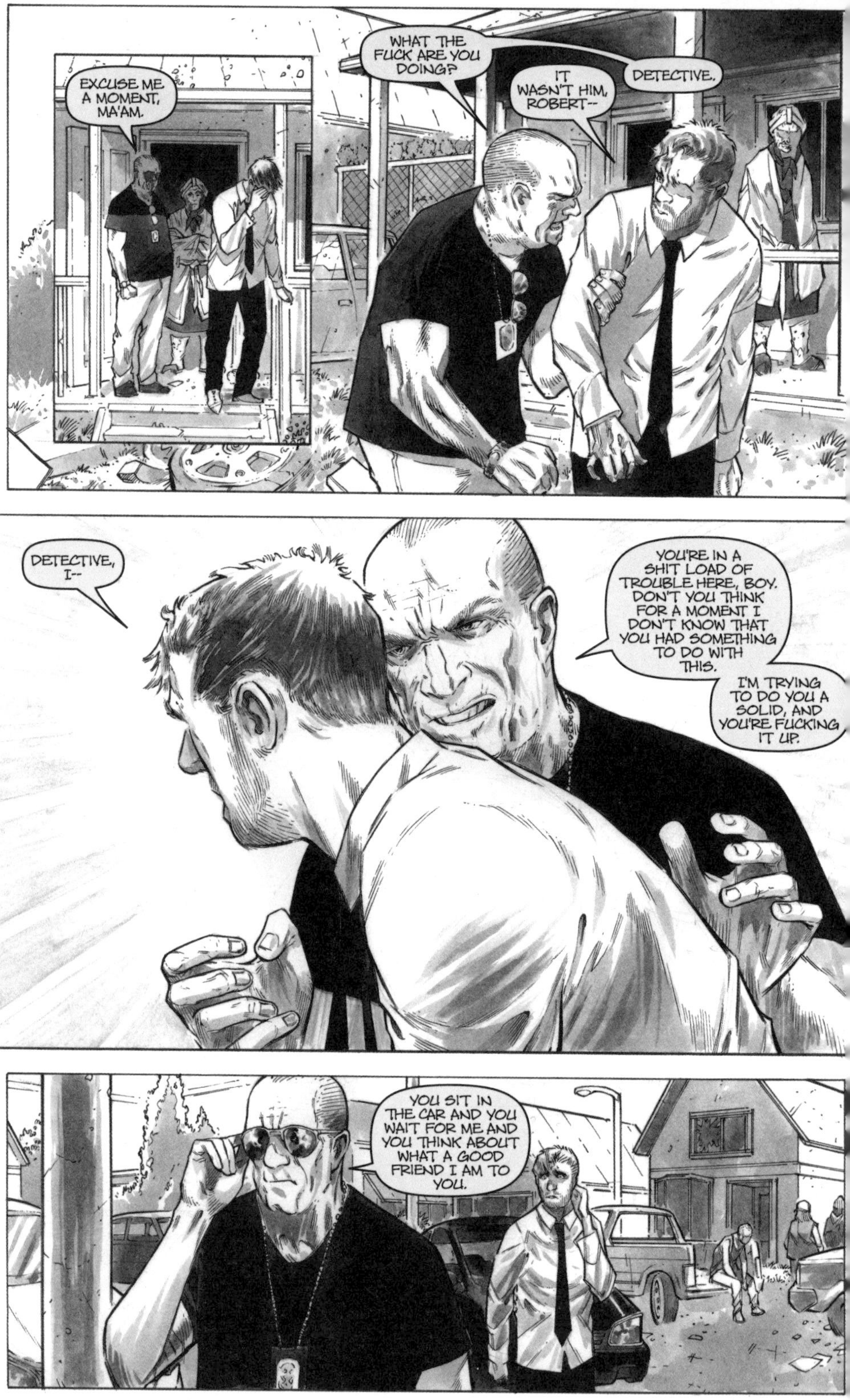
EXCUSE ME A MOMENT, MA'AM.
WHAT THE FUCK ARE YOU DOING?
DETECTIVE.
IT WASN'T HIM, ROBERT--
DETECTIVE, I--
YOU'RE IN A SHIT LOAD OF TROUBLE HERE, BOY. DON'T YOU THINK FOR A MOMENT I DON'T KNOW THAT YOU HAD SOMETHING TO DO WITH THIS.
I'M TRYING TO DO YOU A SOLID, AND YOU'RE FUCKING IT UP.
YOU SIT IN THE CAR AND YOU WAIT FOR ME AND YOU THINK ABOUT WHAT A GOOD FRIEND I AM TO YOU.

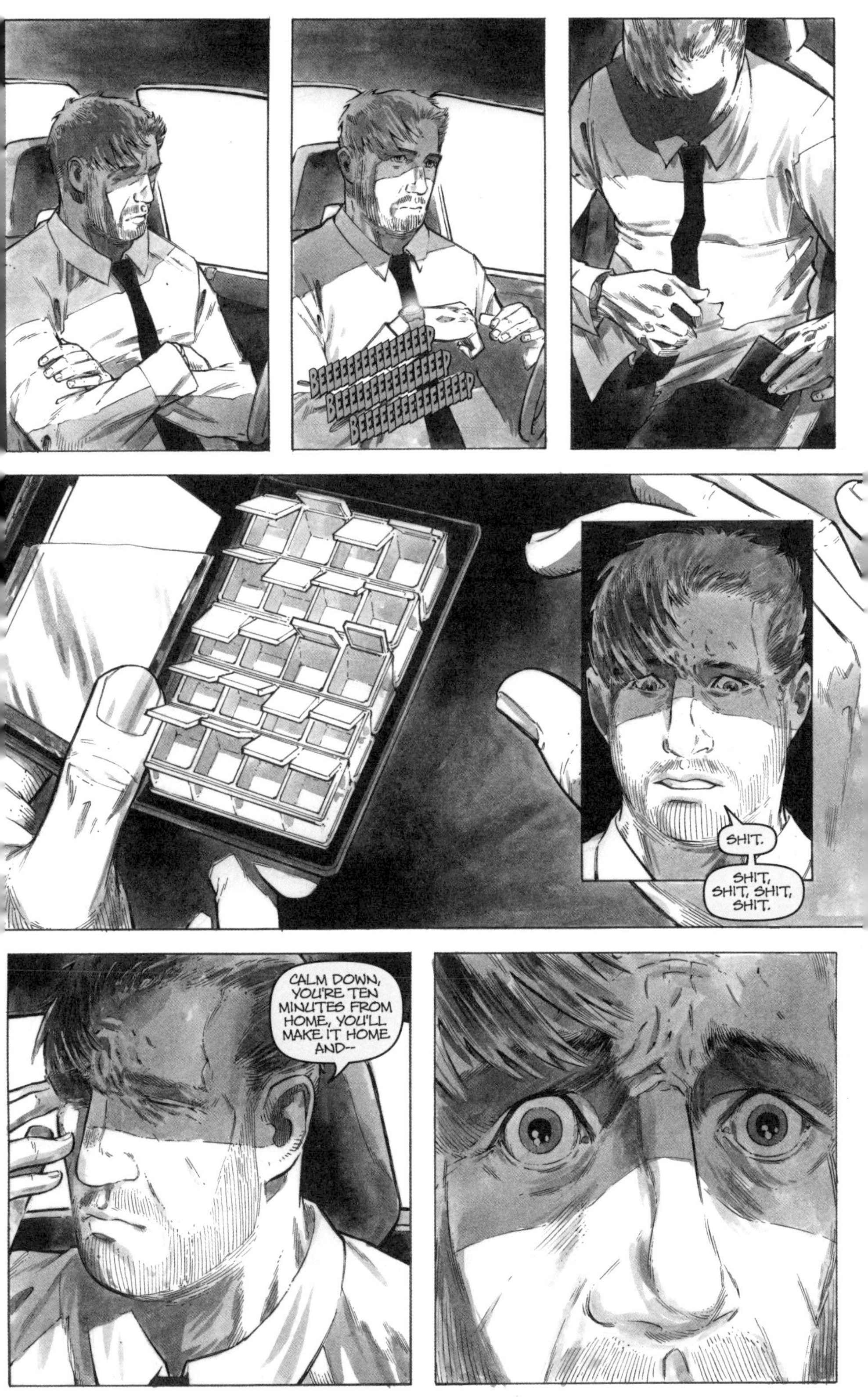
BEEEEEEEEEEEEEEP
BEEEEEEEEEEEEEEEP
BEEEEEEEEEEEEEEEP
SHIT.
SHIT, SHIT, SHIT, SHIT.
CALM DOWN, YOU'RE TEN MINUTES FROM HOME, YOU'LL MAKE IT HOME AND--

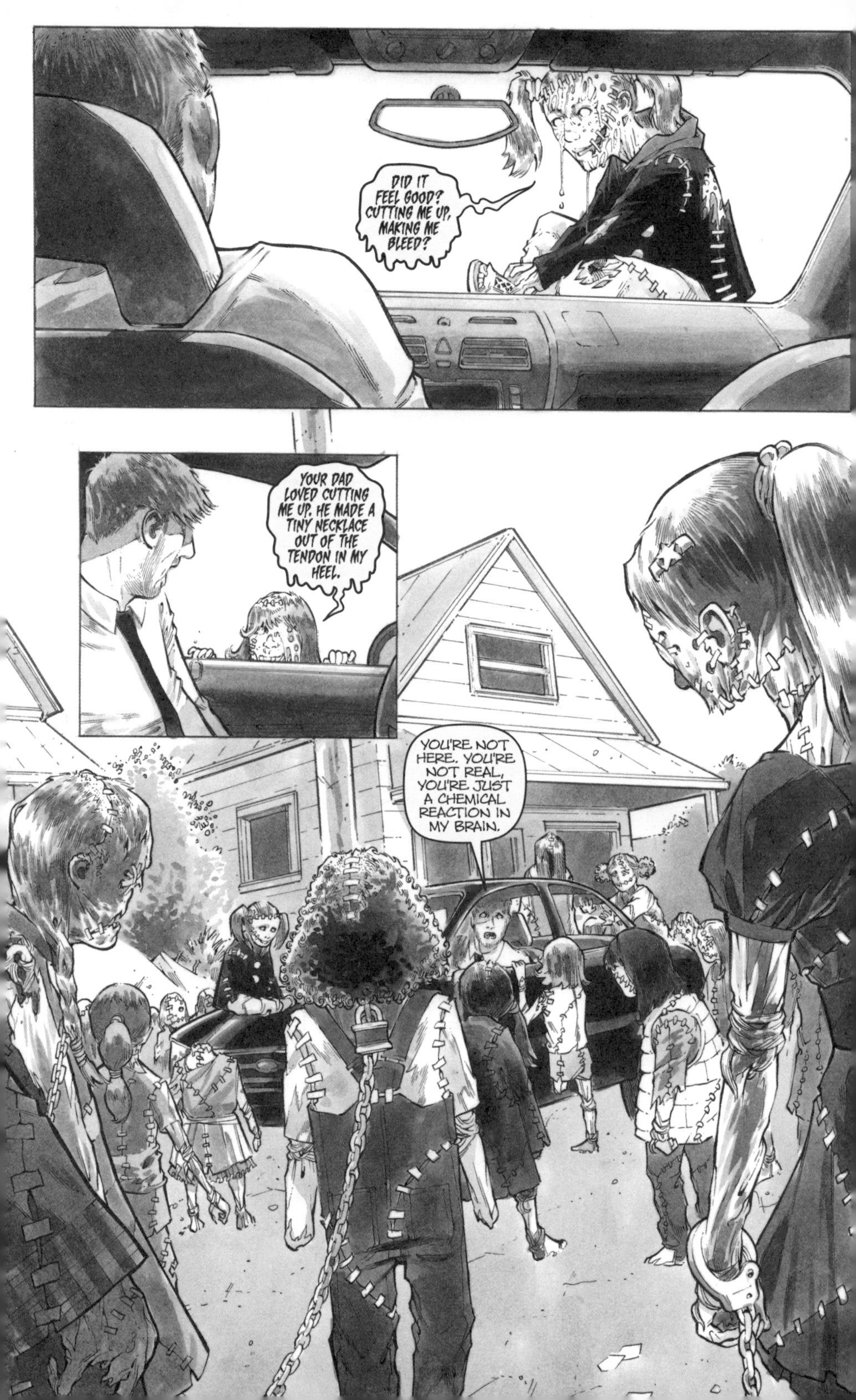
DID IT FEEL GOOD? CUTTING ME UP, MAKING ME BLEED?
YOUR DAD LOVED CUTTING ME UP. HE MADE A TINY NECKLACE OUT OF THE TENDON IN MY HEEL.
YOU'RE NOT HERE. YOU'RE NOT REAL, YOU'RE JUST A CHEMICAL REACTION IN MY BRAIN.

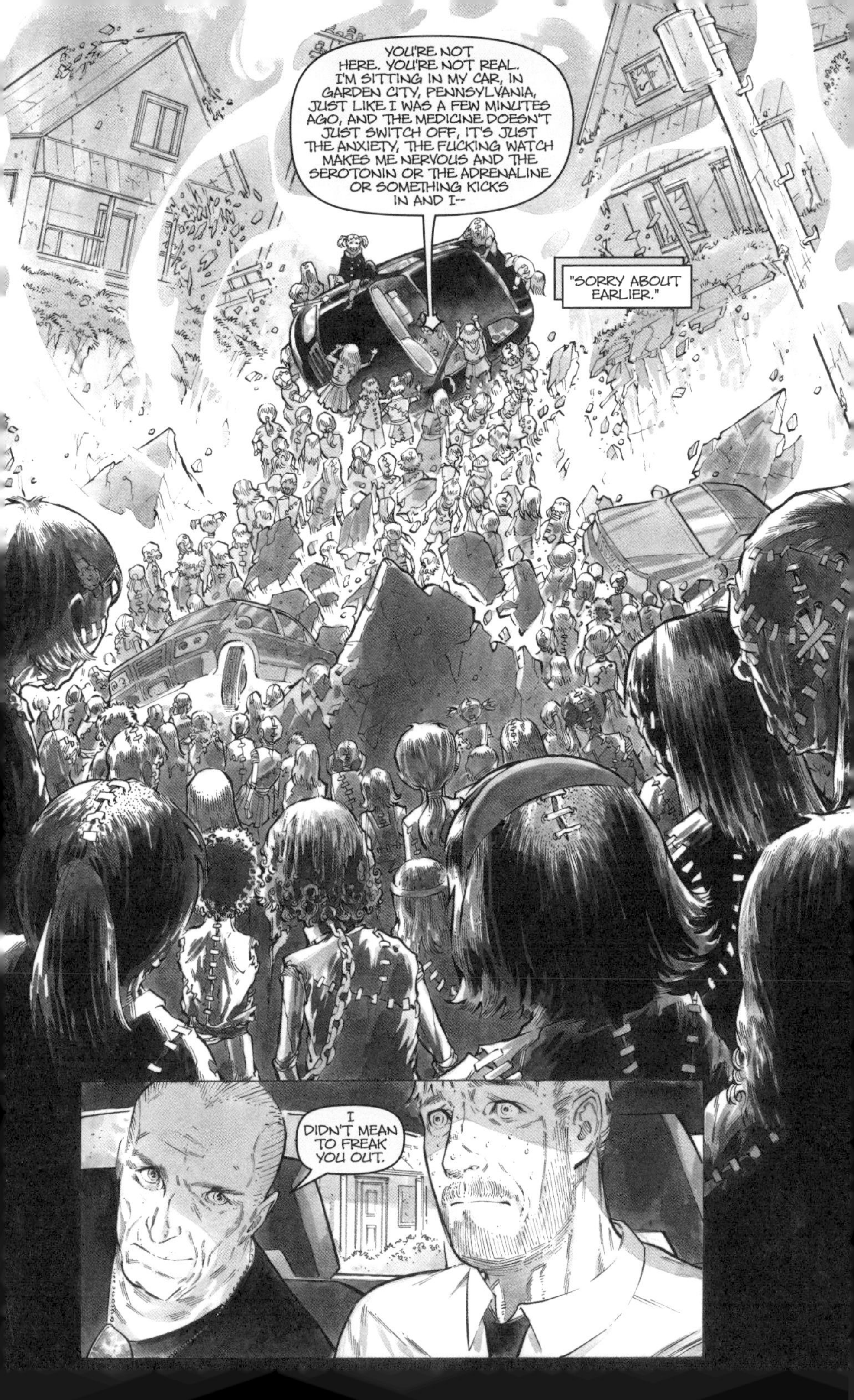
YOU'RE NOT HERE. YOU'RE NOT REAL. I'M SITTING IN MY CAR, IN GARDEN CITY, PENNSYLVANIA, JUST LIKE I WAS A FEW MINUTES AGO, AND THE MEDICINE DOESN'T JUST SWITCH OFF, IT'S JUST THE ANXIETY, THE FUCKING WATCH MAKES ME NERVOUS AND THE SEROTONIN OR THE ADRENALINE OR SOMETHING KICKS IN AND I--
"SORRY ABOUT EARLIER."
I DIDN'T MEAN TO FREAK YOU OUT.

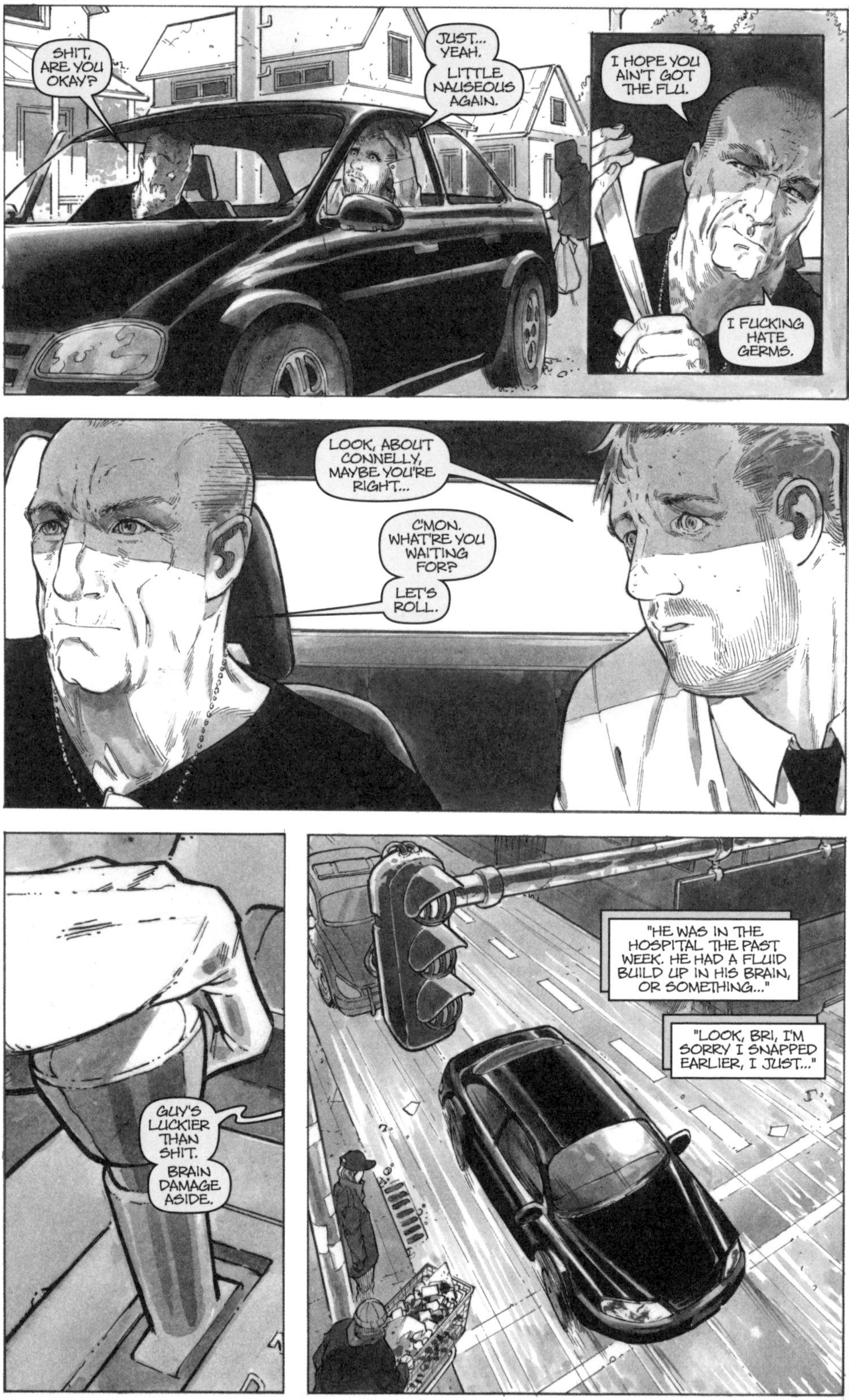
SHIT, ARE YOU OKAY?
JUST... YEAH.
LITTLE NAUSEOUS AGAIN.
I HOPE YOU AIN'T GOT THE FLU.
I FUCKING HATE GERMS.
LOOK, ABOUT CONNELLY, MAYBE YOU'RE RIGHT...
C'MON. WHAT'RE YOU WAITING FOR?
LET'S ROLL.
GUY'S LUCKIER THAN SHIT.
BRAIN DAMAGE ASIDE.
"HE WAS IN THE HOSPITAL THE PAST WEEK. HE HAD A FLUID BUILD UP IN HIS BRAIN, OR SOMETHING..."
"LOOK, BRI, I'M SORRY I SNAPPED EARLIER, I JUST..."

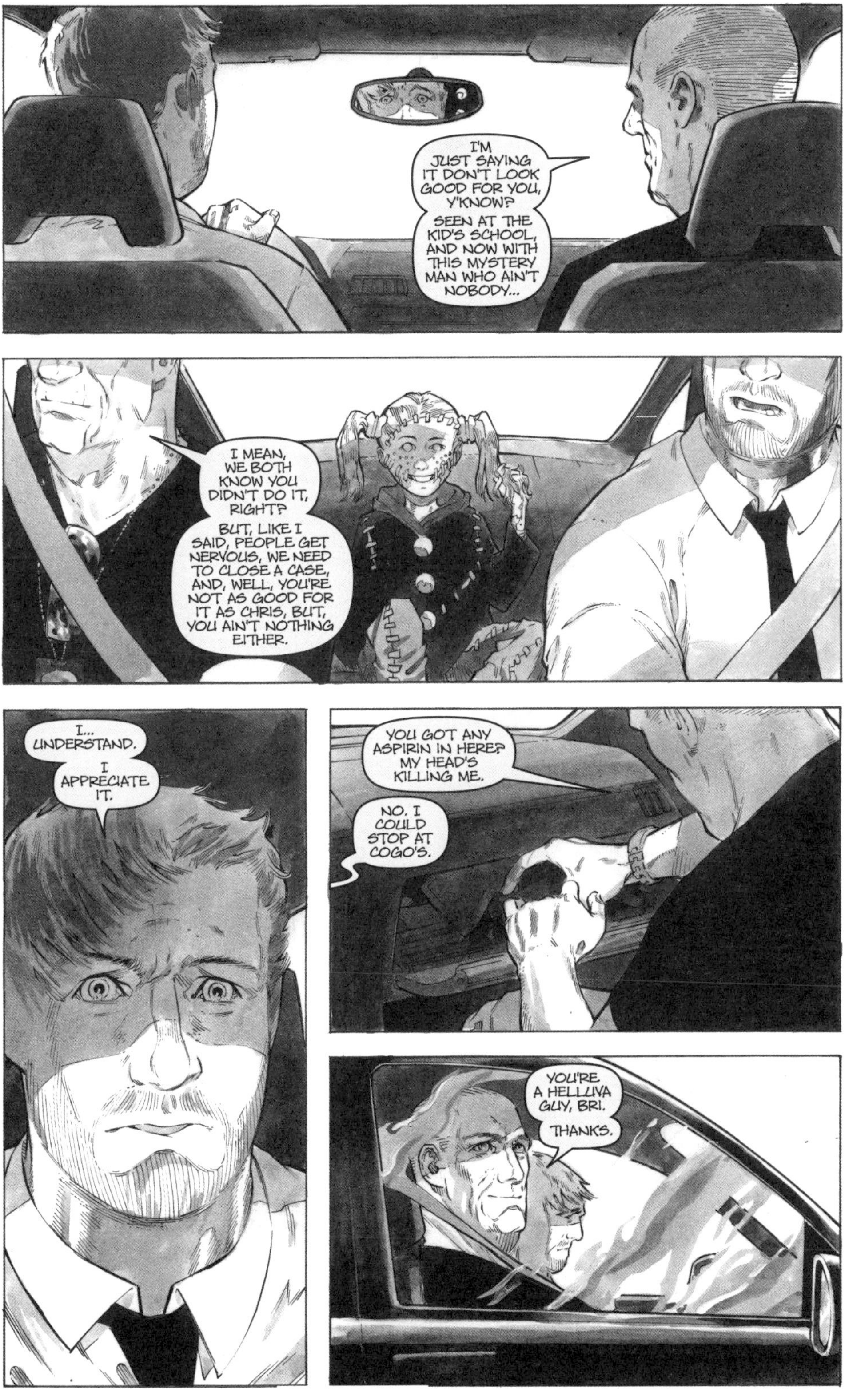
I'M JUST SAYING IT DON'T LOOK GOOD FOR YOU, Y'KNOW?
SEEN AT THE KID'S SCHOOL, AND NOW WITH THIS MYSTERY MAN WHO AIN'T NOBODY...
I MEAN, WE BOTH KNOW YOU DIDN'T DO IT, RIGHT?
BUT, LIKE I SAID, PEOPLE GET NERVOUS, WE NEED TO CLOSE A CASE, AND, WELL, YOU'RE NOT AS GOOD FOR IT AS CHRIS, BUT, YOU AIN'T NOTHING EITHER.
I... UNDERSTAND.
I APPRECIATE IT.
YOU GOT ANY ASPIRIN IN HERE? MY HEAD'S KILLING ME.
NO. I COULD STOP AT COGO'S.
YOU'RE A HELLUVA GUY, BRI.
THANKS.

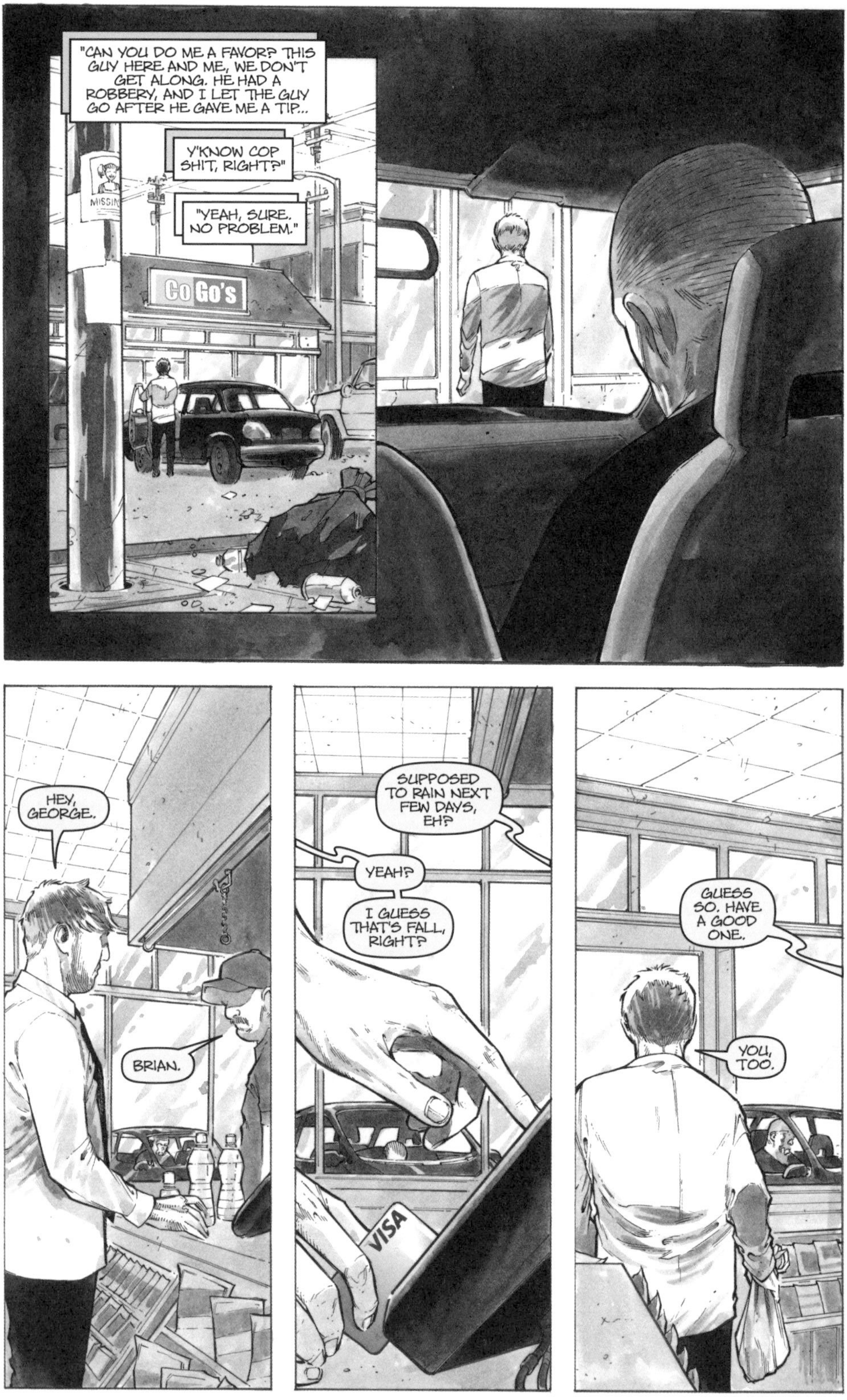
"CAN YOU DO ME A FAVOR? THIS GUY HERE AND ME, WE DON'T GET ALONG. HE HAD A ROBBERY, AND I LET THE GUY GO AFTER HE GAVE ME A TIP...
Y'KNOW COP SHIT, RIGHT?"
"YEAH, SURE. NO PROBLEM."
CoGo's
HEY, GEORGE.
BRIAN.
SUPPOSED TO RAIN NEXT FEW DAYS, EH?
YEAH?
I GUESS THAT'S FALL, RIGHT?
VISA
GUESS SO. HAVE A GOOD ONE.
YOU, TOO.

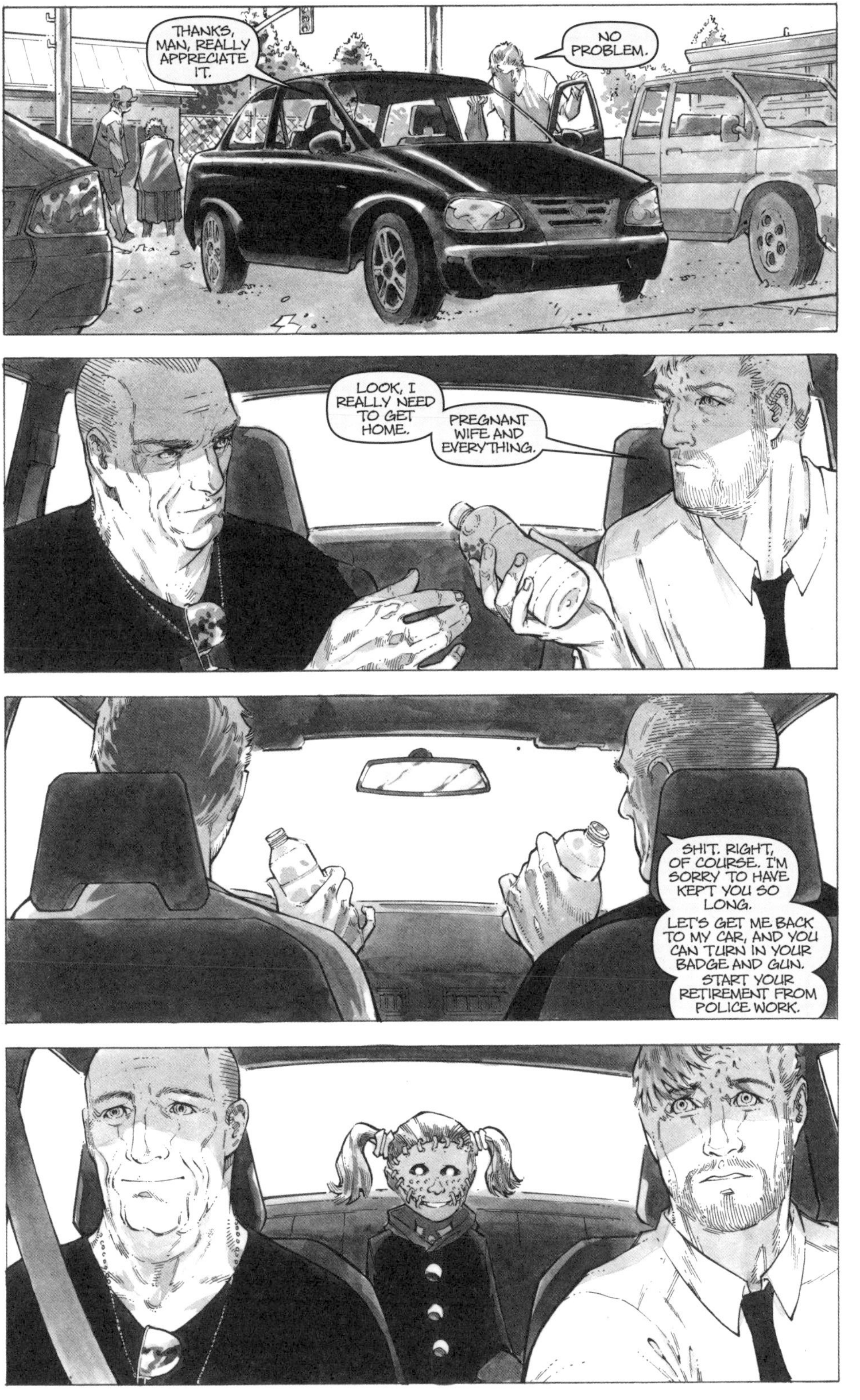
THANKS, MAN, REALLY APPRECIATE IT.
NO PROBLEM.
LOOK, I REALLY NEED TO GET HOME.
PREGNANT WIFE AND EVERYTHING.
SHIT. RIGHT, OF COURSE. I'M SORRY TO HAVE KEPT YOU SO LONG.
LET'S GET ME BACK TO MY CAR, AND YOU CAN TURN IN YOUR BADGE AND GUN.
START YOUR RETIREMENT FROM POLICE WORK.

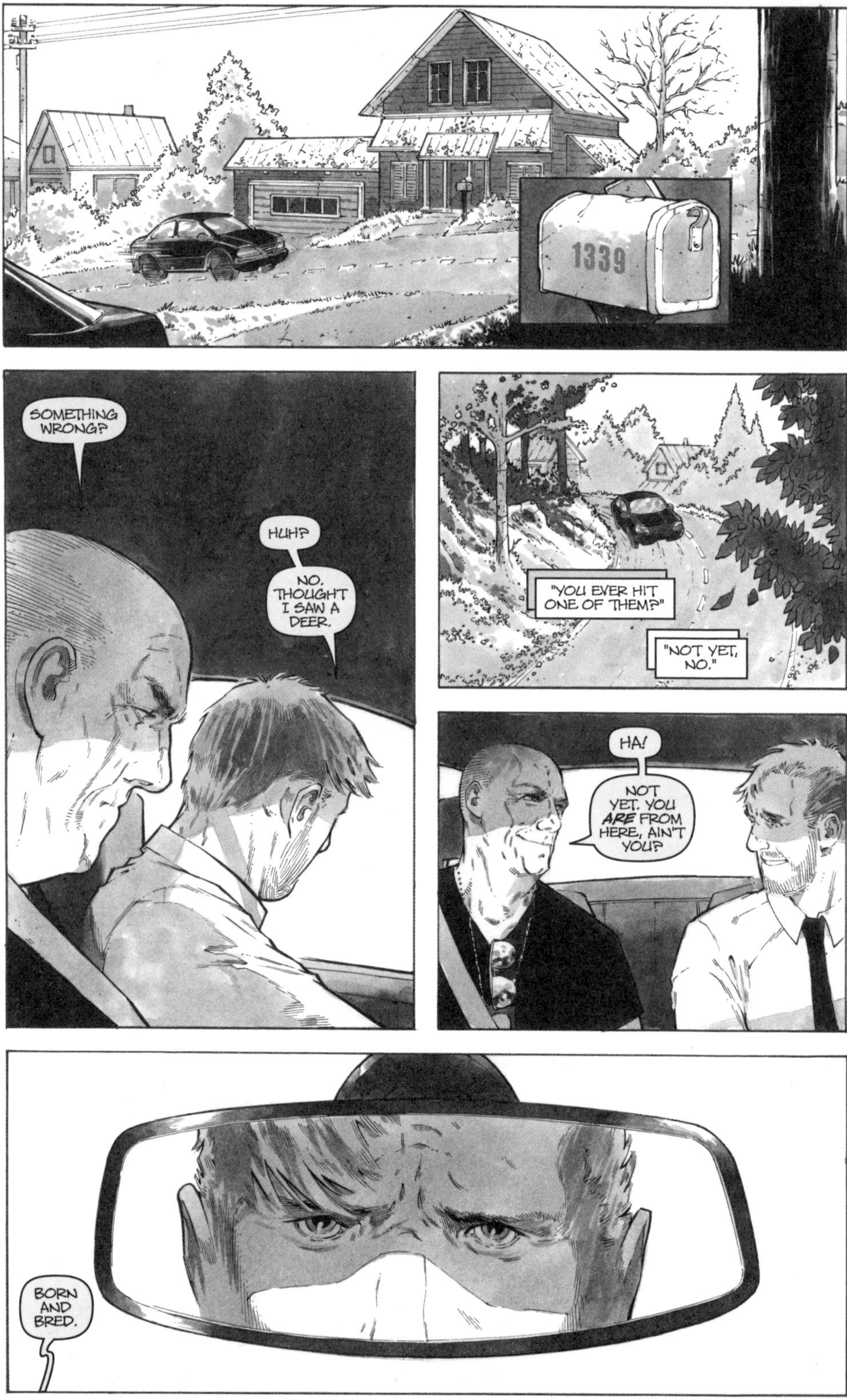
1339
SOMETHING WRONG?
HUH?
NO. THOUGHT I SAW A DEER.
"YOU EVER HIT ONE OF THEM?"
"NOT YET, NO."
HA!
NOT YET. YOU *ARE* FROM HERE, AIN'T YOU?
BORN AND BRED.

"WELL, ALRIGHT, HERE WE ARE."

AGAIN, I'M SORRY ABOUT BEFORE--

NO, NO, FORGET IT.

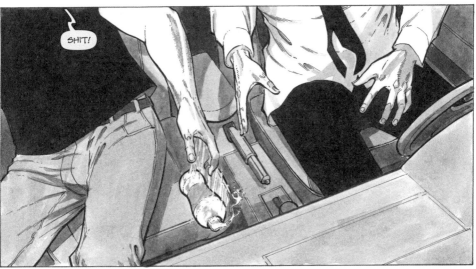

SHIT!

I'M SORRY, BRIAN, I SPILLED THE WHOLE DAMN THING. Y'KNOW, LET ME GO GET SOME NAPKINS OR--

NO, NO, THAT'S FINE. YOU GO CATCH THIS GUY. I'LL TAKE CARE OF IT.

WELL, SHIT, BRIAN, YOU PUT IT THAT WAY...

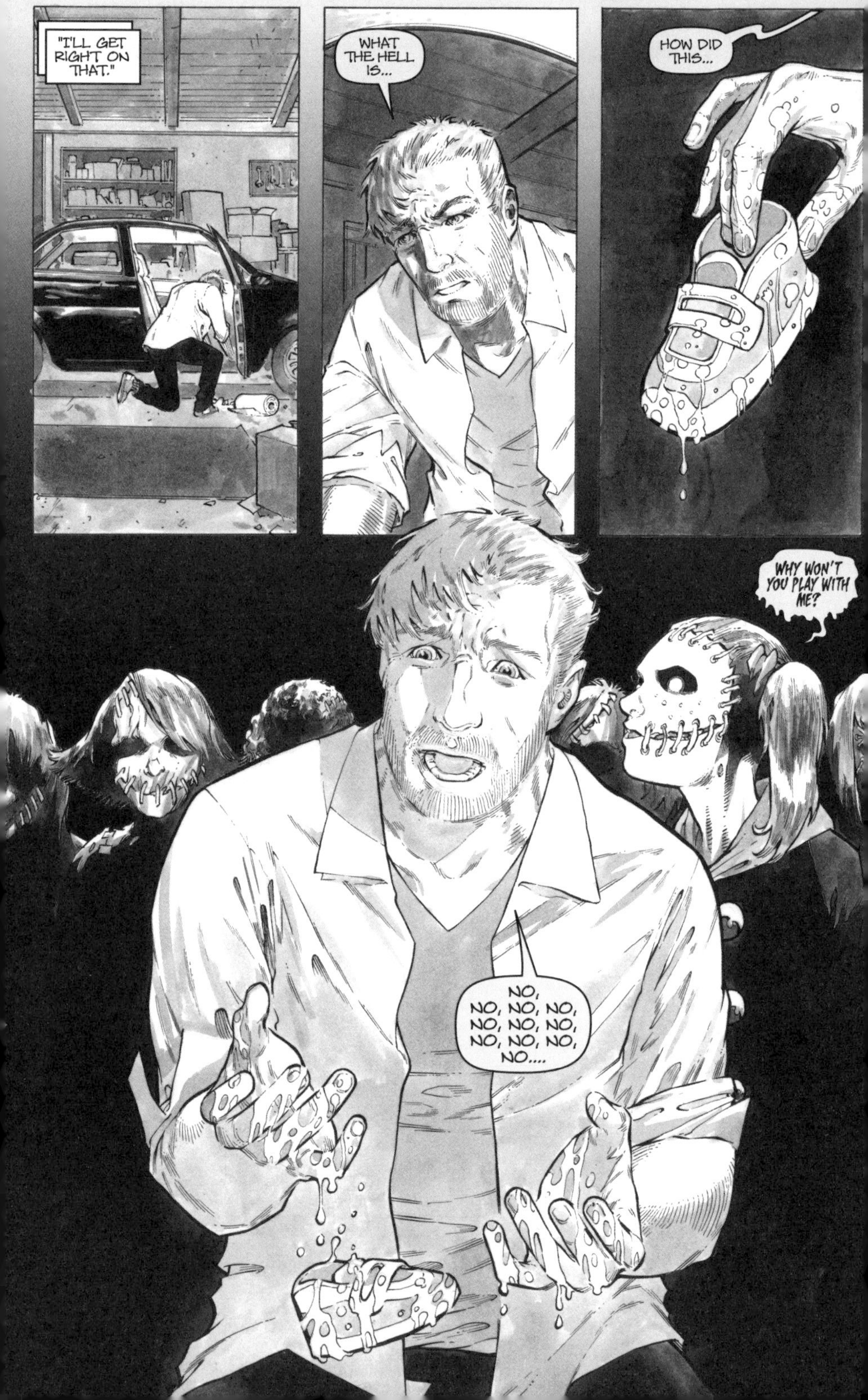
"I'LL GET RIGHT ON THAT."
WHAT THE HELL IS...
HOW DID THIS...
WHY WON'T YOU PLAY WITH ME?
NO, NO, NO, NO, NO, NO, NO, NO, NO, NO, NO....

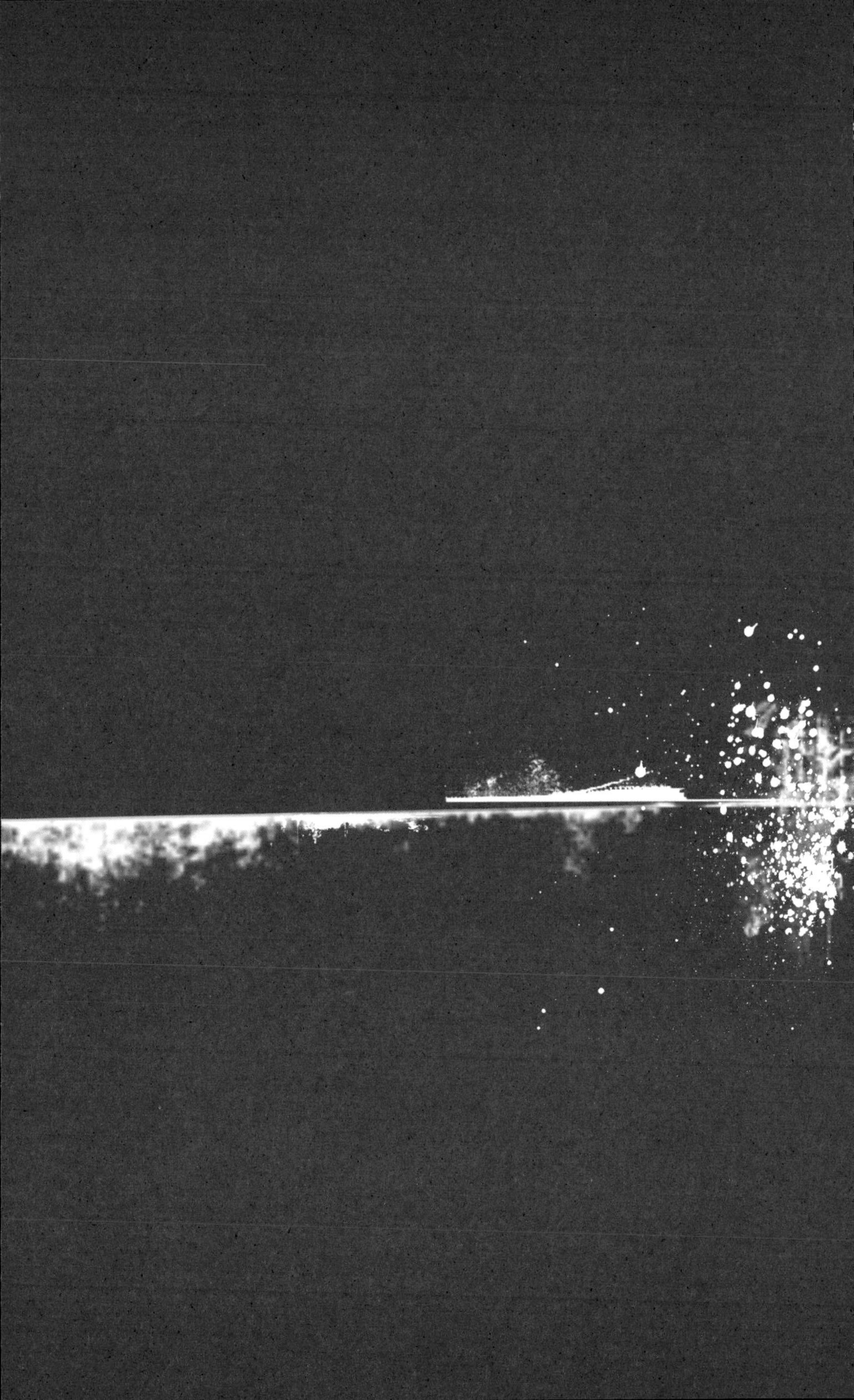

ECHOES™

CHAPTER FOUR

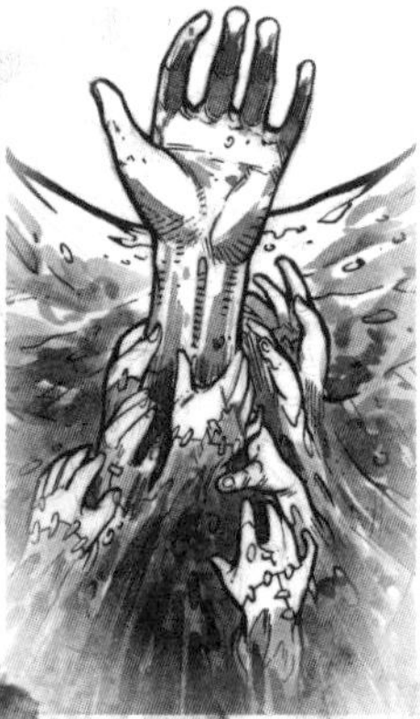

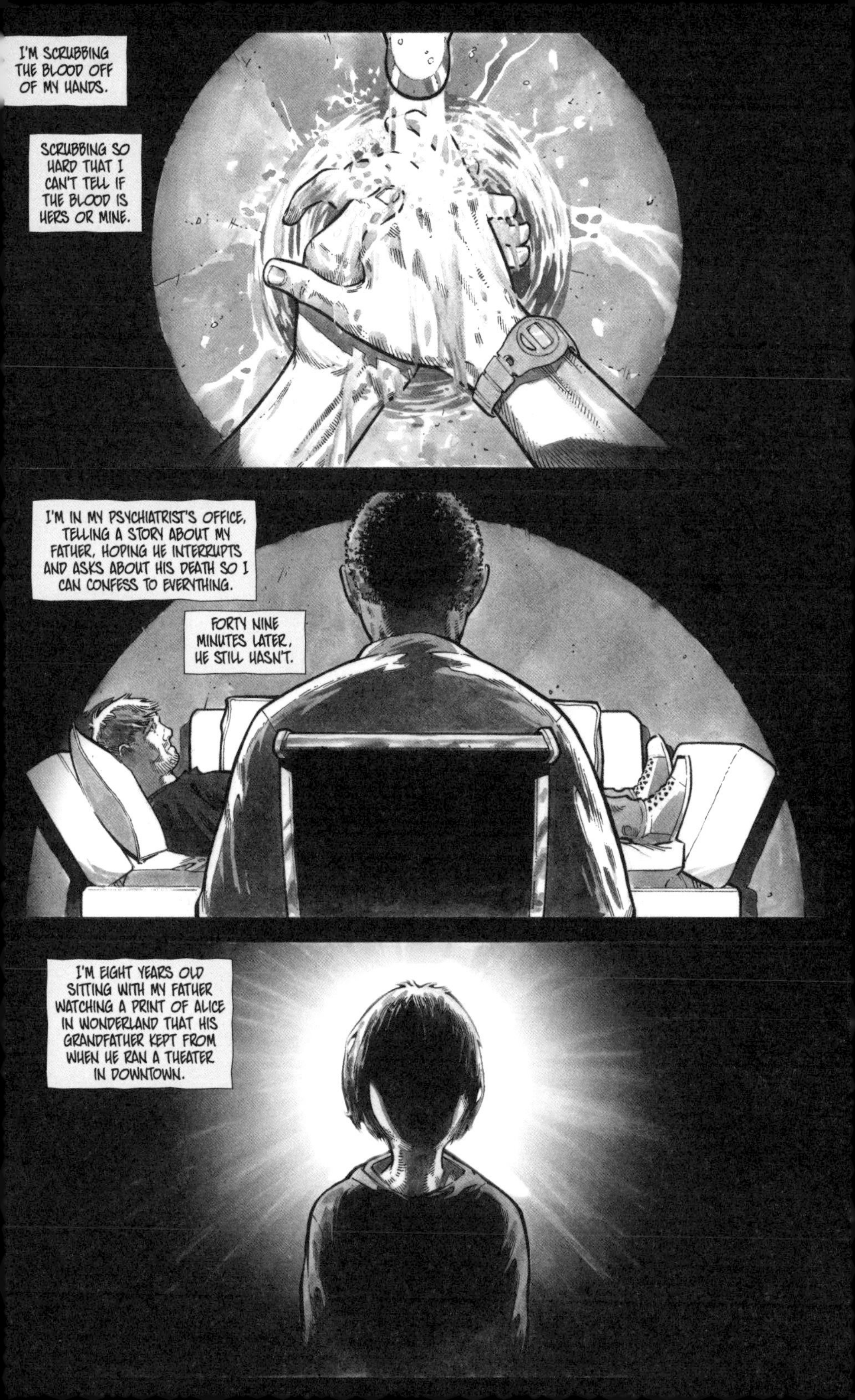

I'M SCRUBBING THE BLOOD OFF OF MY HANDS.
SCRUBBING SO HARD THAT I CAN'T TELL IF THE BLOOD IS HERS OR MINE.
I'M IN MY PSYCHIATRIST'S OFFICE, TELLING A STORY ABOUT MY FATHER, HOPING HE INTERRUPTS AND ASKS ABOUT HIS DEATH SO I CAN CONFESS TO EVERYTHING.
FORTY NINE MINUTES LATER, HE STILL HASN'T.
I'M EIGHT YEARS OLD SITTING WITH MY FATHER WATCHING A PRINT OF ALICE IN WONDERLAND THAT HIS GRANDFATHER KEPT FROM WHEN HE RAN A THEATER IN DOWNTOWN.

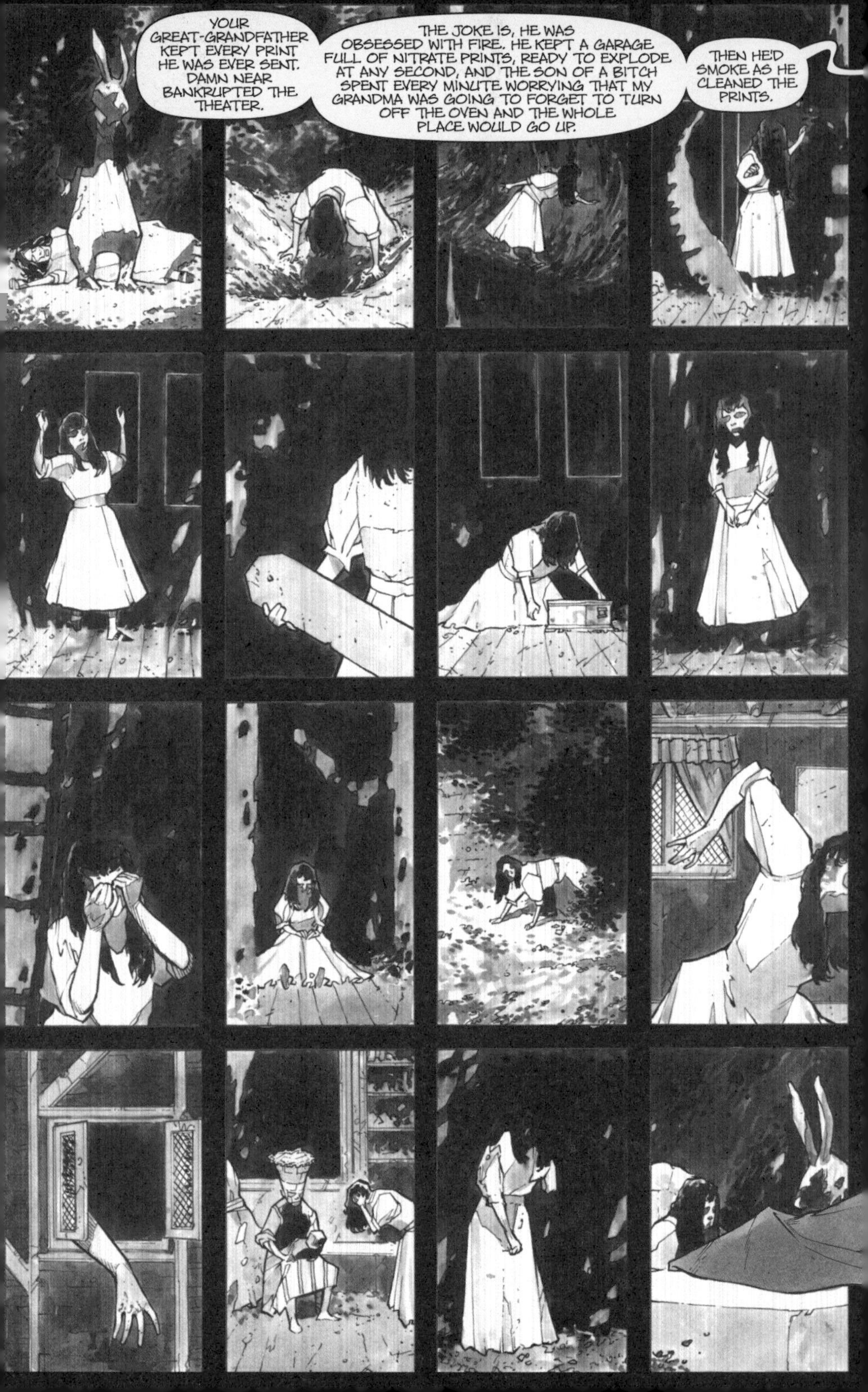
YOUR GREAT-GRANDFATHER KEPT EVERY PRINT HE WAS EVER SENT. DAMN NEAR BANKRUPTED THE THEATER.
THE JOKE IS, HE WAS OBSESSED WITH FIRE. HE KEPT A GARAGE FULL OF NITRATE PRINTS, READY TO EXPLODE AT ANY SECOND, AND THE SON OF A BITCH SPENT EVERY MINUTE WORRYING THAT MY GRANDMA WAS GOING TO FORGET TO TURN OFF THE OVEN AND THE WHOLE PLACE WOULD GO UP.
THEN HE'D SMOKE AS HE CLEANED THE PRINTS.

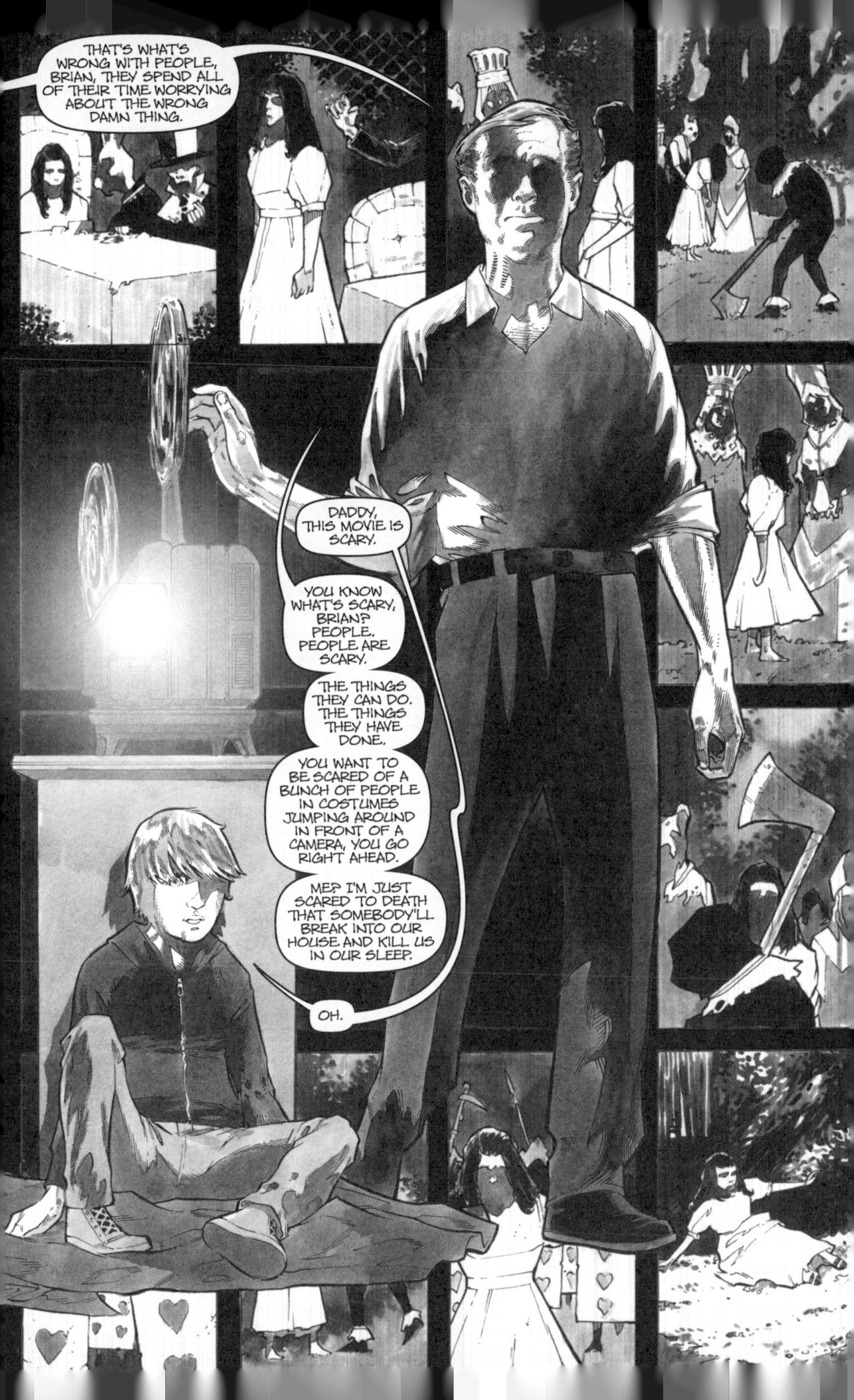
THAT'S WHAT'S WRONG WITH PEOPLE, BRIAN, THEY SPEND ALL OF THEIR TIME WORRYING ABOUT THE WRONG DAMN THING.
DADDY, THIS MOVIE IS SCARY.
YOU KNOW WHAT'S SCARY, BRIAN? PEOPLE. PEOPLE ARE SCARY.
THE THINGS THEY CAN DO. THE THINGS THEY HAVE DONE.
YOU WANT TO BE SCARED OF A BUNCH OF PEOPLE IN COSTUMES JUMPING AROUND IN FRONT OF A CAMERA, YOU GO RIGHT AHEAD.
ME? I'M JUST SCARED TO DEATH THAT SOMEBODY'LL BREAK INTO OUR HOUSE AND KILL US IN OUR SLEEP.
OH.

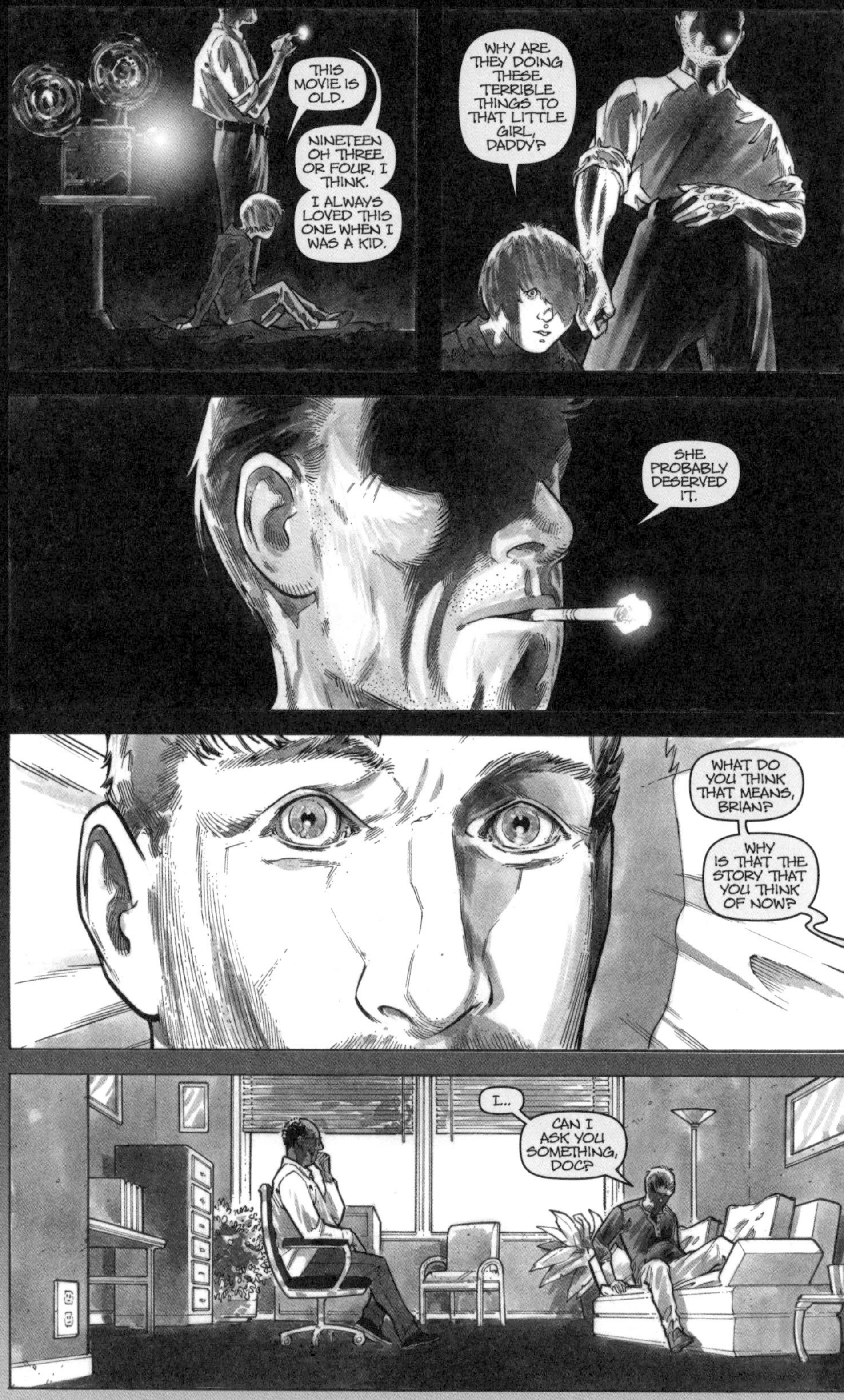
THIS MOVIE IS OLD.
NINETEEN OH THREE OR FOUR, I THINK.
I ALWAYS LOVED THIS ONE WHEN I WAS A KID.
WHY ARE THEY DOING THESE TERRIBLE THINGS TO THAT LITTLE GIRL, DADDY?
SHE PROBABLY DESERVED IT.
WHAT DO YOU THINK THAT MEANS, BRIAN?
WHY IS THAT THE STORY THAT YOU THINK OF NOW?
I...
CAN I ASK YOU SOMETHING, DOC?

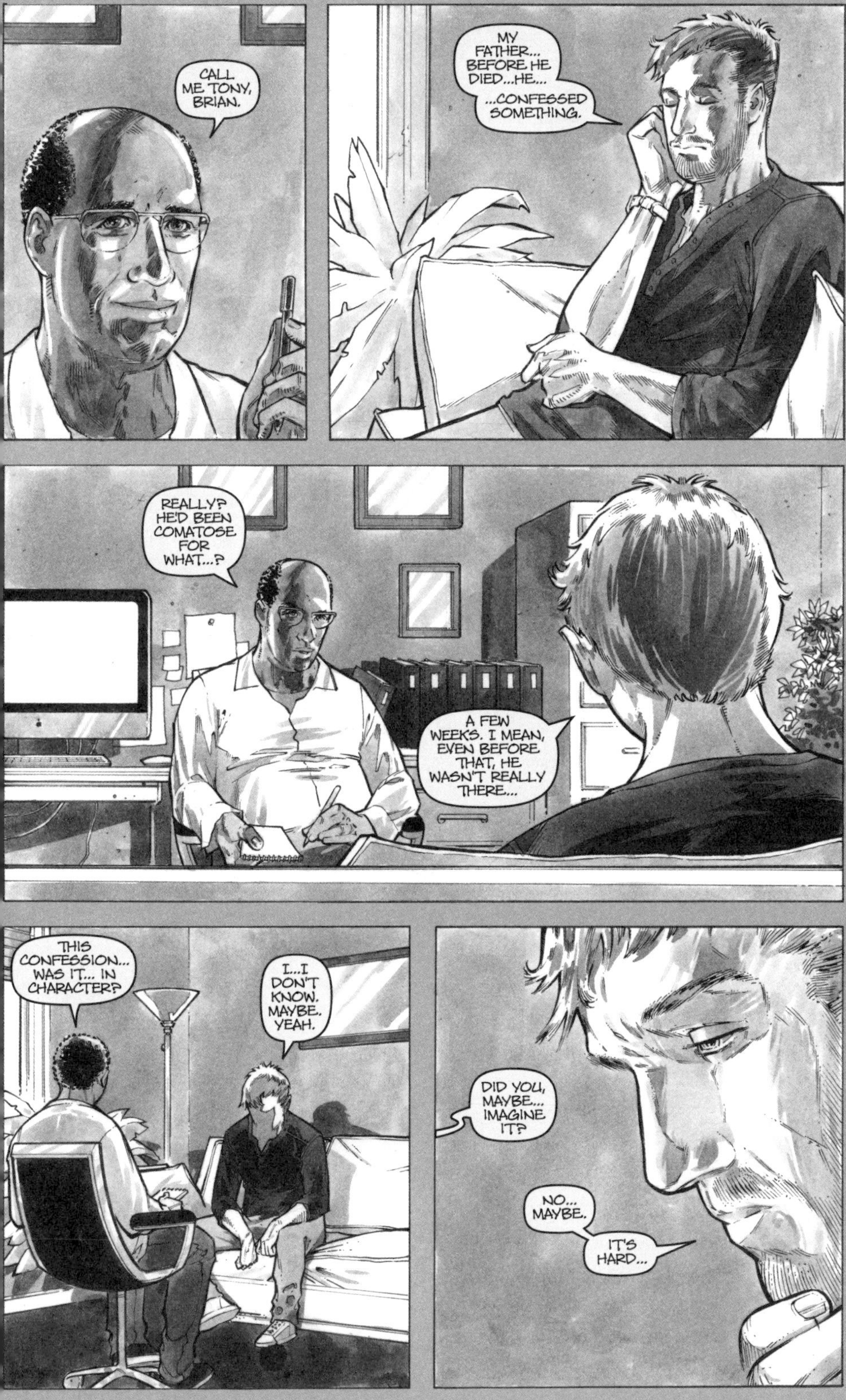
CALL ME TONY, BRIAN.
MY FATHER... BEFORE HE DIED...HE...
...CONFESSED SOMETHING.
REALLY? HE'D BEEN COMATOSE FOR WHAT...?
A FEW WEEKS. I MEAN, EVEN BEFORE THAT, HE WASN'T REALLY THERE...
THIS CONFESSION... WAS IT... IN CHARACTER?
I...I DON'T KNOW. MAYBE. YEAH.
DID YOU, MAYBE... IMAGINE IT?
NO... MAYBE.
IT'S HARD...

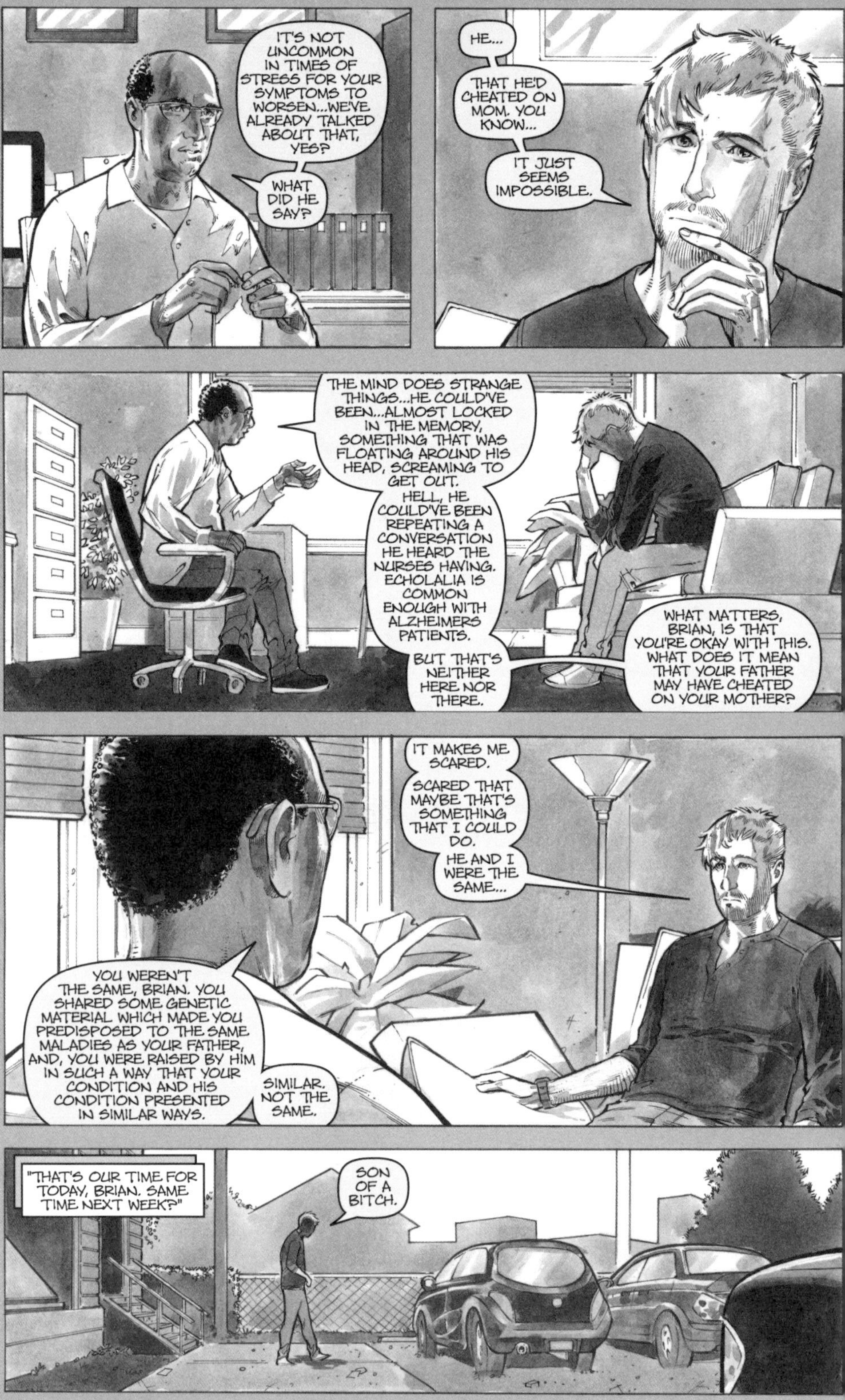
IT'S NOT UNCOMMON IN TIMES OF STRESS FOR YOUR SYMPTOMS TO WORSEN...WE'VE ALREADY TALKED ABOUT THAT, YES?
WHAT DID HE SAY?
HE...
THAT HE'D CHEATED ON MOM. YOU KNOW...
IT JUST SEEMS IMPOSSIBLE.
THE MIND DOES STRANGE THINGS...HE COULD'VE BEEN...ALMOST LOCKED IN THE MEMORY, SOMETHING THAT WAS FLOATING AROUND HIS HEAD, SCREAMING TO GET OUT.
HELL, HE COULD'VE BEEN REPEATING A CONVERSATION HE HEARD THE NURSES HAVING. ECHOLALIA IS COMMON ENOUGH WITH ALZHEIMERS PATIENTS.
BUT THAT'S NEITHER HERE NOR THERE.
WHAT MATTERS, BRIAN, IS THAT YOU'RE OKAY WITH THIS. WHAT DOES IT MEAN THAT YOUR FATHER MAY HAVE CHEATED ON YOUR MOTHER?
IT MAKES ME SCARED.
SCARED THAT MAYBE THAT'S SOMETHING THAT I COULD DO.
HE AND I WERE THE SAME...
YOU WEREN'T THE SAME, BRIAN. YOU SHARED SOME GENETIC MATERIAL WHICH MADE YOU PREDISPOSED TO THE SAME MALADIES AS YOUR FATHER, AND, YOU WERE RAISED BY HIM IN SUCH A WAY THAT YOUR CONDITION AND HIS CONDITION PRESENTED IN SIMILAR WAYS.
SIMILAR. NOT THE SAME.
"THAT'S OUR TIME FOR TODAY, BRIAN. SAME TIME NEXT WEEK?"
SON OF A BITCH.

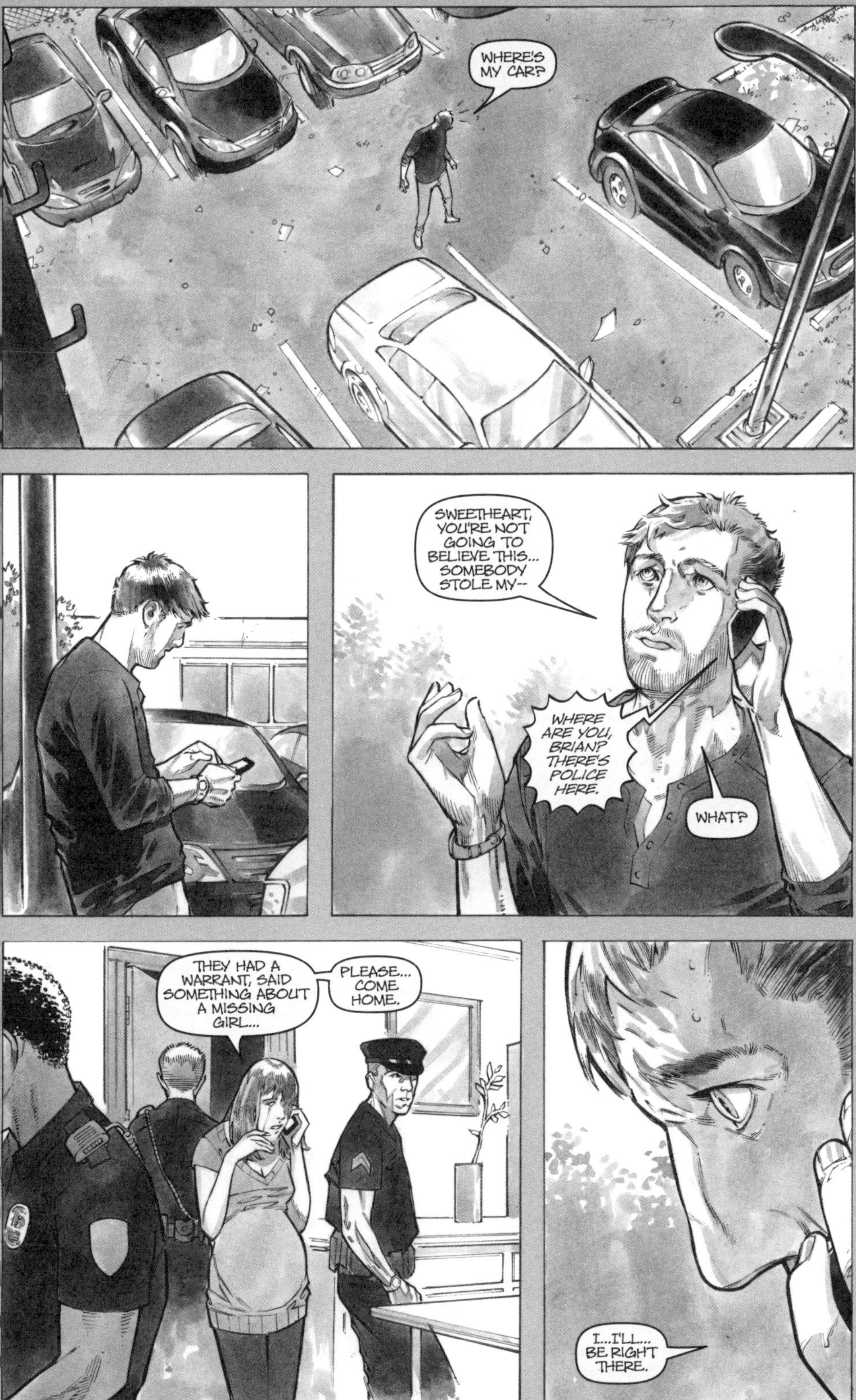
WHERE'S MY CAR?
SWEETHEART, YOU'RE NOT GOING TO BELIEVE THIS... SOMEBODY STOLE MY--
WHERE ARE YOU, BRIAN? THERE'S POLICE HERE.
WHAT?
THEY HAD A WARRANT, SAID SOMETHING ABOUT A MISSING GIRL...
PLEASE... COME HOME.
I...I'LL... BE RIGHT THERE.

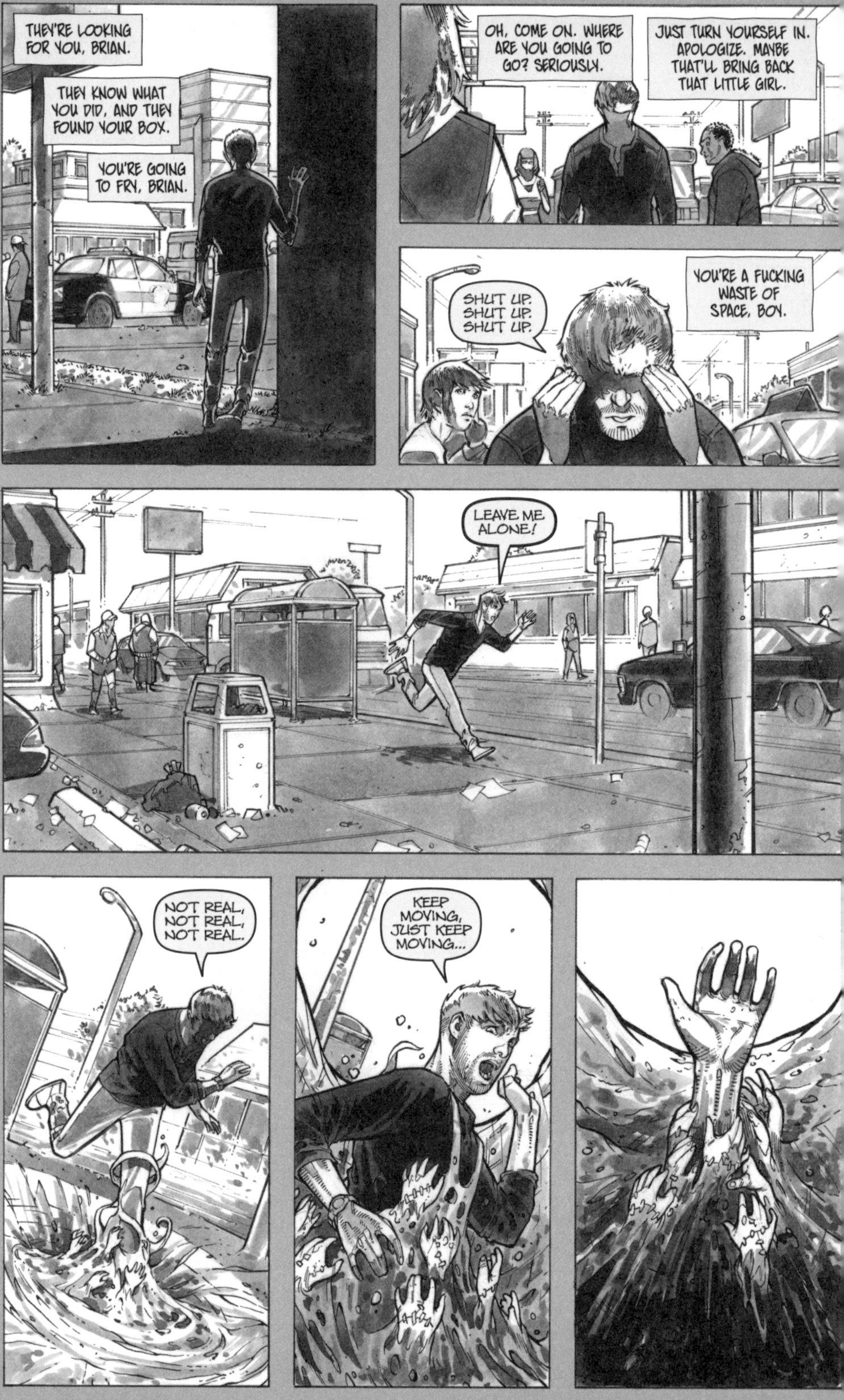
THEY'RE LOOKING FOR YOU, BRIAN.
THEY KNOW WHAT YOU DID, AND THEY FOUND YOUR BOX.
YOU'RE GOING TO FRY, BRIAN.
OH, COME ON. WHERE ARE YOU GOING TO GO? SERIOUSLY.
JUST TURN YOURSELF IN. APOLOGIZE. MAYBE THAT'LL BRING BACK THAT LITTLE GIRL.
SHUT UP. SHUT UP. SHUT UP.
YOU'RE A FUCKING WASTE OF SPACE, BOY.
LEAVE ME ALONE!
NOT REAL, NOT REAL, NOT REAL.
KEEP MOVING, JUST KEEP MOVING...

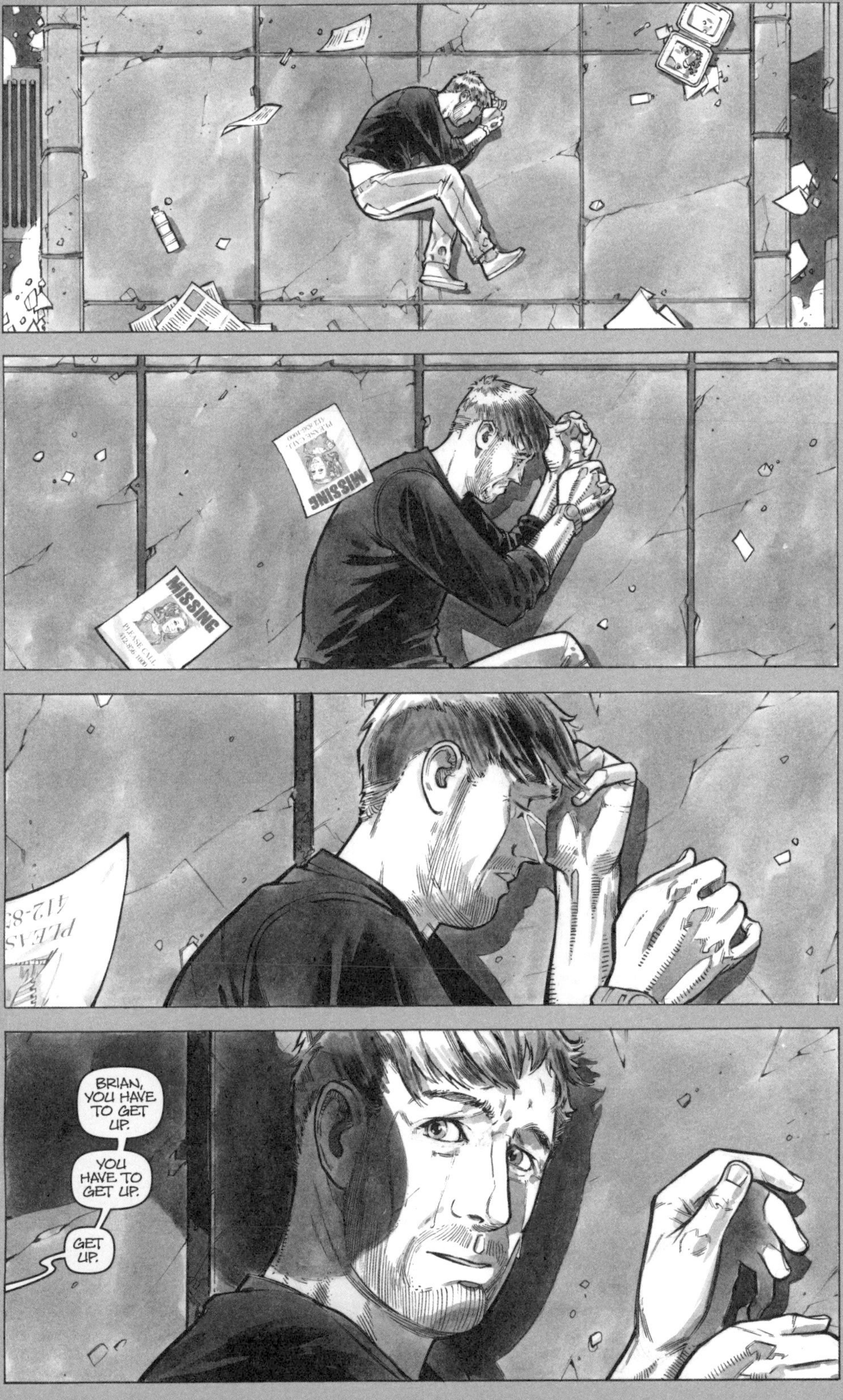
MISSING
PLEASE CALL
BRIAN, YOU HAVE TO GET UP.
YOU HAVE TO GET UP.
GET UP.

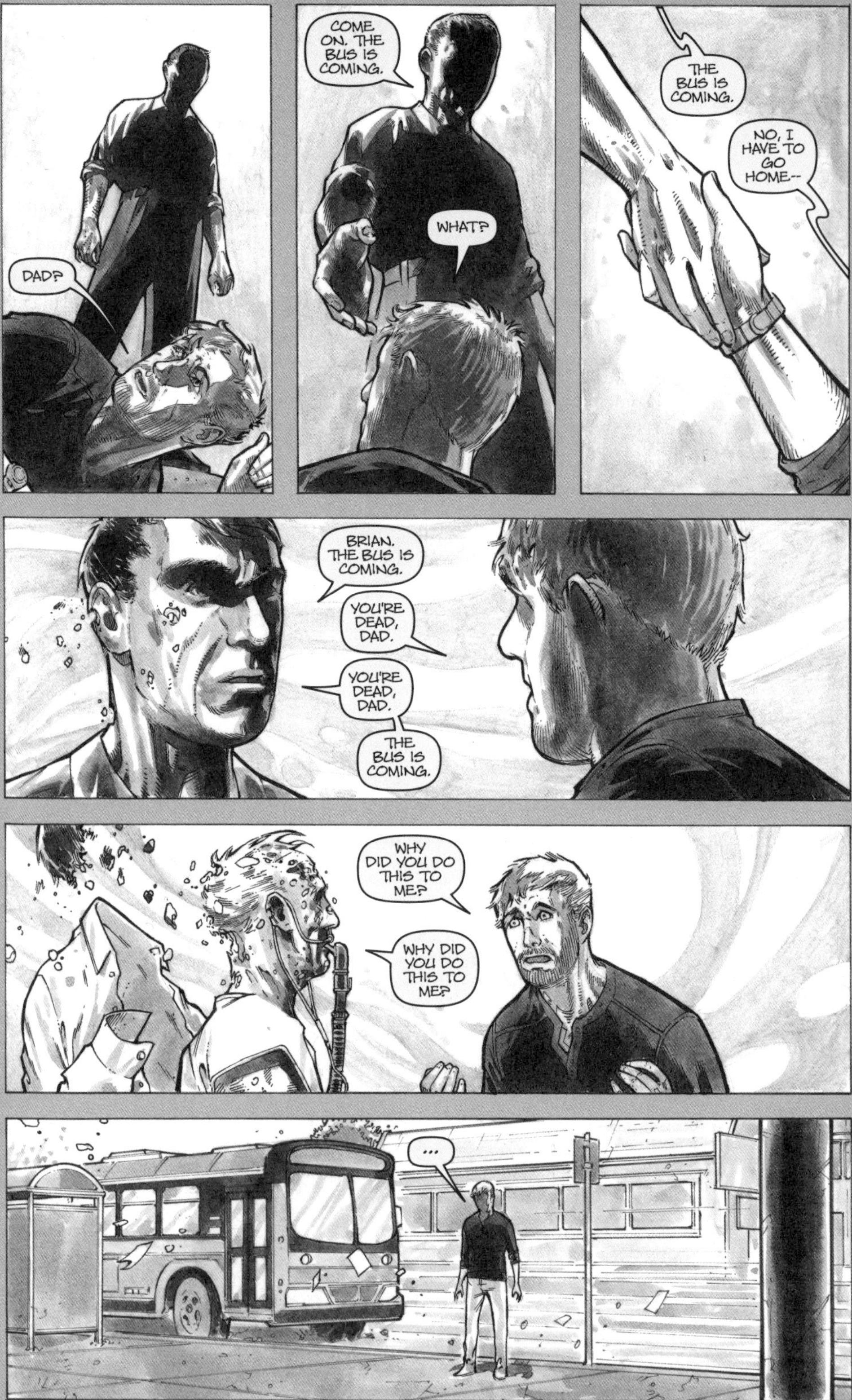
DAD?
COME ON. THE BUS IS COMING.
WHAT?
THE BUS IS COMING.
NO, I HAVE TO GO HOME--
BRIAN. THE BUS IS COMING.
YOU'RE DEAD, DAD.
YOU'RE DEAD, DAD.
THE BUS IS COMING.
WHY DID YOU DO THIS TO ME?
WHY DID YOU DO THIS TO ME?
...

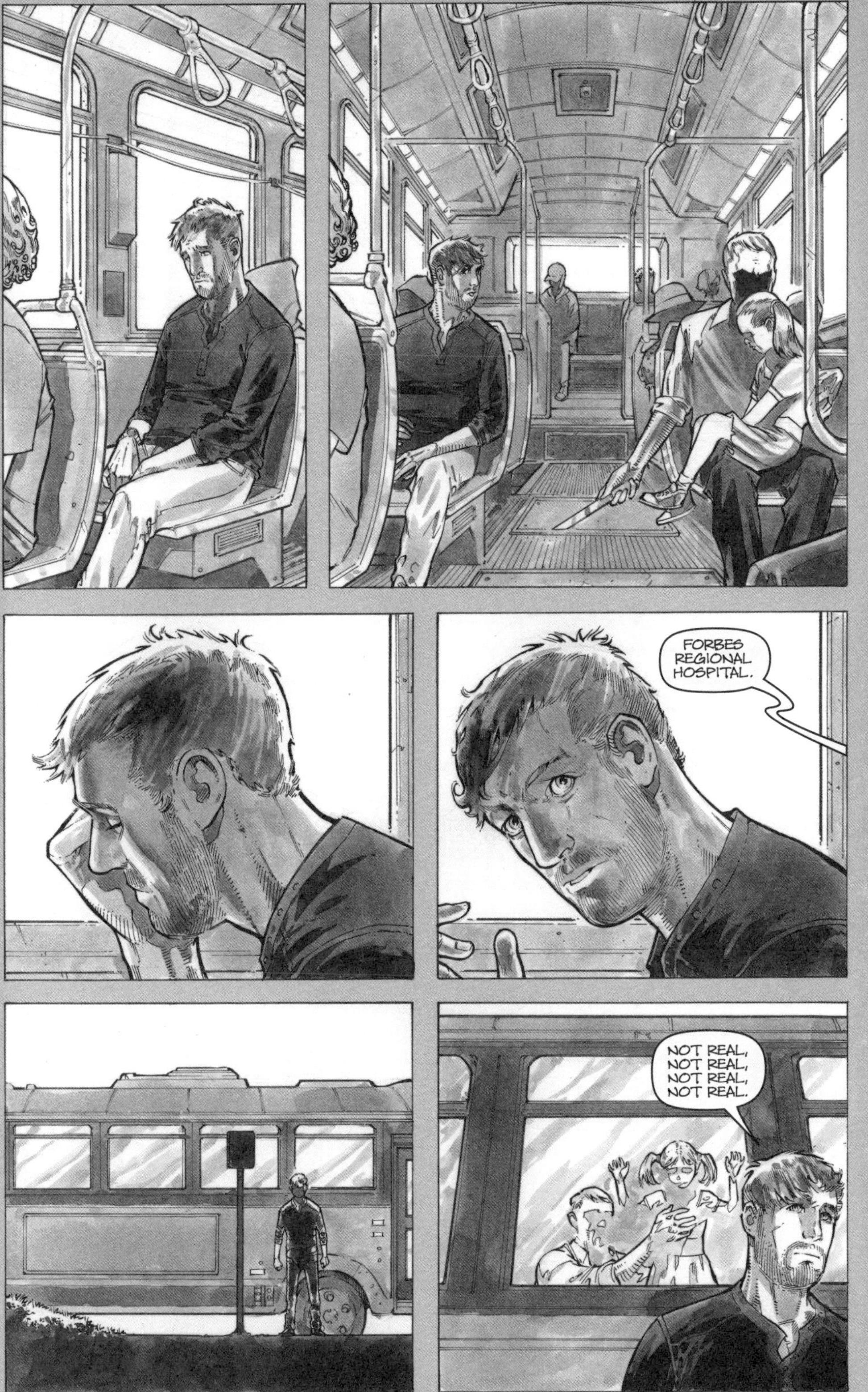
FORBES REGIONAL HOSPITAL.
NOT REAL, NOT REAL, NOT REAL, NOT REAL.

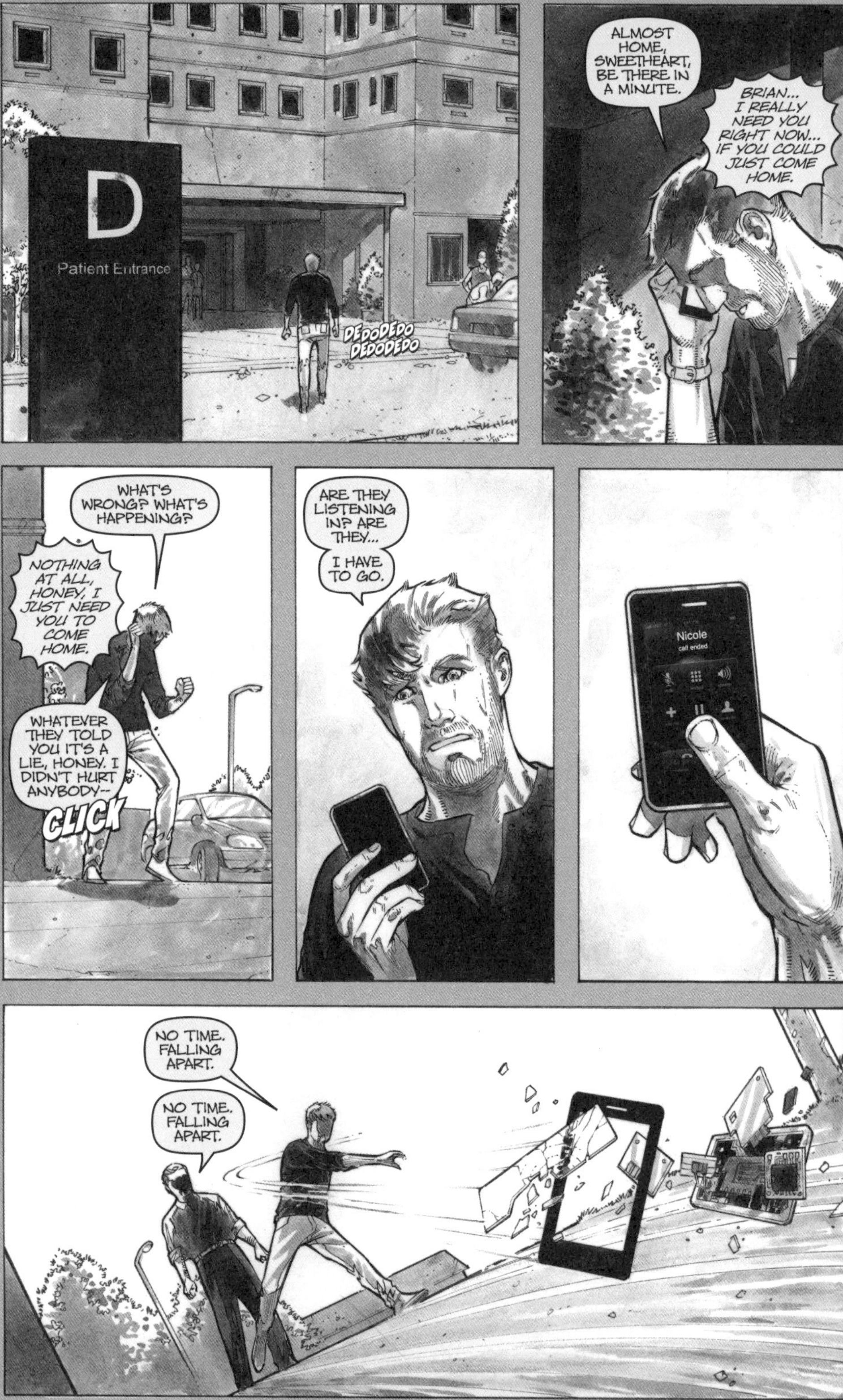
D
Patient Entrance
DEDODEDO DEDODEDO
ALMOST HOME, SWEETHEART, BE THERE IN A MINUTE.
BRIAN... I REALLY NEED YOU RIGHT NOW... IF YOU COULD JUST COME HOME.
WHAT'S WRONG? WHAT'S HAPPENING?
NOTHING AT ALL, HONEY, I JUST NEED YOU TO COME HOME.
WHATEVER THEY TOLD YOU IT'S A LIE, HONEY. I DIDN'T HURT ANYBODY--
CLICK
ARE THEY LISTENING IN? ARE THEY...
I HAVE TO GO.
Nicole
call ended
NO TIME. FALLING APART.
NO TIME. FALLING APART.

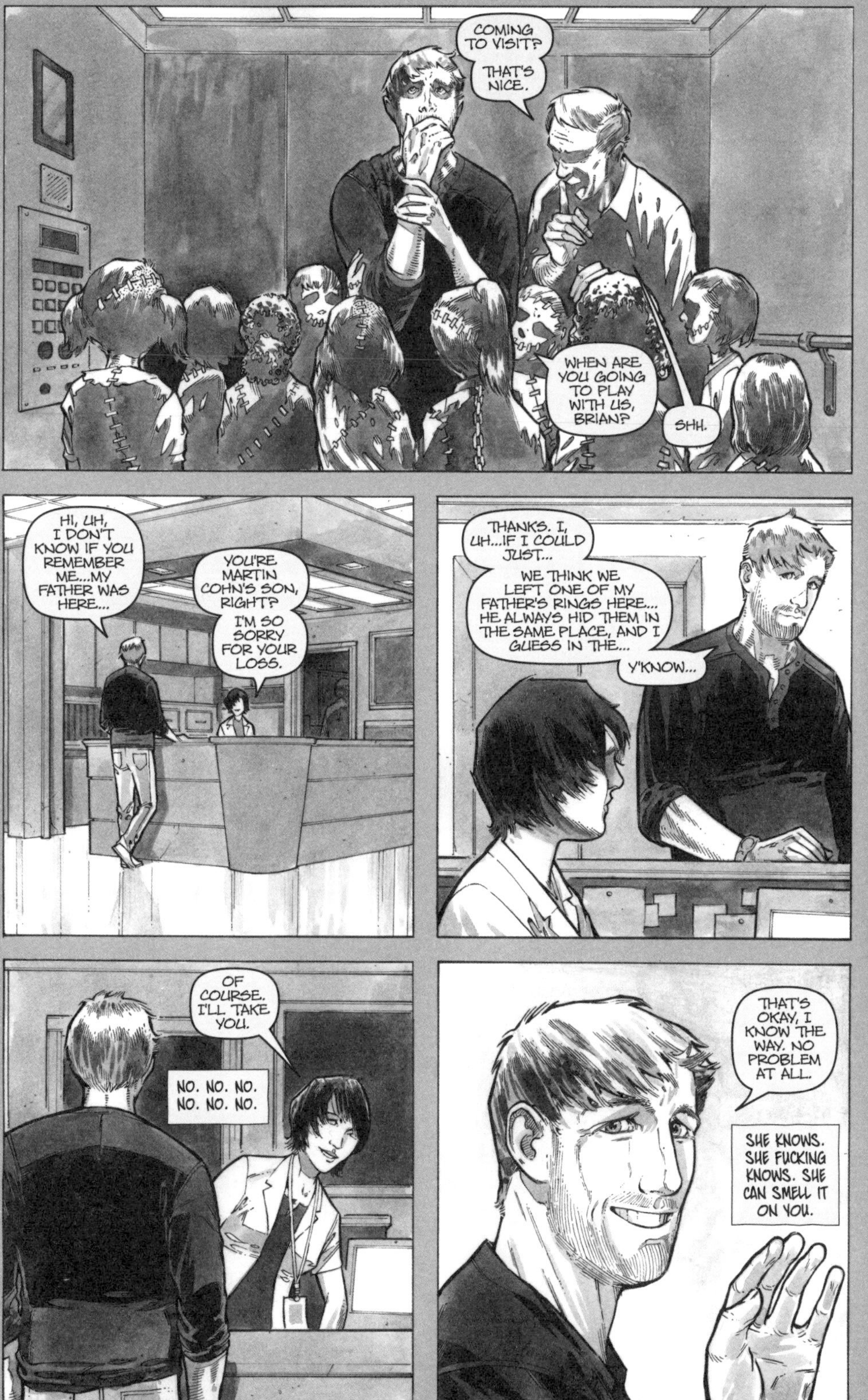
COMING TO VISIT?
THAT'S NICE.
WHEN ARE YOU GOING TO PLAY WITH US, BRIAN?
SHH.
HI, UH, I DON'T KNOW IF YOU REMEMBER ME...MY FATHER WAS HERE...
YOU'RE MARTIN COHN'S SON, RIGHT?
I'M SO SORRY FOR YOUR LOSS.
THANKS. I, UH...IF I COULD JUST...
WE THINK WE LEFT ONE OF MY FATHER'S RINGS HERE... HE ALWAYS HID THEM IN THE SAME PLACE, AND I GUESS IN THE...
Y'KNOW...
OF COURSE. I'LL TAKE YOU.
NO. NO. NO. NO. NO. NO.
THAT'S OKAY, I KNOW THE WAY. NO PROBLEM AT ALL.
SHE KNOWS. SHE FUCKING KNOWS. SHE CAN SMELL IT ON YOU.

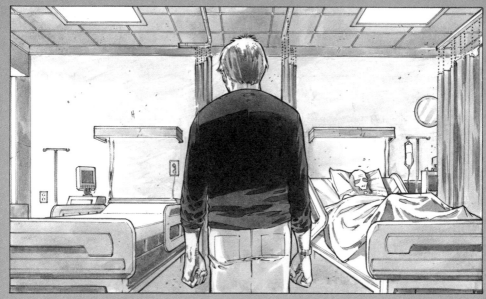

WHAT THE FUCK ARE YOU DOING?

SORRY...

MY DAD WAS IN HERE...

YEAH, I REMEMBER YOU.

YOU WERE HERE.

YOU WERE HIS ROOMMATE, RIGHT?

THE MUTTERING GUY...

WAS, YEAH.

YOU'RE NOT HERE.

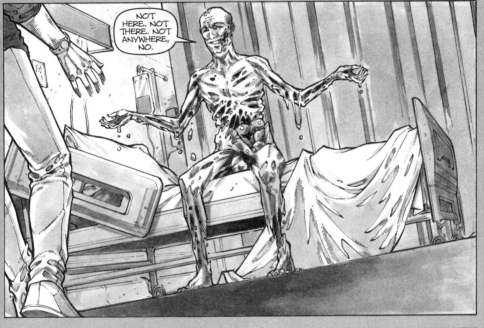

NOT HERE. NOT THERE. NOT ANYWHERE, NO.

THEN GO AWAY.

YOU'RE NOT REAL.

MAYBE *YOU'RE* NOT REAL.

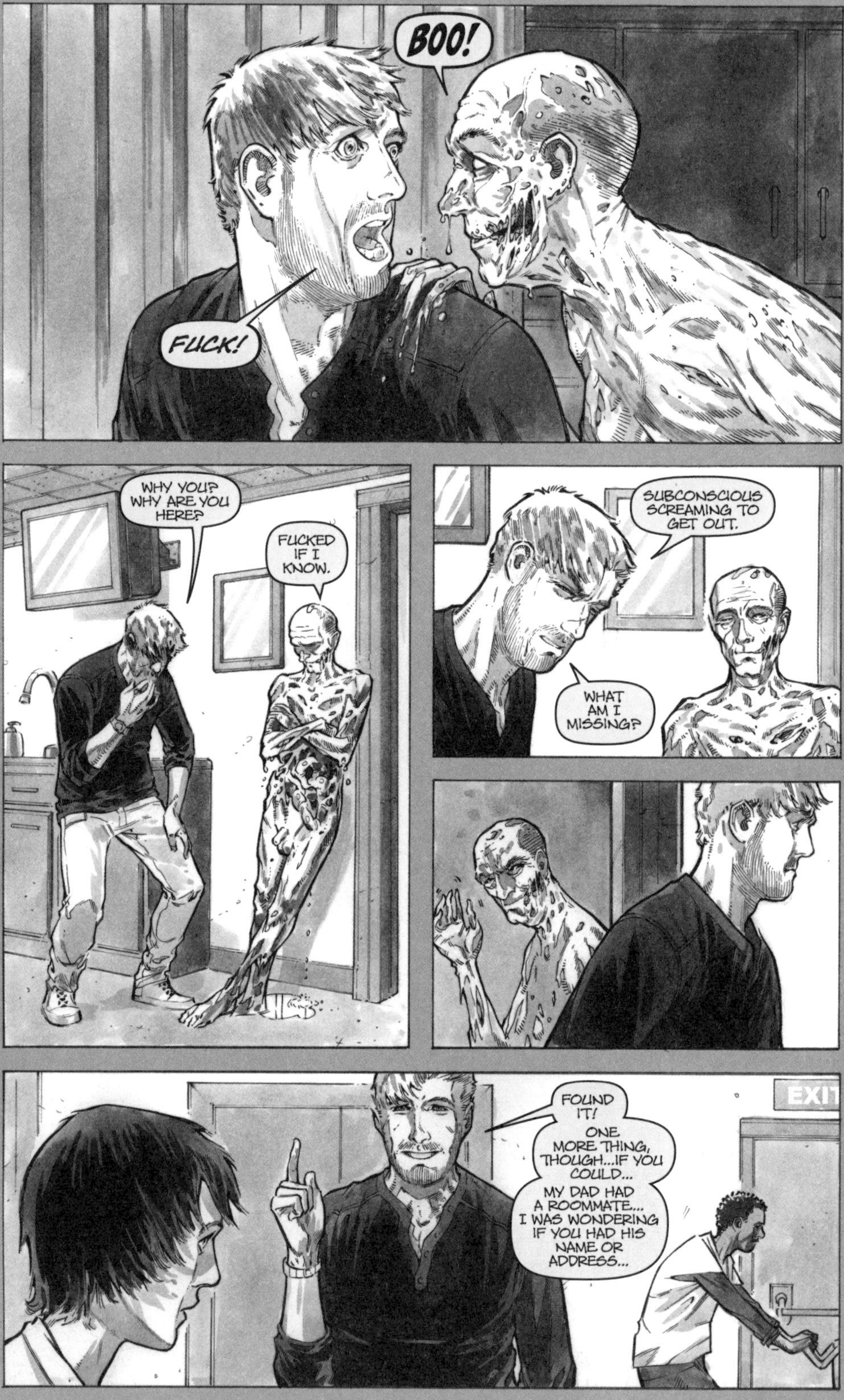
BOO!
FUCK!
WHY YOU? WHY ARE YOU HERE?
FUCKED IF I KNOW.
SUBCONSCIOUS SCREAMING TO GET OUT.
WHAT AM I MISSING?
FOUND IT!
ONE MORE THING, THOUGH...IF YOU COULD...
MY DAD HAD A ROOMMATE... I WAS WONDERING IF YOU HAD HIS NAME OR ADDRESS...
EXIT

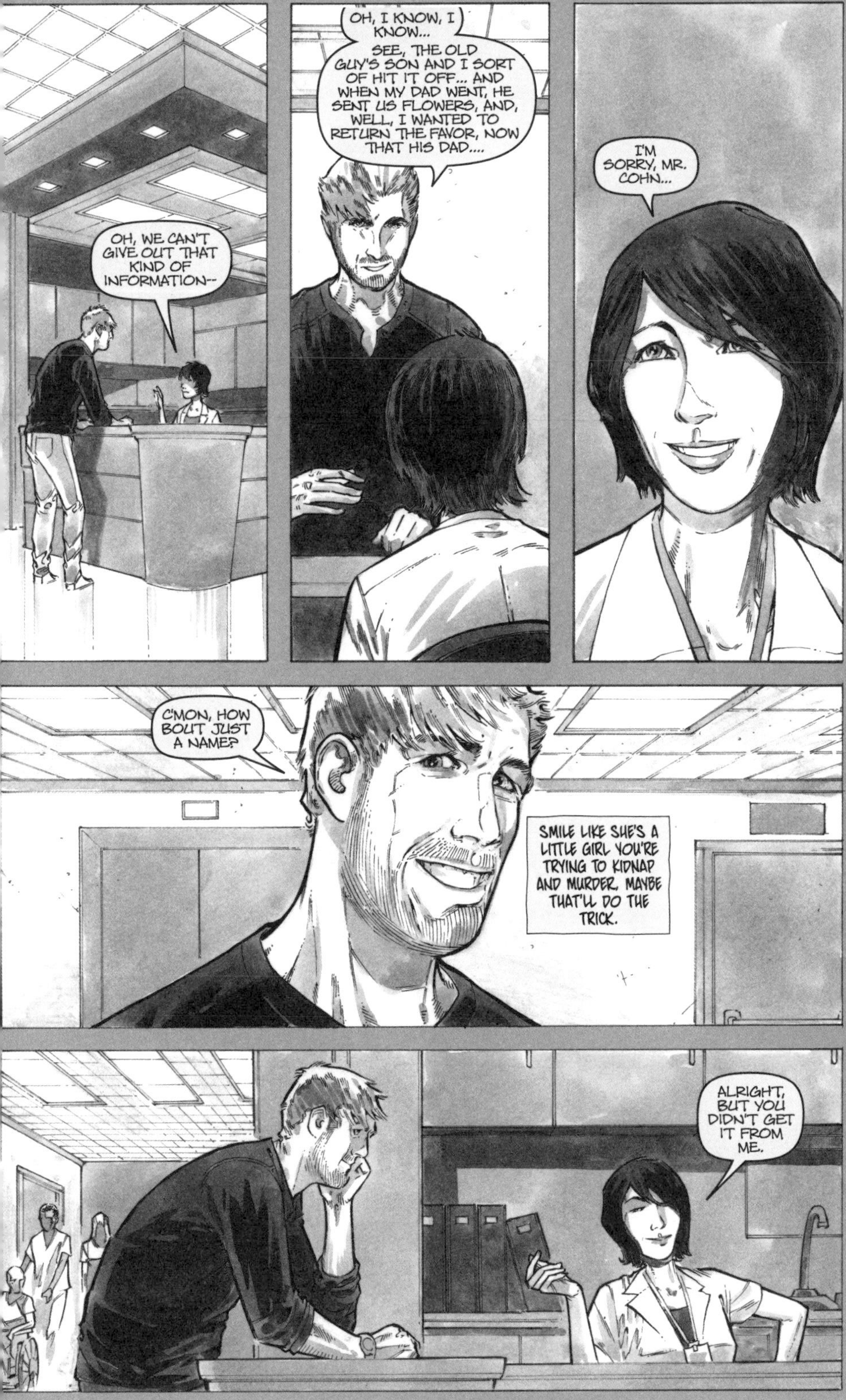
OH, WE CAN'T GIVE OUT THAT KIND OF INFORMATION--
OH, I KNOW, I KNOW... SEE, THE OLD GUY'S SON AND I SORT OF HIT IT OFF... AND WHEN MY DAD WENT, HE SENT US FLOWERS, AND, WELL, I WANTED TO RETURN THE FAVOR, NOW THAT HIS DAD....
I'M SORRY, MR. COHN...
C'MON, HOW BOUT JUST A NAME?
SMILE LIKE SHE'S A LITTLE GIRL YOU'RE TRYING TO KIDNAP AND MURDER, MAYBE THAT'LL DO THE TRICK.
ALRIGHT, BUT YOU DIDN'T GET IT FROM ME.

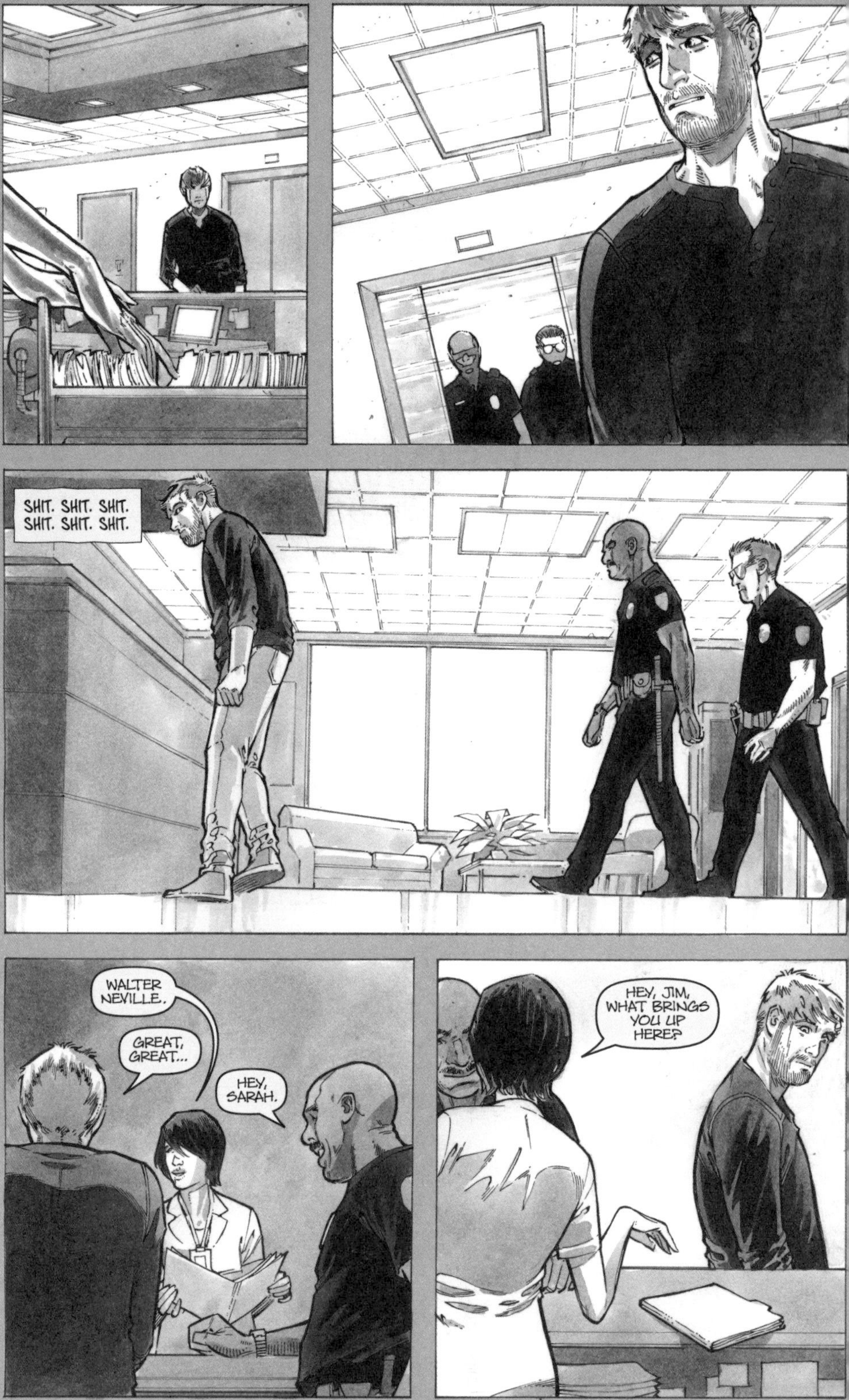
SHIT. SHIT. SHIT.
SHIT. SHIT. SHIT.
WALTER NEVILLE.
GREAT, GREAT...
HEY, SARAH.
HEY, JIM, WHAT BRINGS YOU UP HERE?

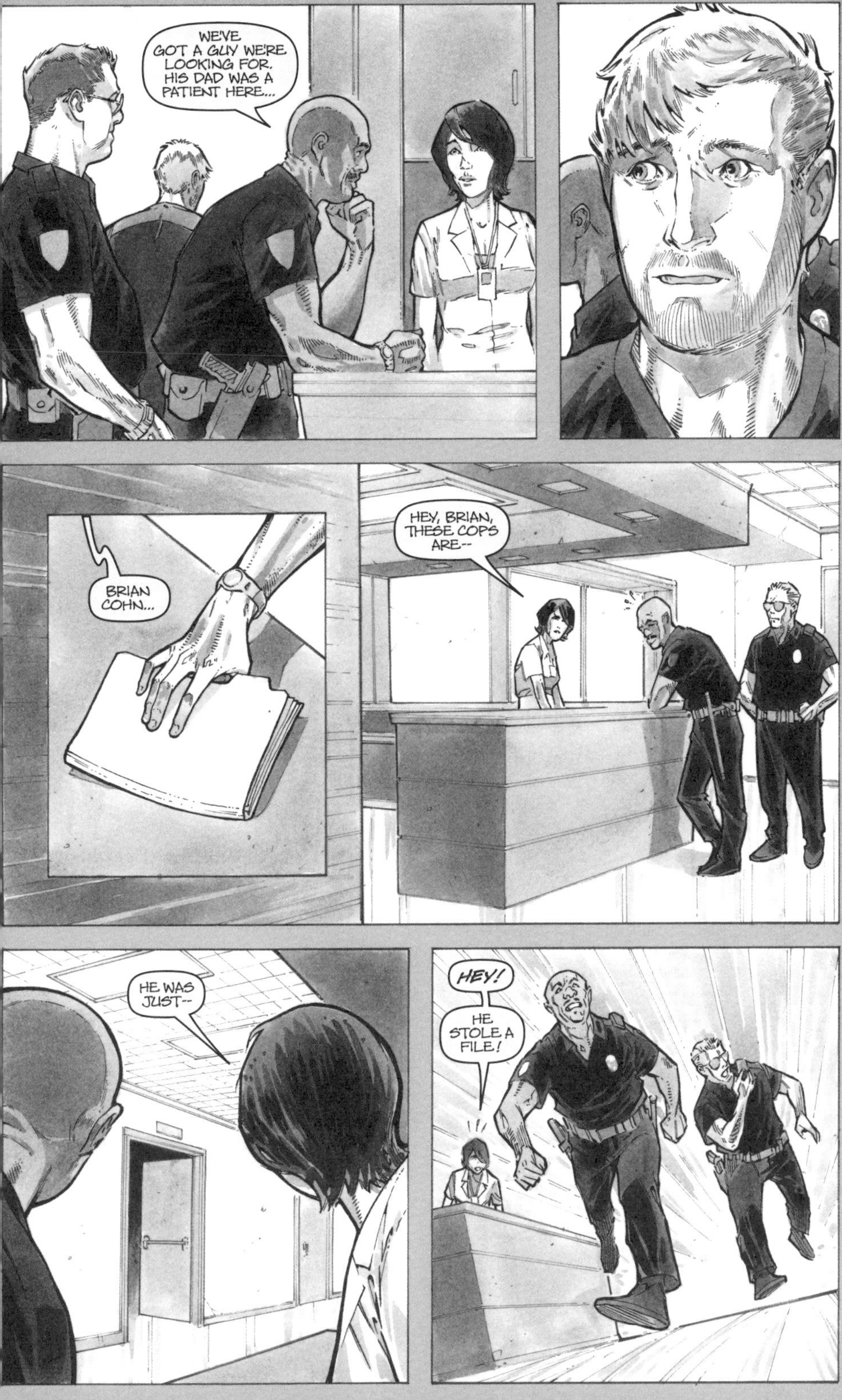
WE'VE GOT A GUY WE'RE LOOKING FOR. HIS DAD WAS A PATIENT HERE...
BRIAN COHN...
HEY, BRIAN, THESE COPS ARE--
HE WAS JUST--
HEY!
HE STOLE A FILE!

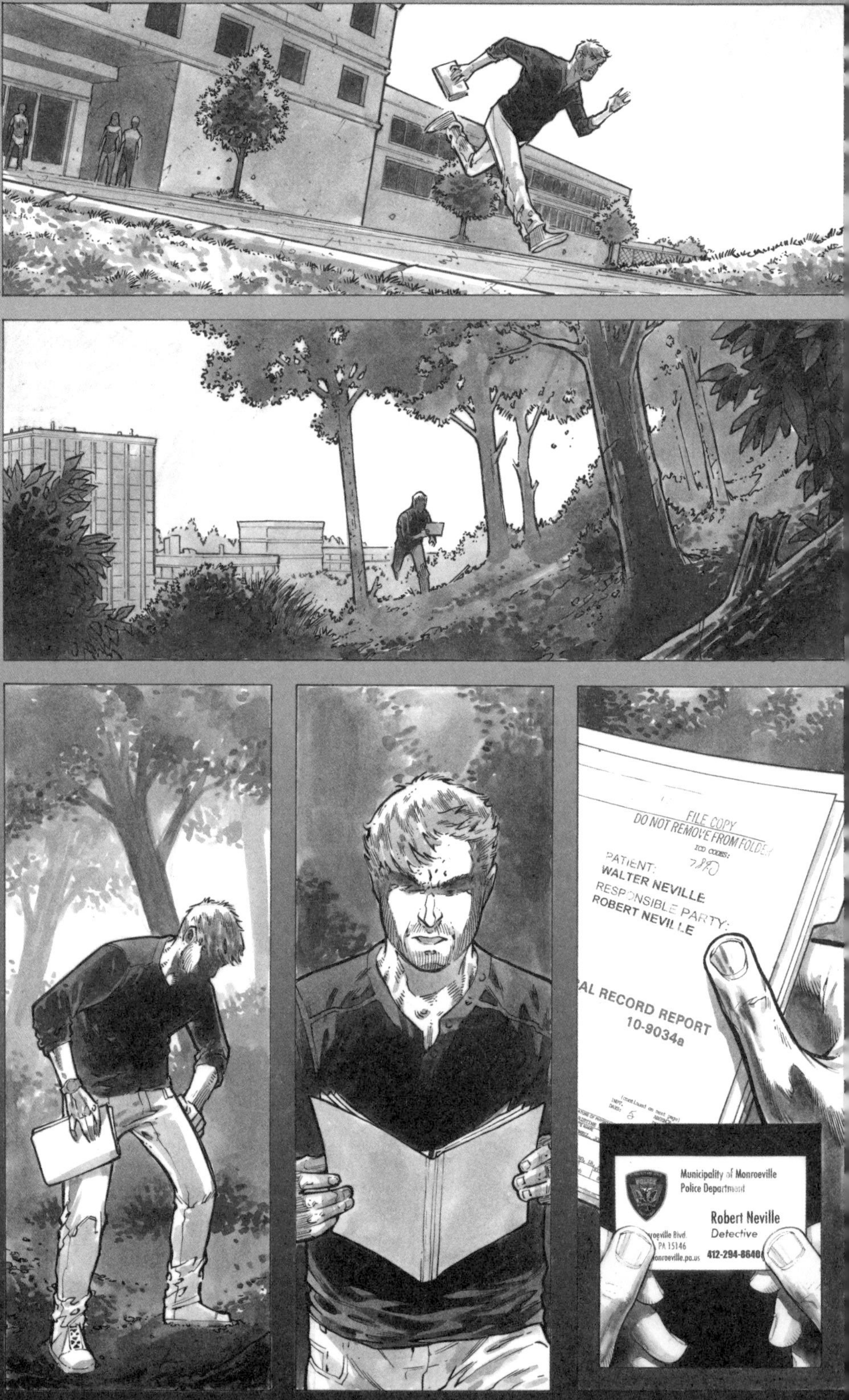
FILE COPY
DO NOT REMOVE FROM FOLDER
ICD CODES:
PATIENT:
WALTER NEVILLE
RESPONSIBLE PARTY:
ROBERT NEVILLE
AL RECORD REPORT
10-9034a
(continued on next page)
Municipality of Monroeville
Police Department
Robert Neville
Detective
roeville Blvd.
PA 15146
onroeville.pa.us
412-294-8640

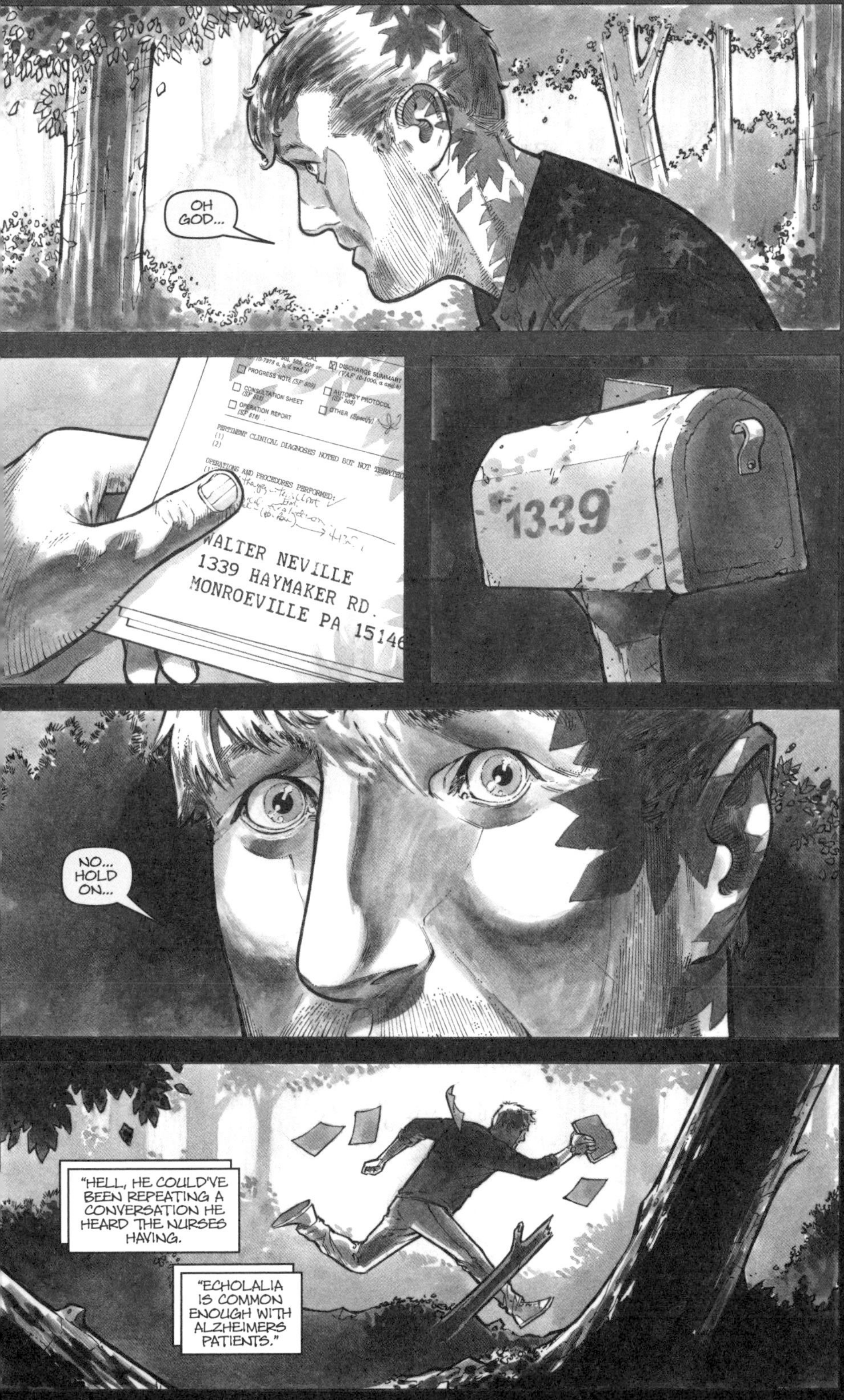
OH GOD...
PROGRESS NOTE (SF 509)
DISCHARGE SUMMARY
CONSULTATION SHEET
AUTOPSY PROTOCOL
OPERATION REPORT
OTHER (Specify)
PERTINENT CLINICAL DIAGNOSES NOTED BUT NOT TREATED
OPERATIONS AND PROCEDURES PERFORMED:
WALTER NEVILLE
1339 HAYMAKER RD.
MONROEVILLE PA 15146
1339
NO... HOLD ON...
"HELL, HE COULD'VE BEEN REPEATING A CONVERSATION HE HEARD THE NURSES HAVING.
"ECHOLALIA IS COMMON ENOUGH WITH ALZHEIMERS PATIENTS."

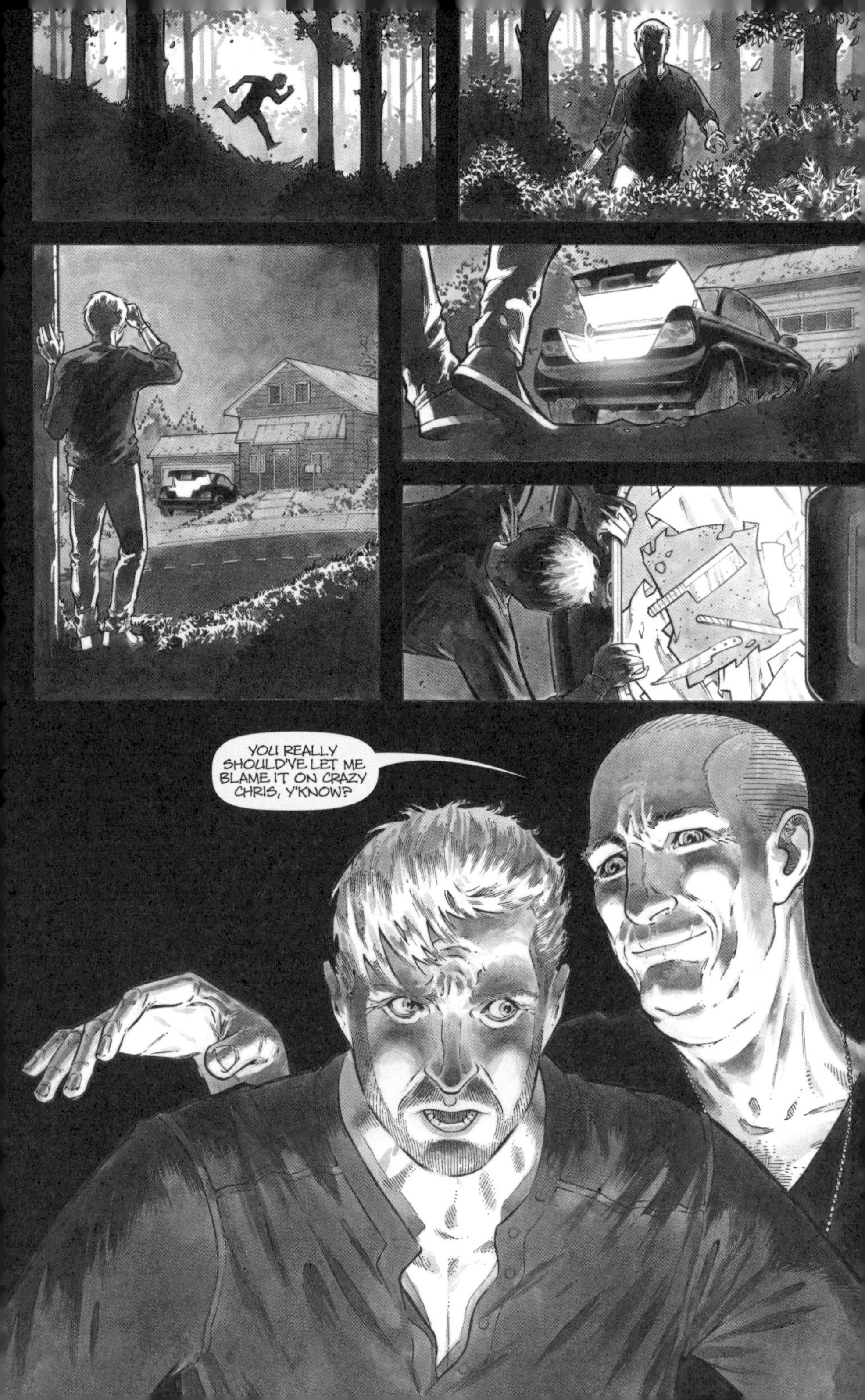
YOU REALLY SHOULD'VE LET ME BLAME IT ON CRAZY CHRIS, Y'KNOW?

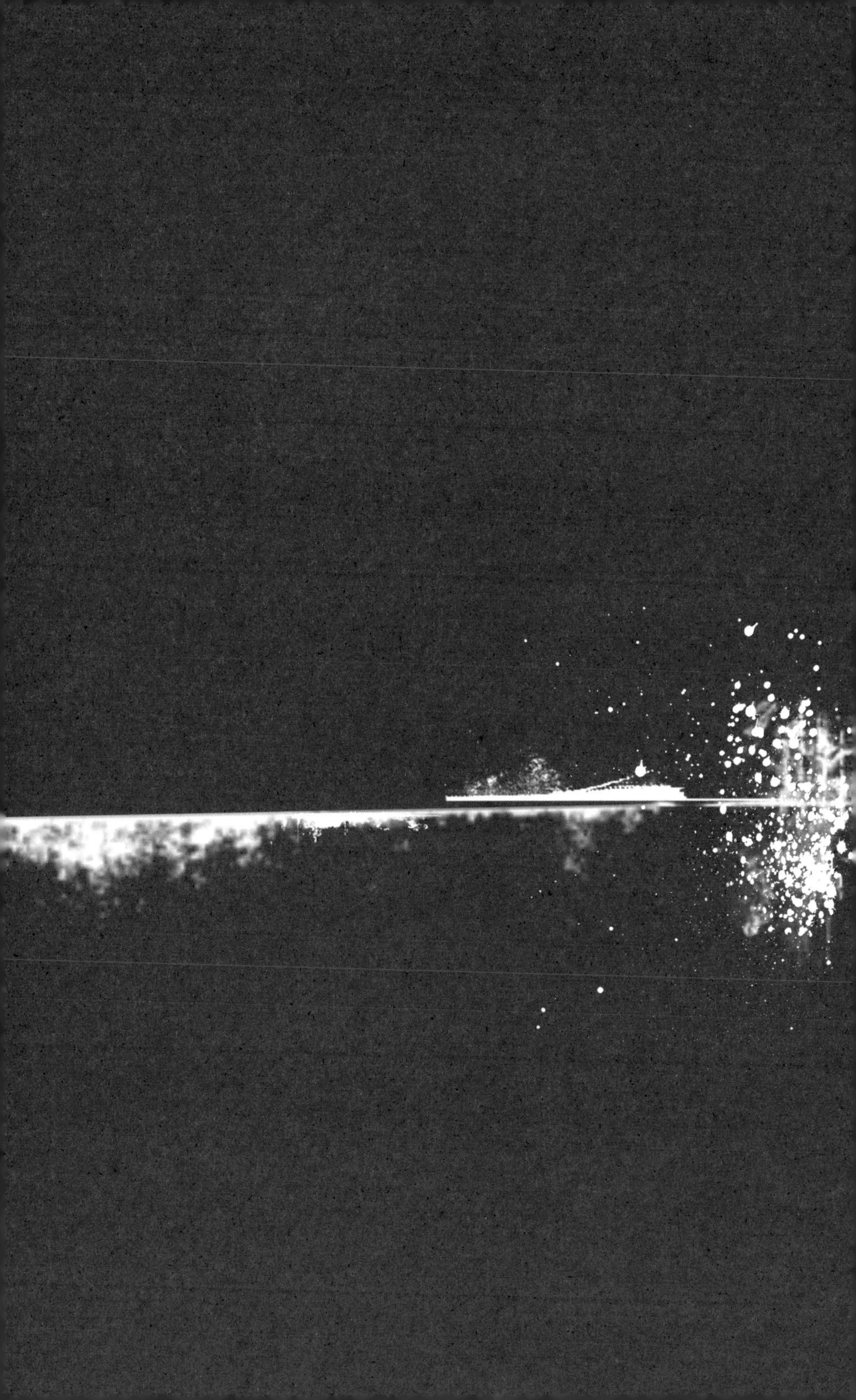

ECHOES™

CHAPTER FIVE

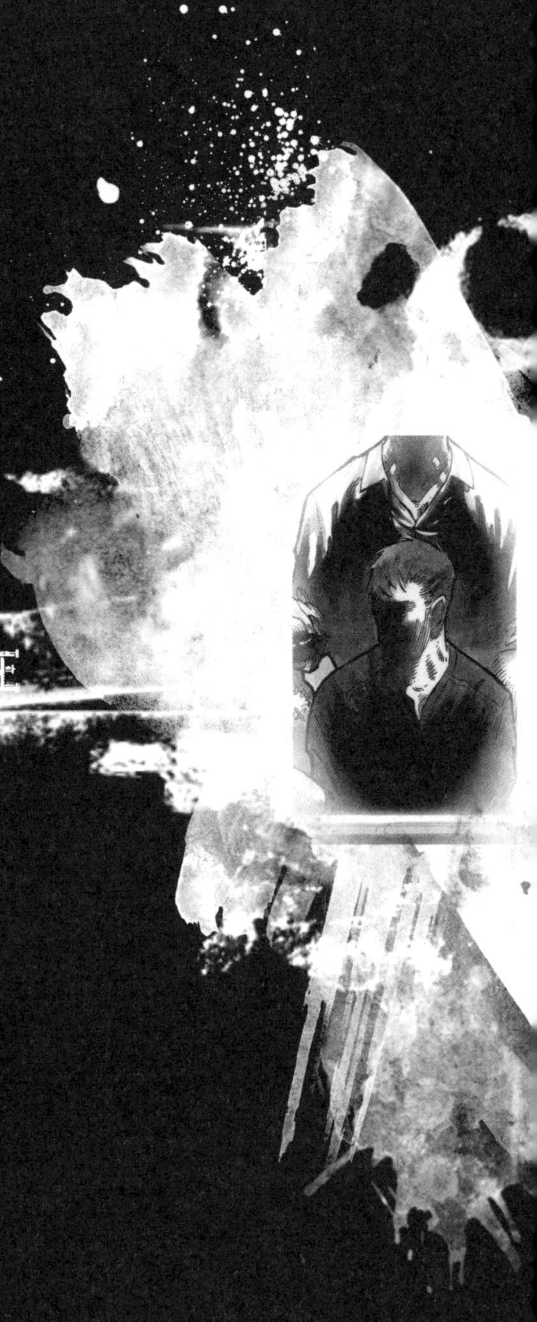

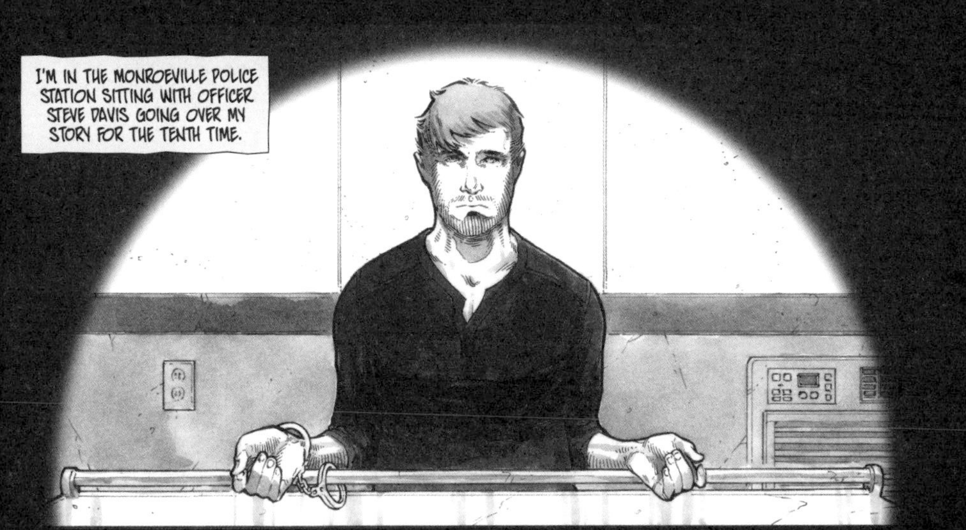
I'M IN THE MONROEVILLE POLICE STATION SITTING WITH OFFICER STEVE DAVIS GOING OVER MY STORY FOR THE TENTH TIME.

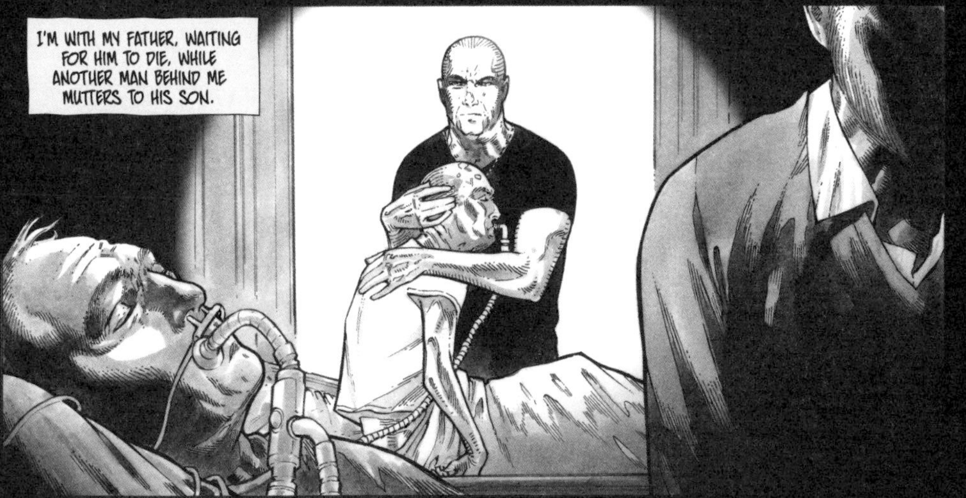
I'M WITH MY FATHER, WAITING FOR HIM TO DIE, WHILE ANOTHER MAN BEHIND ME MUTTERS TO HIS SON.

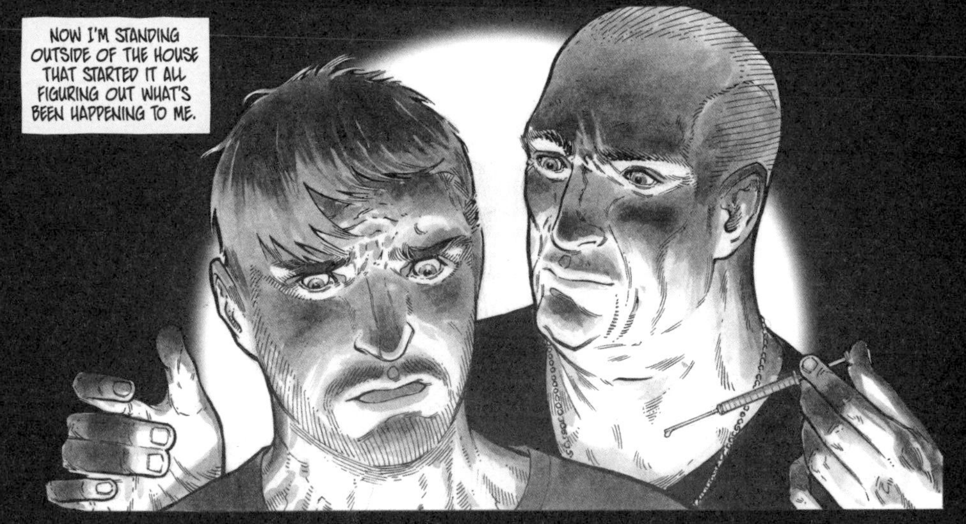
NOW I'M STANDING OUTSIDE OF THE HOUSE THAT STARTED IT ALL FIGURING OUT WHAT'S BEEN HAPPENING TO ME.

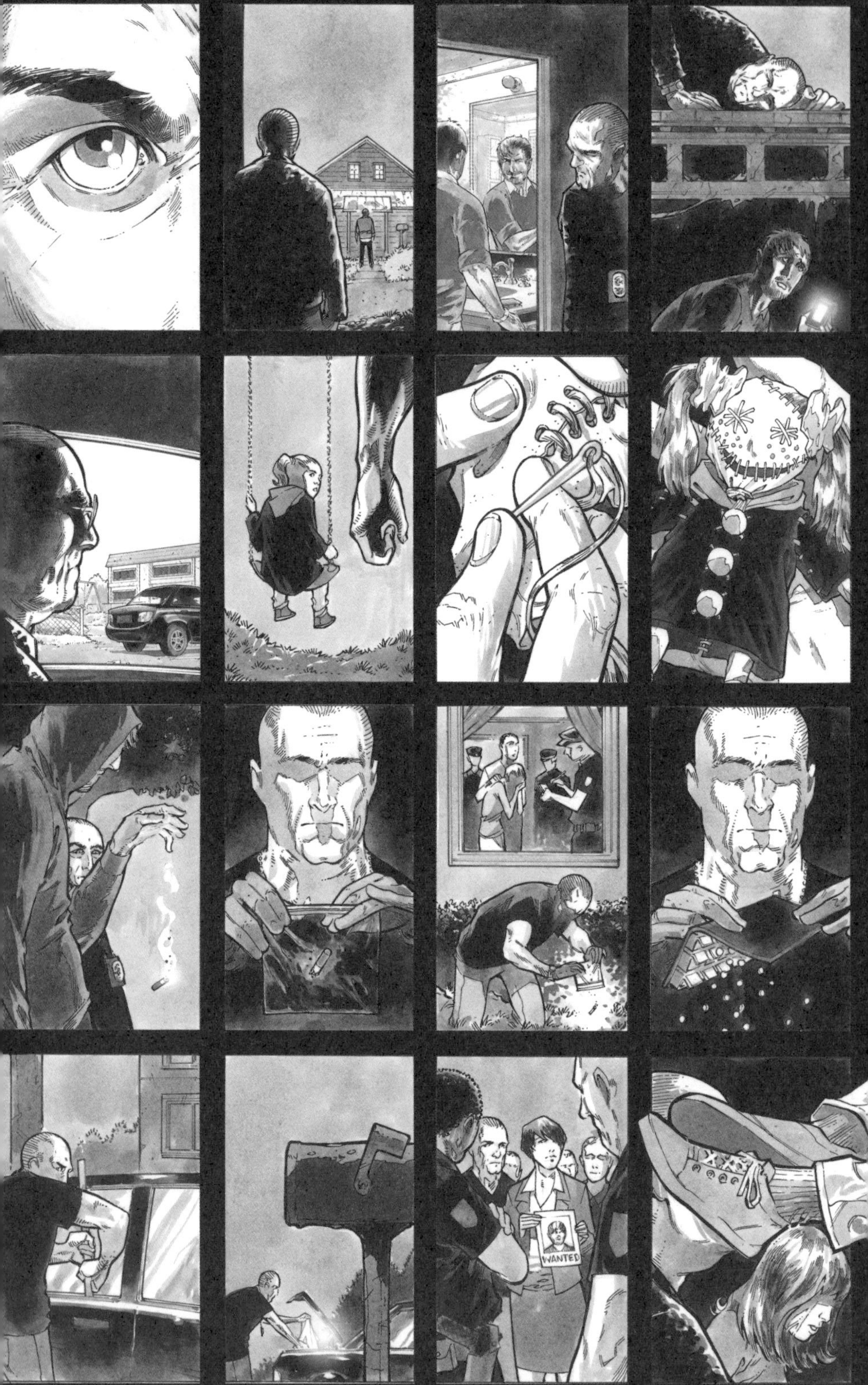
WANTED

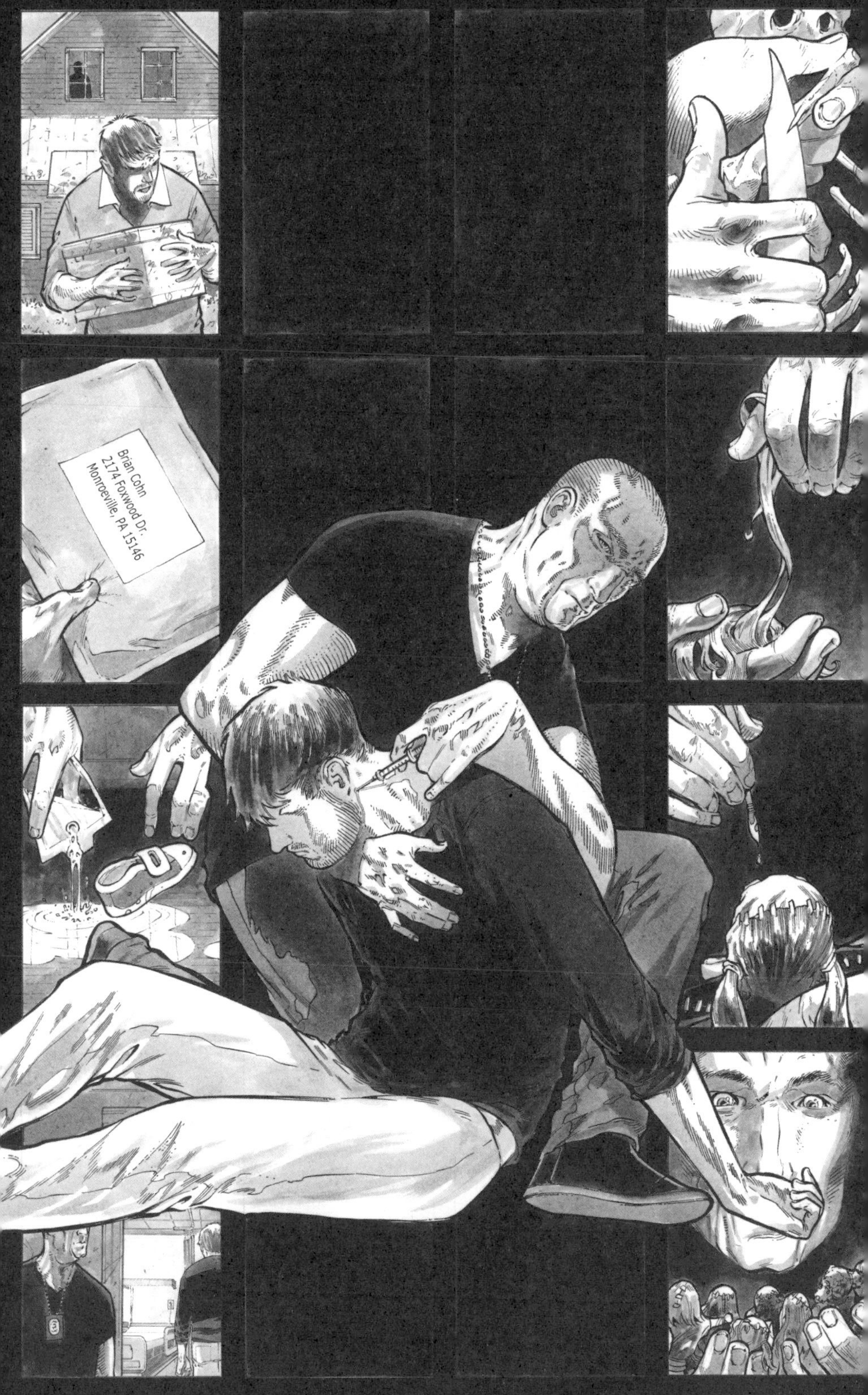
Brian Cohn
2174 Foxwood Dr.
Monroeville, PA 15146

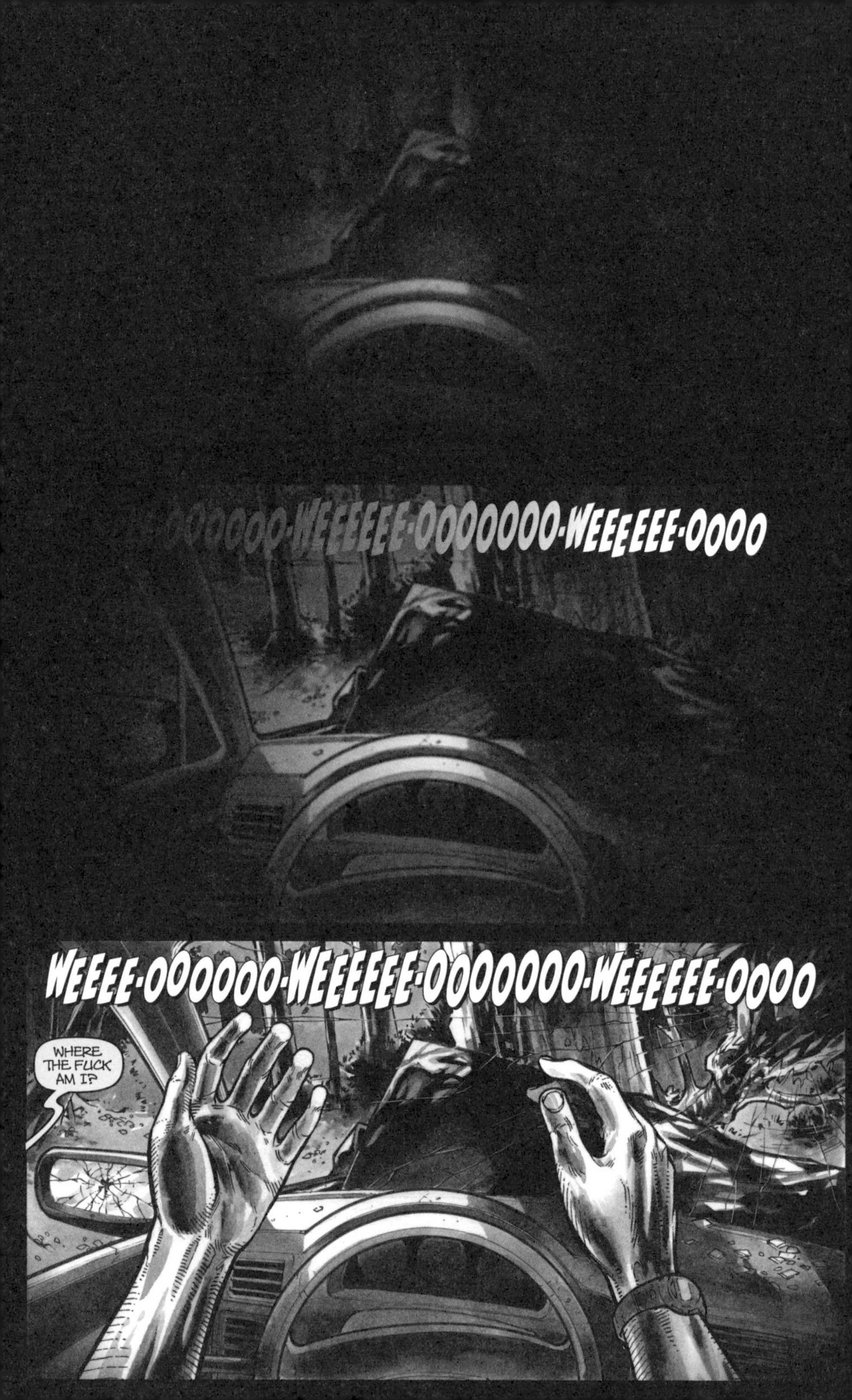
OOOOOO-WEEEEEE-OOOOOOO-WEEEEEE-OOOO
WEEEE-OOOOOO-WEEEEEE-OOOOOOO-WEEEEEE-OOOO
WHERE THE FUCK AM I?

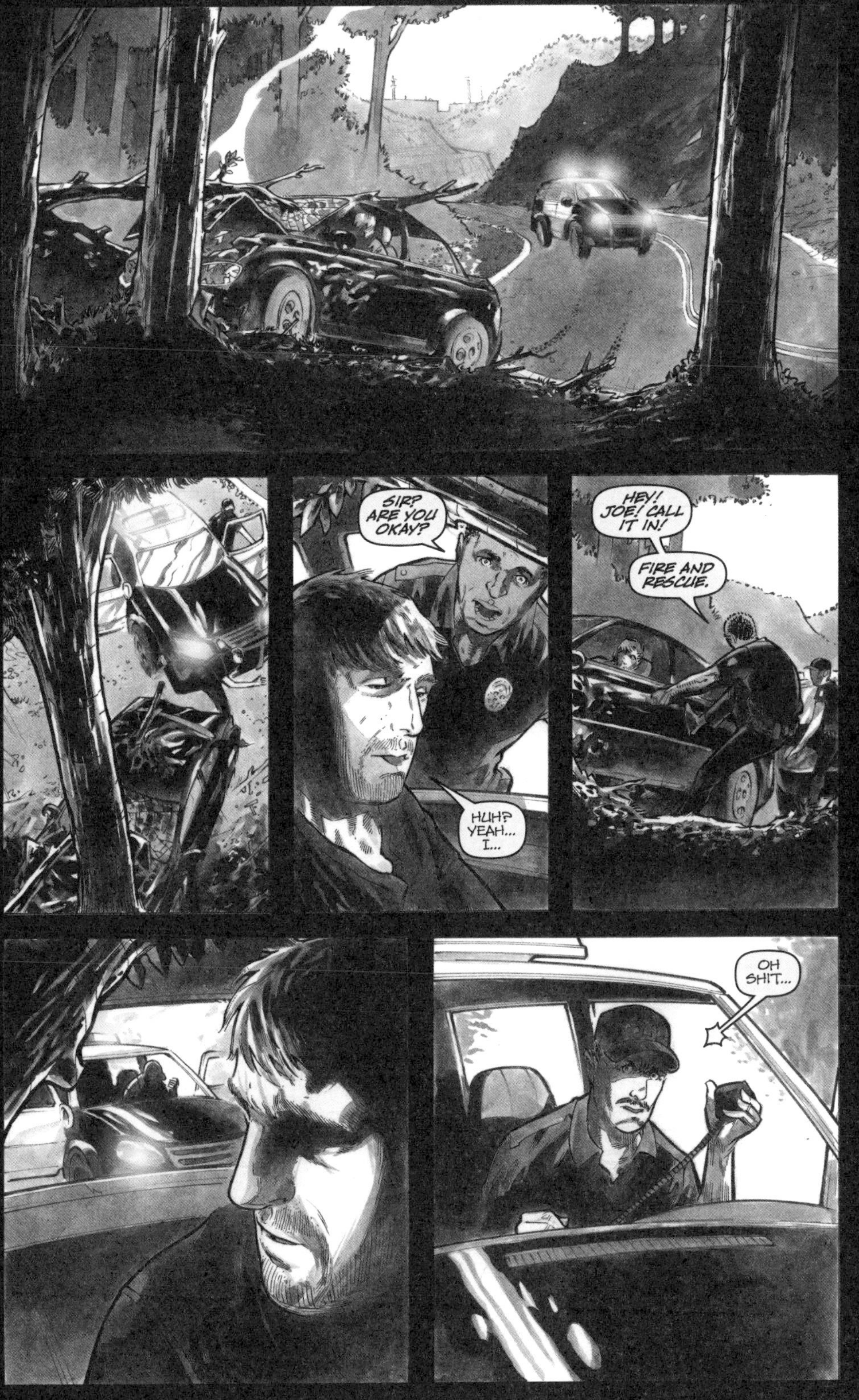
SIR? ARE YOU OKAY?
HUH? YEAH... I...
HEY! JOE! CALL IT IN!
FIRE AND RESCUE.
OH SHIT...

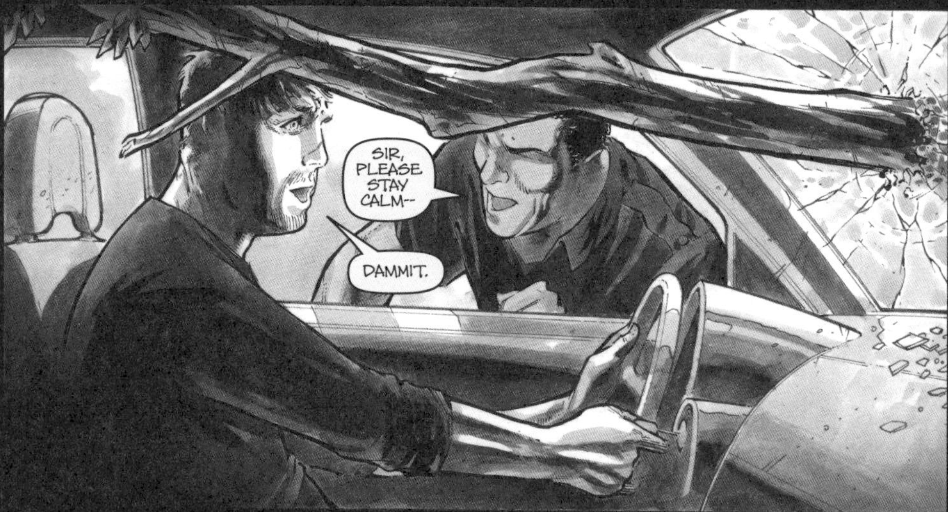
SIR, PLEASE STAY CALM--
DAMMIT.
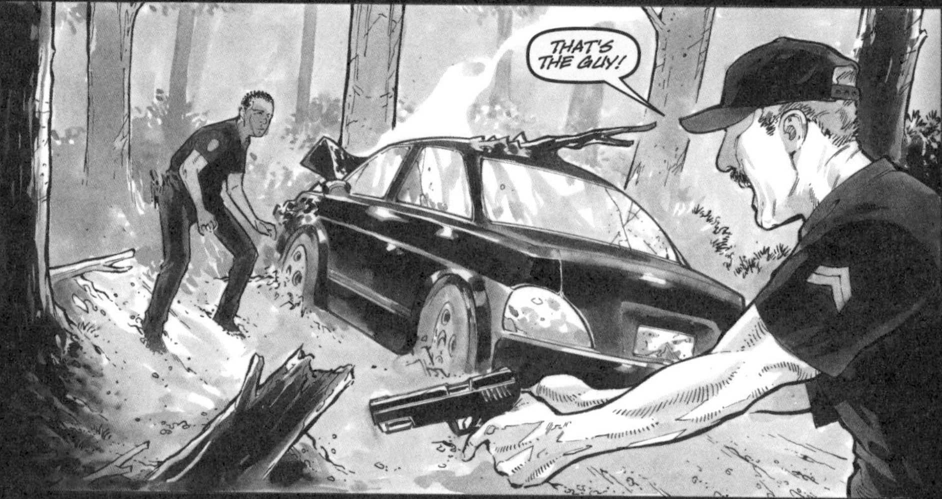
THAT'S THE GUY!
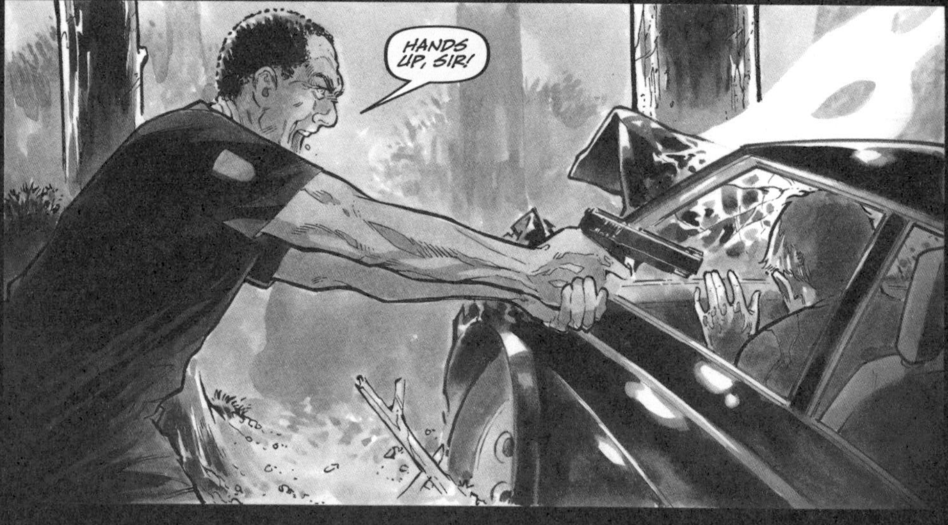
HANDS UP, SIR!

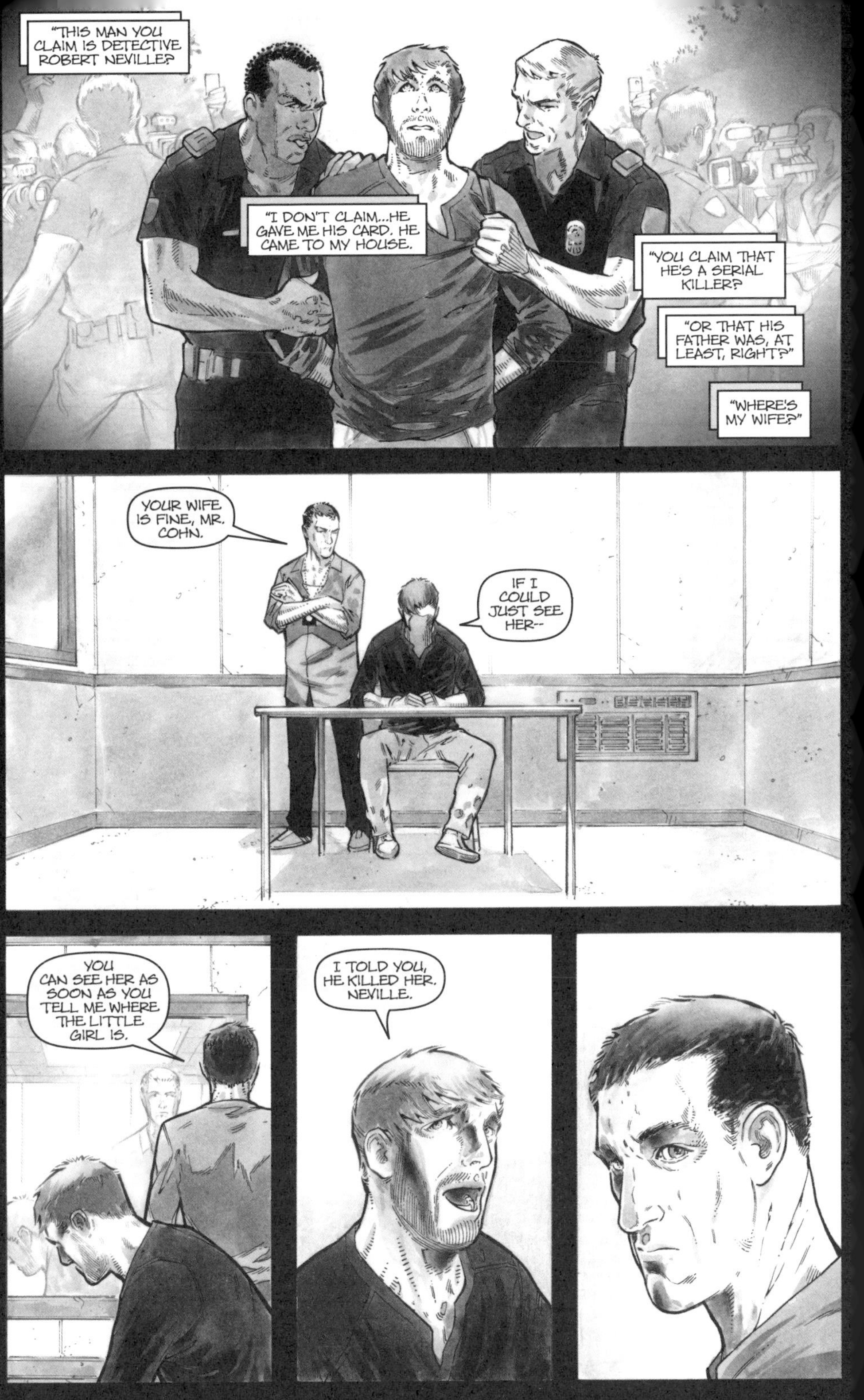
"THIS MAN YOU CLAIM IS DETECTIVE ROBERT NEVILLE?
"I DON'T CLAIM...HE GAVE ME HIS CARD. HE CAME TO MY HOUSE.
"YOU CLAIM THAT HE'S A SERIAL KILLER?
"OR THAT HIS FATHER WAS, AT LEAST, RIGHT?"
"WHERE'S MY WIFE?"
YOUR WIFE IS FINE, MR. COHN.
IF I COULD JUST SEE HER--
YOU CAN SEE HER AS SOON AS YOU TELL ME WHERE THE LITTLE GIRL IS.
I TOLD YOU, HE KILLED HER. NEVILLE.

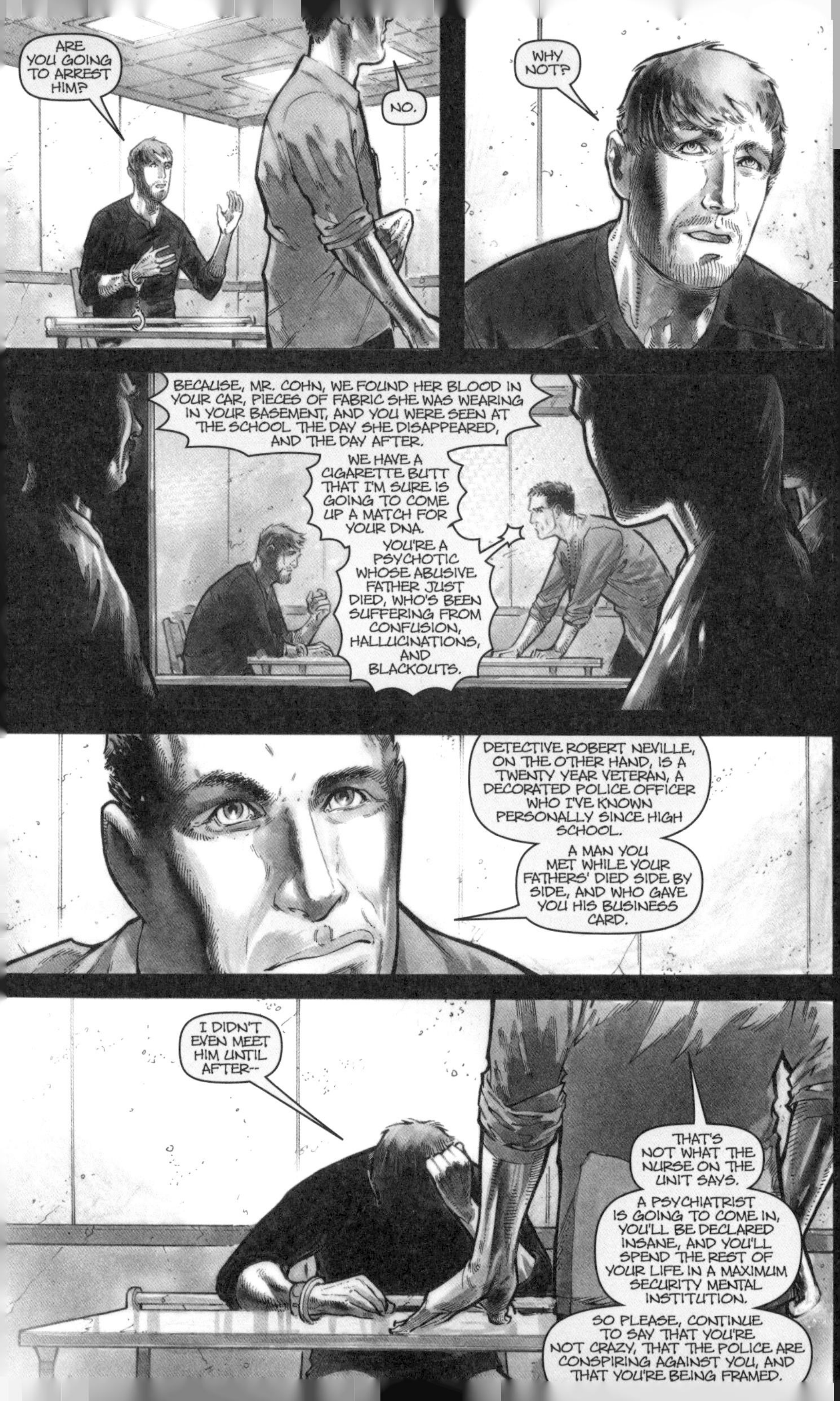
ARE YOU GOING TO ARREST HIM?
NO.
WHY NOT?
BECAUSE, MR. COHN, WE FOUND HER BLOOD IN YOUR CAR, PIECES OF FABRIC SHE WAS WEARING IN YOUR BASEMENT, AND YOU WERE SEEN AT THE SCHOOL THE DAY SHE DISAPPEARED, AND THE DAY AFTER.
WE HAVE A CIGARETTE BUTT THAT I'M SURE IS GOING TO COME UP A MATCH FOR YOUR DNA.
YOU'RE A PSYCHOTIC WHOSE ABUSIVE FATHER JUST DIED, WHO'S BEEN SUFFERING FROM CONFUSION, HALLUCINATIONS, AND BLACKOUTS.
DETECTIVE ROBERT NEVILLE, ON THE OTHER HAND, IS A TWENTY YEAR VETERAN, A DECORATED POLICE OFFICER WHO I'VE KNOWN PERSONALLY SINCE HIGH SCHOOL.
A MAN YOU MET WHILE YOUR FATHERS' DIED SIDE BY SIDE, AND WHO GAVE YOU HIS BUSINESS CARD.
I DIDN'T EVEN MEET HIM UNTIL AFTER--
THAT'S NOT WHAT THE NURSE ON THE UNIT SAYS.
A PSYCHIATRIST IS GOING TO COME IN, YOU'LL BE DECLARED INSANE, AND YOU'LL SPEND THE REST OF YOUR LIFE IN A MAXIMUM SECURITY MENTAL INSTITUTION.
SO PLEASE, CONTINUE TO SAY THAT YOU'RE NOT CRAZY, THAT THE POLICE ARE CONSPIRING AGAINST YOU, AND THAT YOU'RE BEING FRAMED.

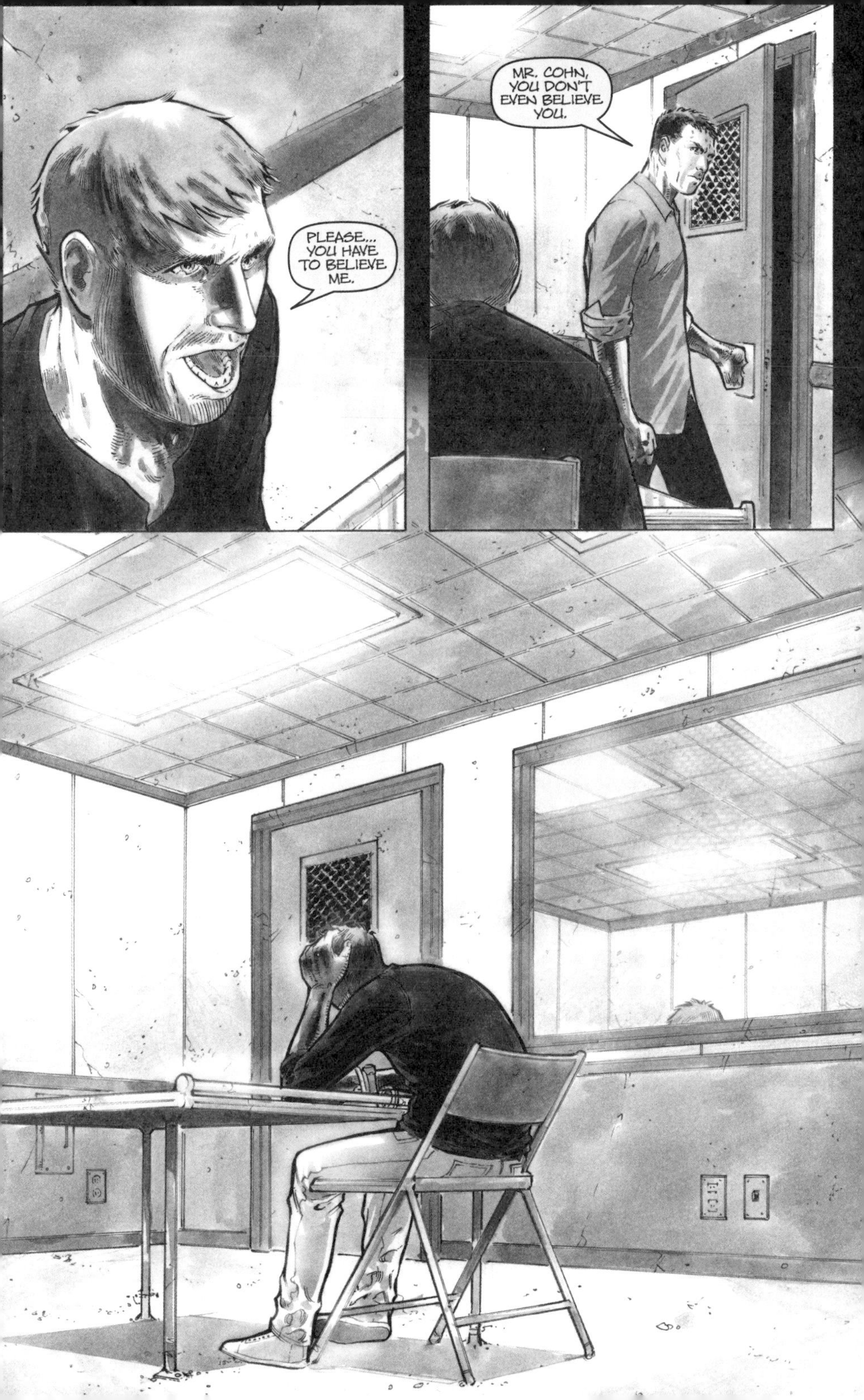
PLEASE... YOU HAVE TO BELIEVE ME.
MR. COHN, YOU DON'T EVEN BELIEVE YOU.

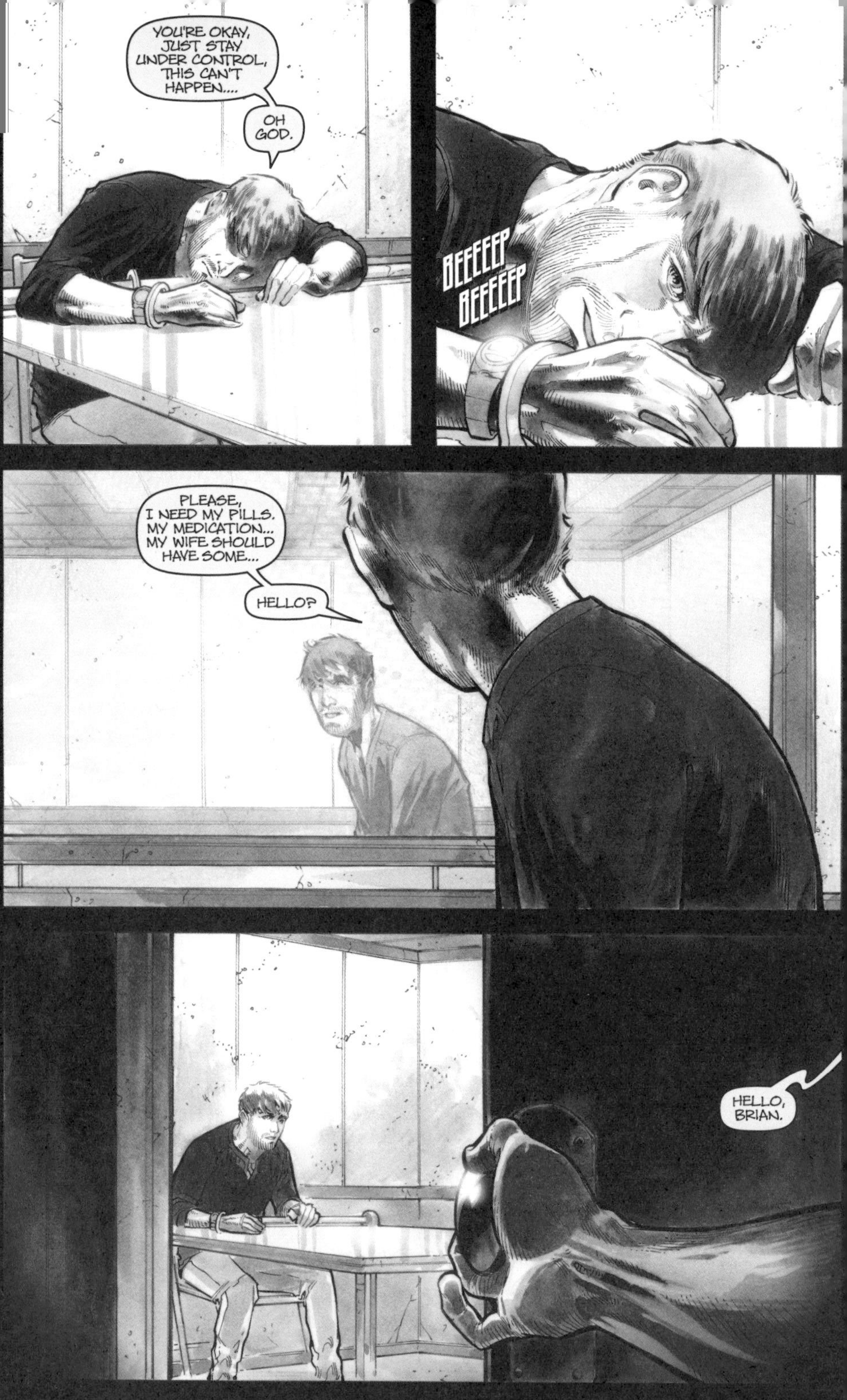
YOU'RE OKAY, JUST STAY UNDER CONTROL, THIS CAN'T HAPPEN....
OH GOD.
BEEEEEP
BEEEEEP
PLEASE, I NEED MY PILLS. MY MEDICATION... MY WIFE SHOULD HAVE SOME...
HELLO?
HELLO, BRIAN.

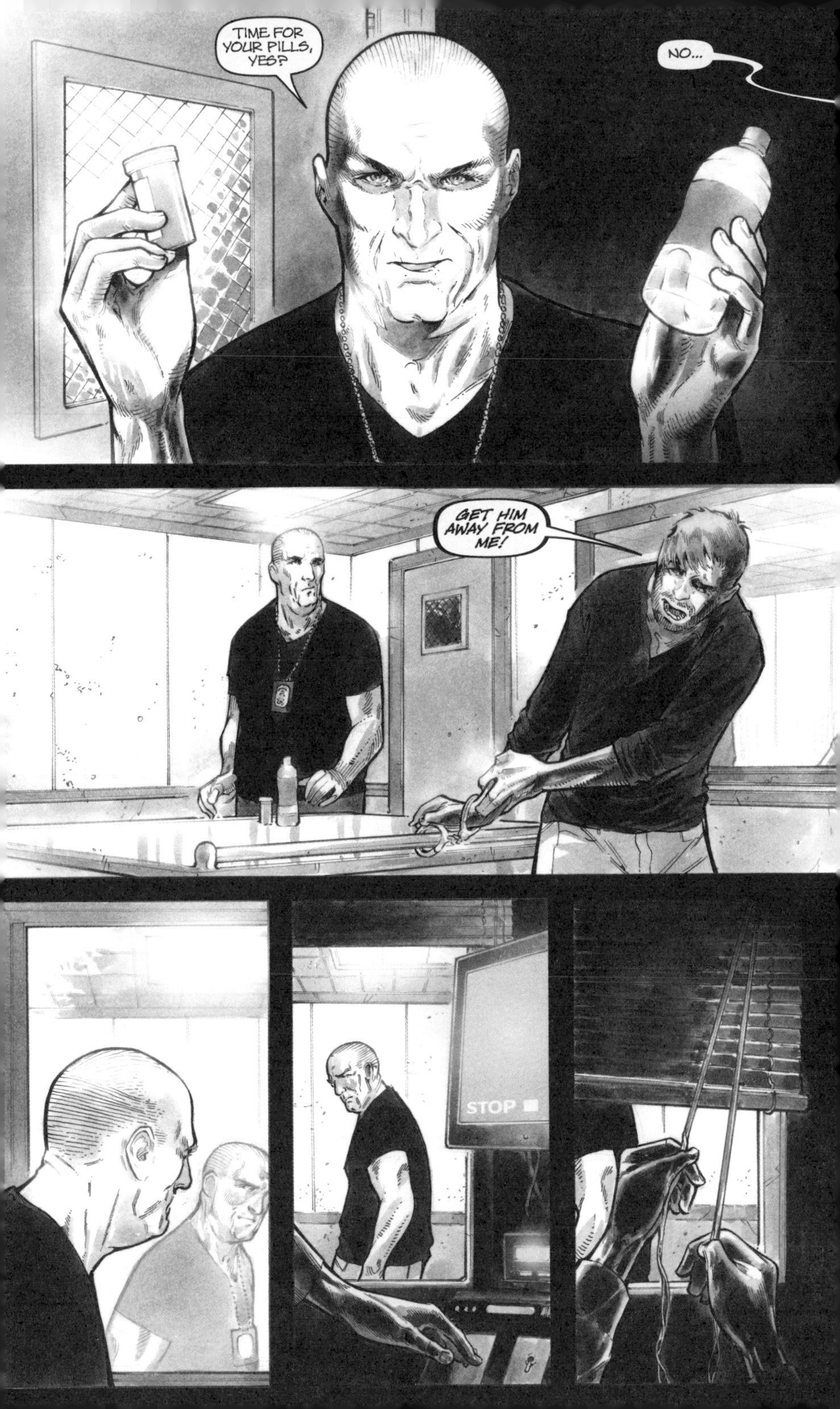
TIME FOR YOUR PILLS, YES?
NO...
GET HIM AWAY FROM ME!
STOP

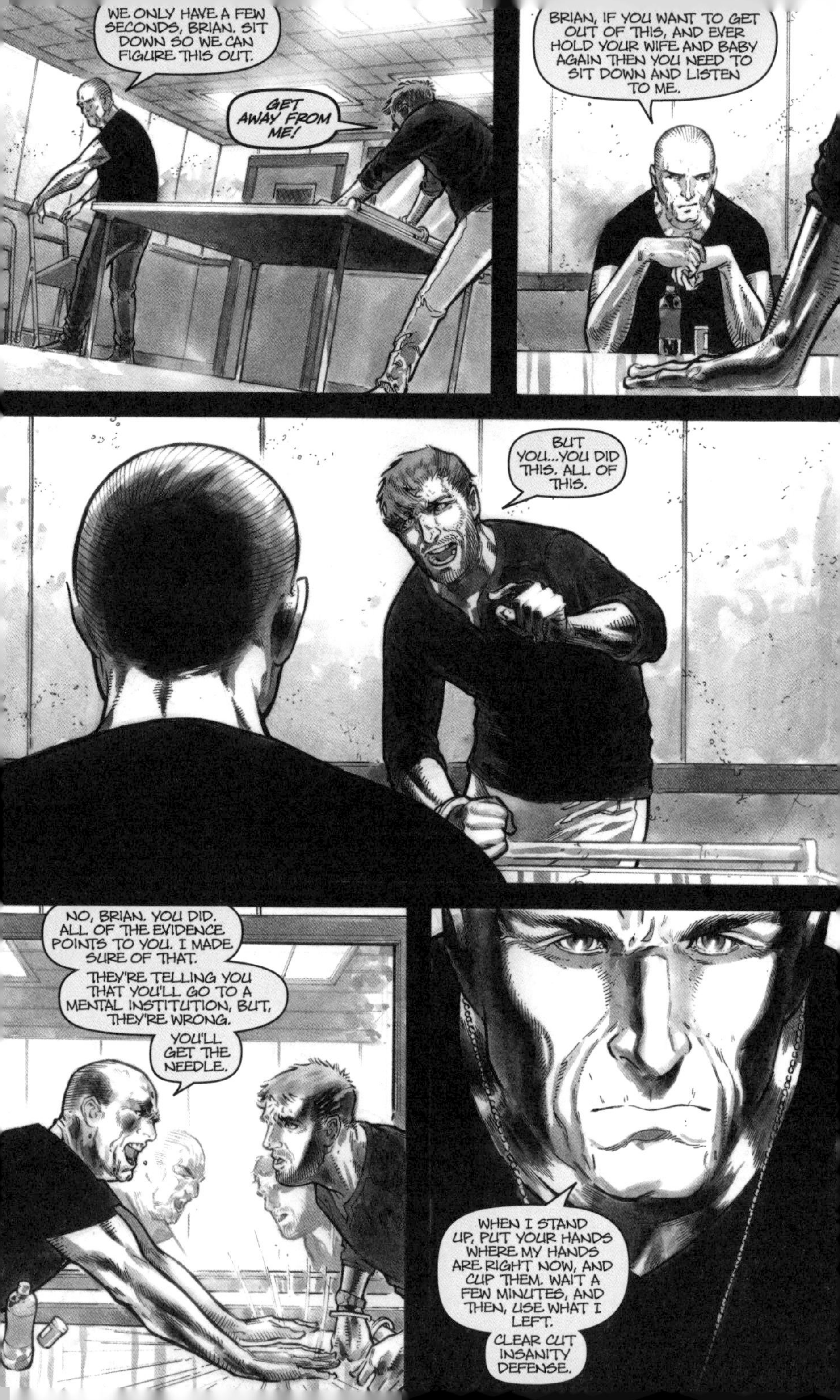
WE ONLY HAVE A FEW SECONDS, BRIAN. SIT DOWN SO WE CAN FIGURE THIS OUT.
GET AWAY FROM ME!
BRIAN, IF YOU WANT TO GET OUT OF THIS, AND EVER HOLD YOUR WIFE AND BABY AGAIN THEN YOU NEED TO SIT DOWN AND LISTEN TO ME.
BUT YOU...YOU DID THIS. ALL OF THIS.
NO, BRIAN. YOU DID. ALL OF THE EVIDENCE POINTS TO YOU. I MADE SURE OF THAT.
THEY'RE TELLING YOU THAT YOU'LL GO TO A MENTAL INSTITUTION, BUT, THEY'RE WRONG.
YOU'LL GET THE NEEDLE.
WHEN I STAND UP, PUT YOUR HANDS WHERE MY HANDS ARE RIGHT NOW, AND CUP THEM. WAIT A FEW MINUTES, AND THEN, USE WHAT I LEFT.
CLEAR CUT INSANITY DEFENSE.

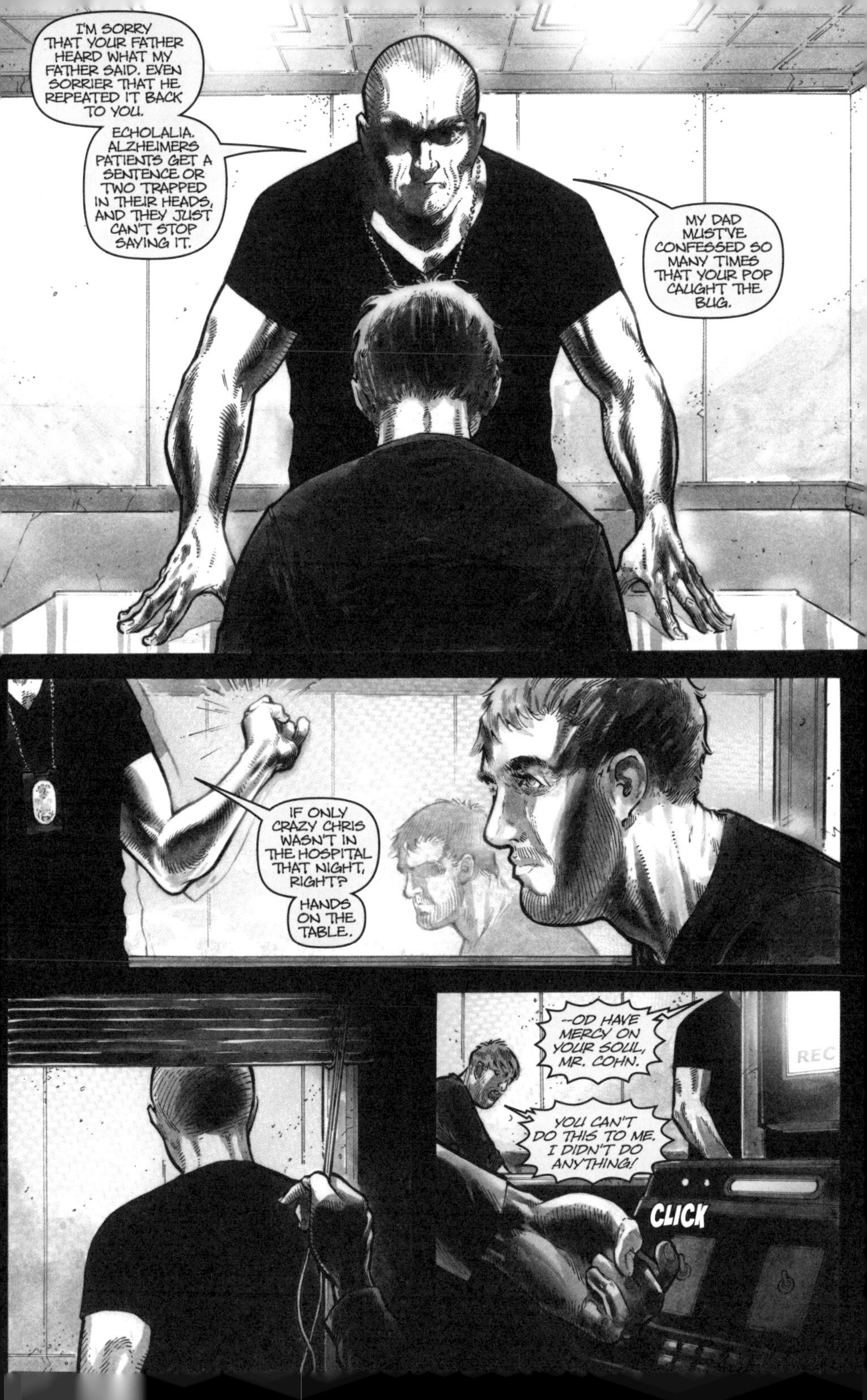
I'M SORRY THAT YOUR FATHER HEARD WHAT MY FATHER SAID. EVEN SORRIER THAT HE REPEATED IT BACK TO YOU.
ECHOLALIA. ALZHEIMERS PATIENTS GET A SENTENCE OR TWO TRAPPED IN THEIR HEADS, AND THEY JUST CAN'T STOP SAYING IT.
MY DAD MUST'VE CONFESSED SO MANY TIMES THAT YOUR POP CAUGHT THE BUG.
IF ONLY CRAZY CHRIS WASN'T IN THE HOSPITAL THAT NIGHT, RIGHT?
HANDS ON THE TABLE.
--OD HAVE MERCY ON YOUR SOUL, MR. COHN.
YOU CAN'T DO THIS TO ME. I DIDN'T DO ANYTHING!
REC
CLICK

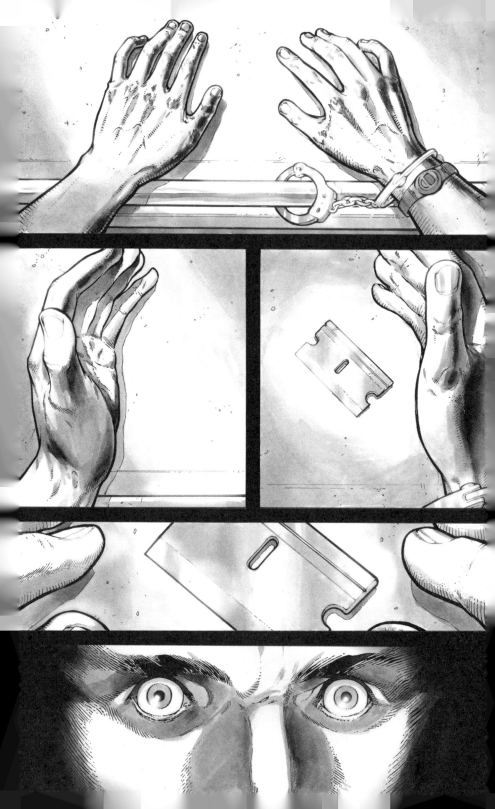

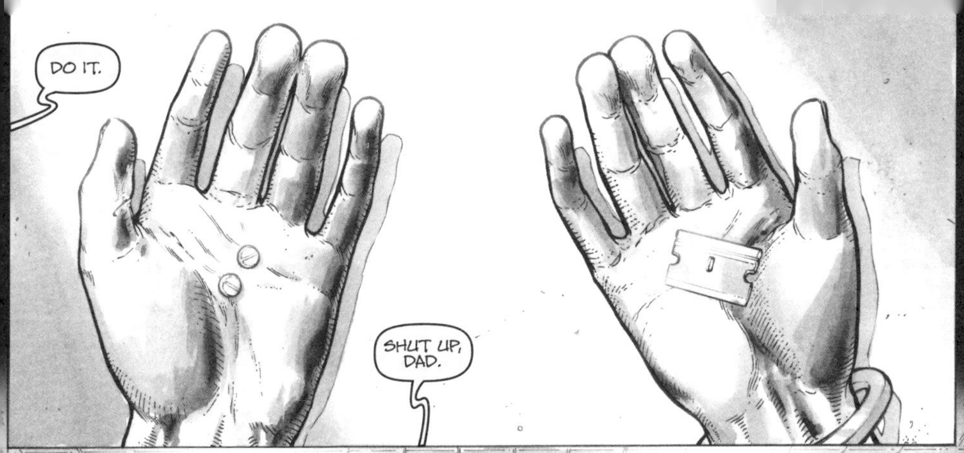
DO IT.
SHUT UP, DAD.

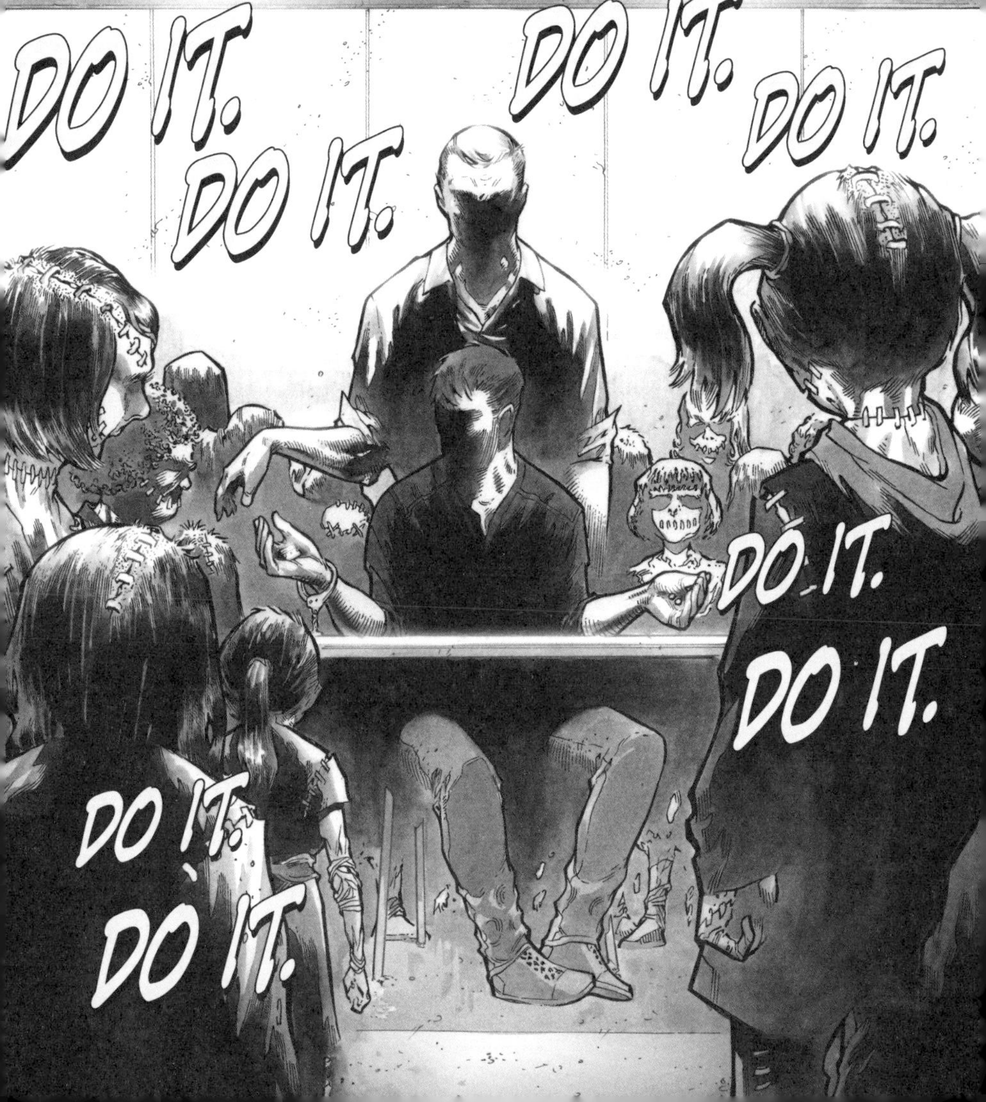
DO IT.
DO IT.
DO IT.
DO IT.
DO IT.
DO IT.
DO IT.
DO IT.

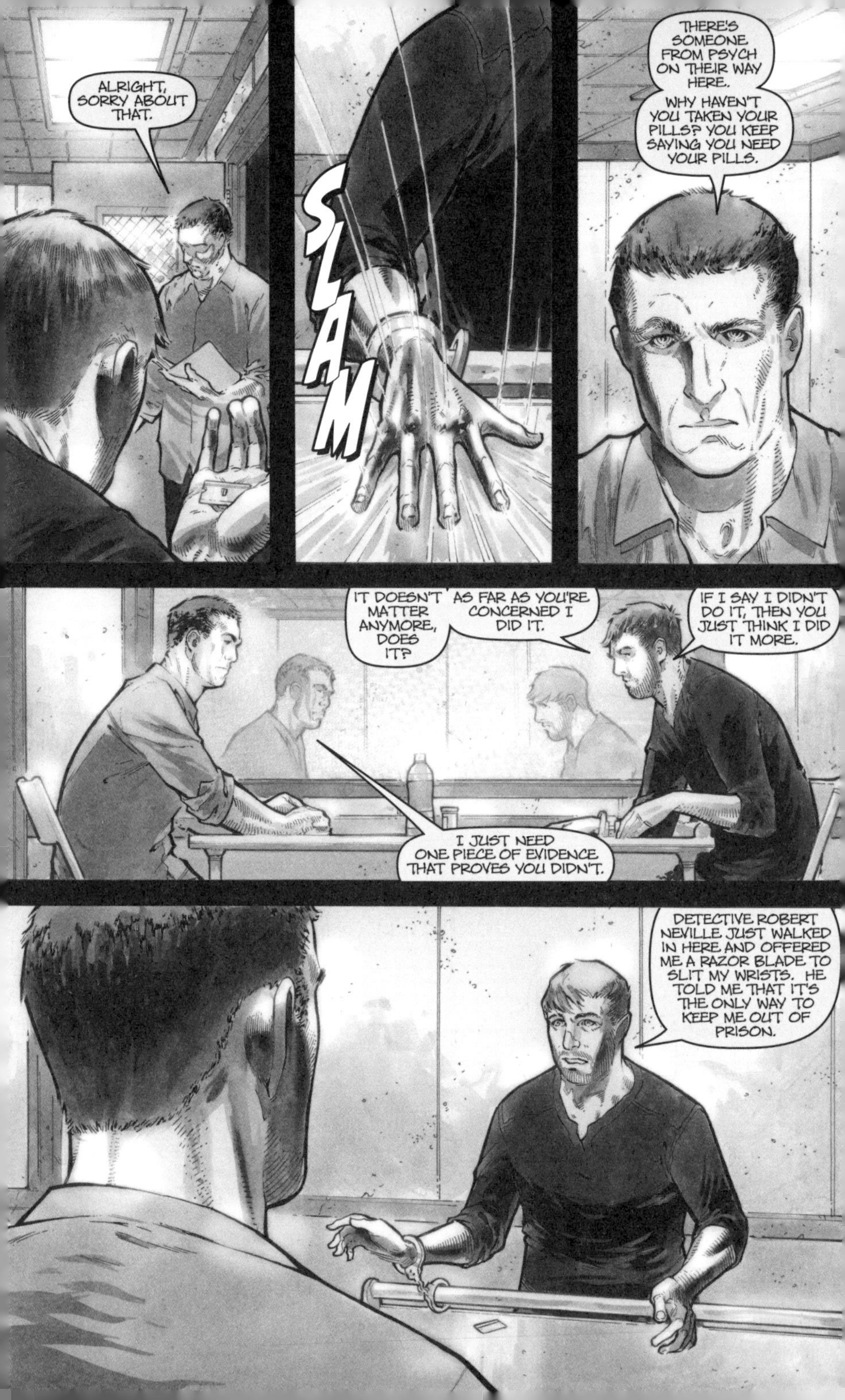
ALRIGHT, SORRY ABOUT THAT.
SLAM
THERE'S SOMEONE FROM PSYCH ON THEIR WAY HERE.
WHY HAVEN'T YOU TAKEN YOUR PILLS? YOU KEEP SAYING YOU NEED YOUR PILLS.
IT DOESN'T MATTER ANYMORE, DOES IT?
AS FAR AS YOU'RE CONCERNED I DID IT.
IF I SAY I DIDN'T DO IT, THEN YOU JUST THINK I DID IT MORE.
I JUST NEED ONE PIECE OF EVIDENCE THAT PROVES YOU DIDN'T.
DETECTIVE ROBERT NEVILLE JUST WALKED IN HERE AND OFFERED ME A RAZOR BLADE TO SLIT MY WRISTS. HE TOLD ME THAT IT'S THE ONLY WAY TO KEEP ME OUT OF PRISON.

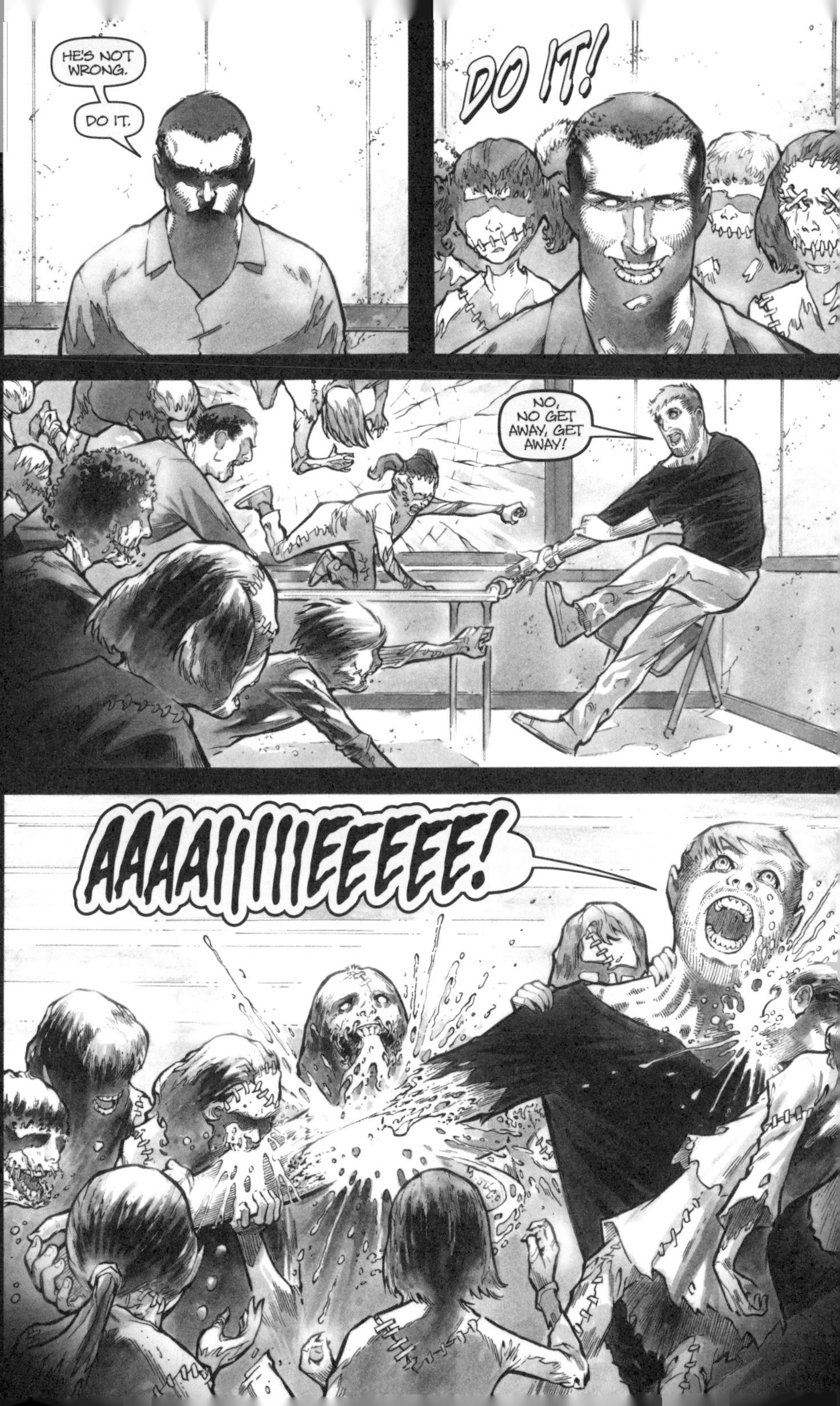
HE'S NOT WRONG.
DO IT.
DO IT!
NO, NO GET AWAY, GET AWAY!
AAAAIIIIIEEEEEE!

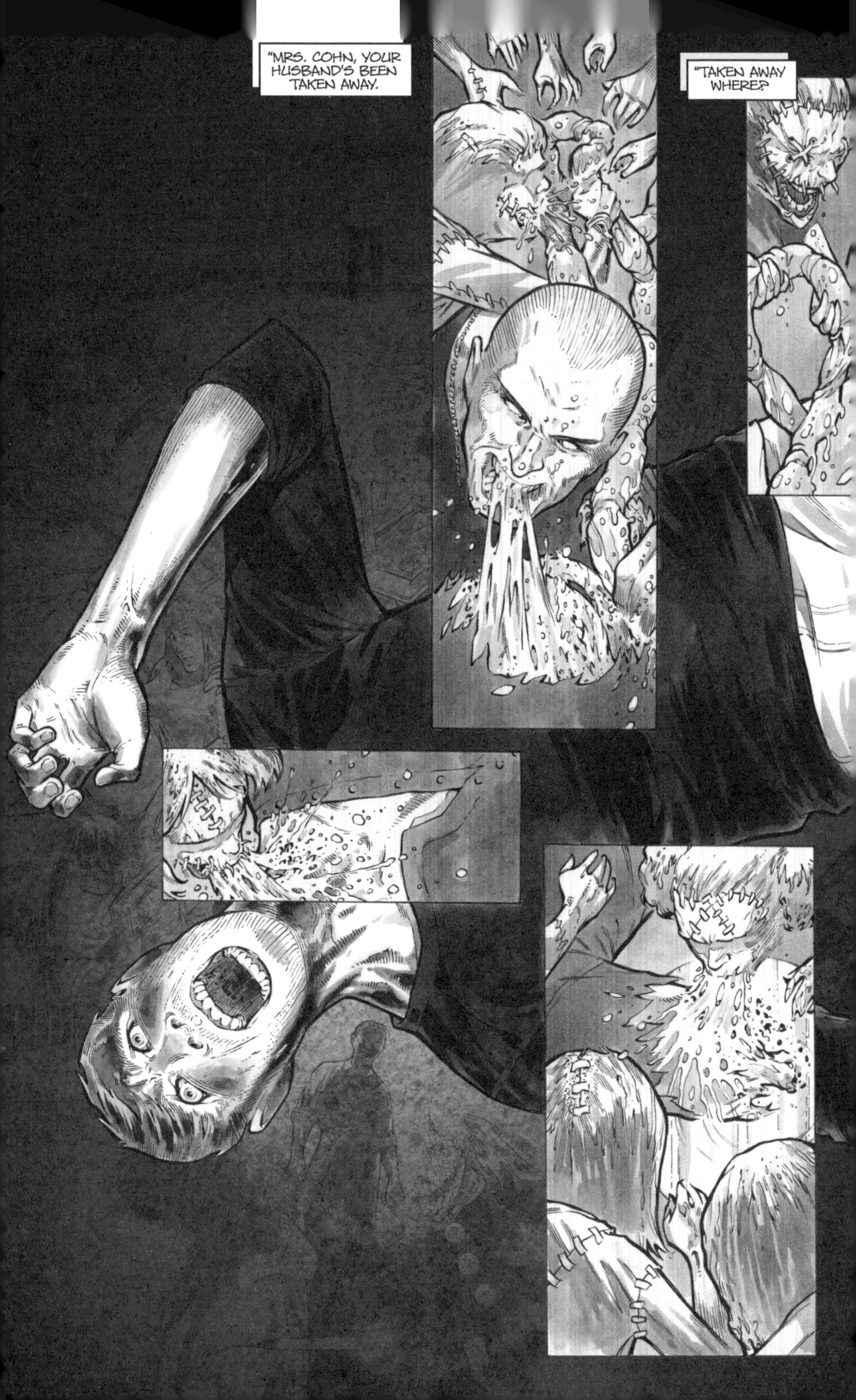
"MRS. COHN, YOUR HUSBAND'S BEEN TAKEN AWAY.
"TAKEN AWAY WHERE?

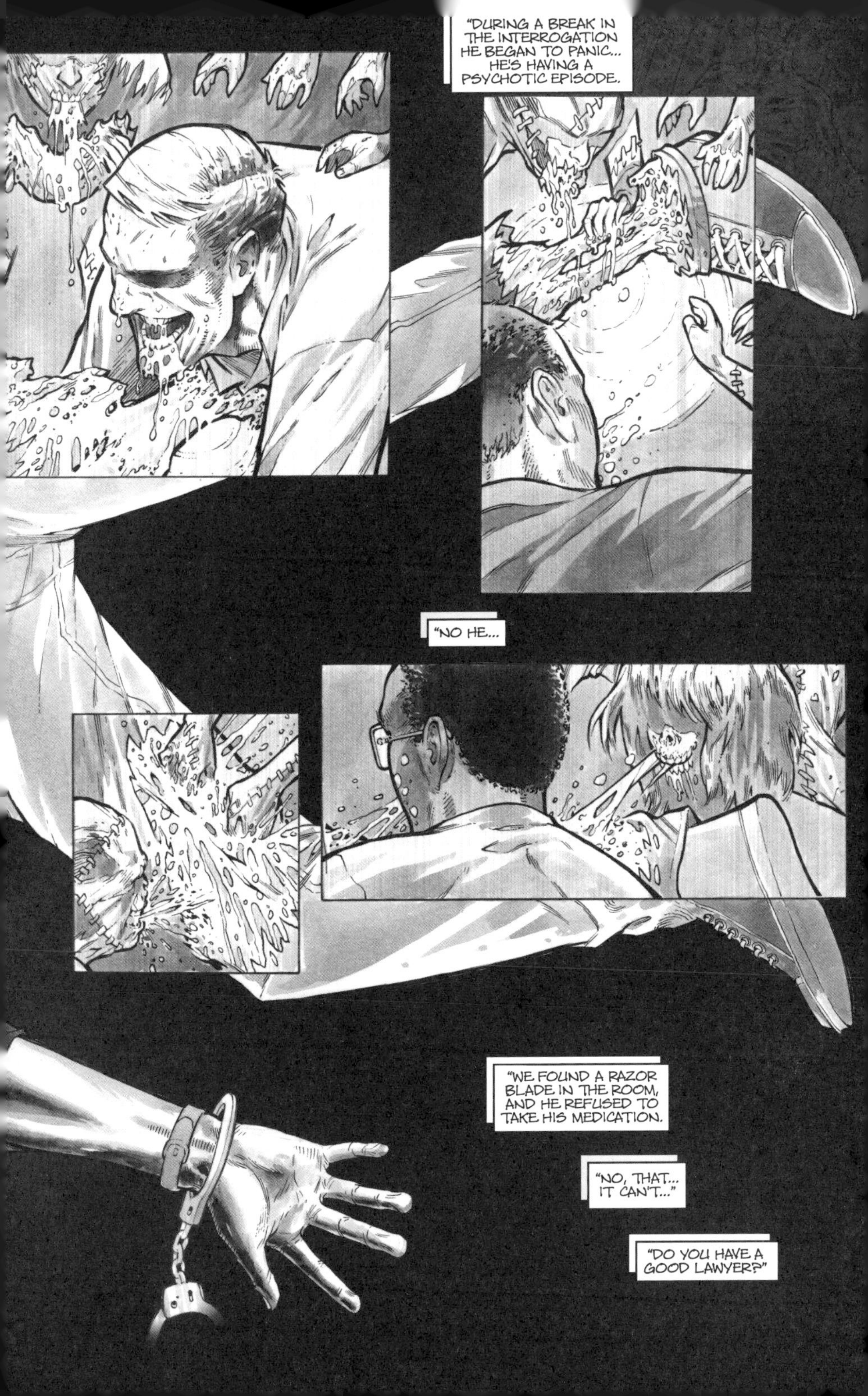
"DURING A BREAK IN THE INTERROGATION HE BEGAN TO PANIC... HE'S HAVING A PSYCHOTIC EPISODE.
"NO HE...
"WE FOUND A RAZOR BLADE IN THE ROOM, AND HE REFUSED TO TAKE HIS MEDICATION.
"NO, THAT... IT CAN'T..."
"DO YOU HAVE A GOOD LAWYER?"

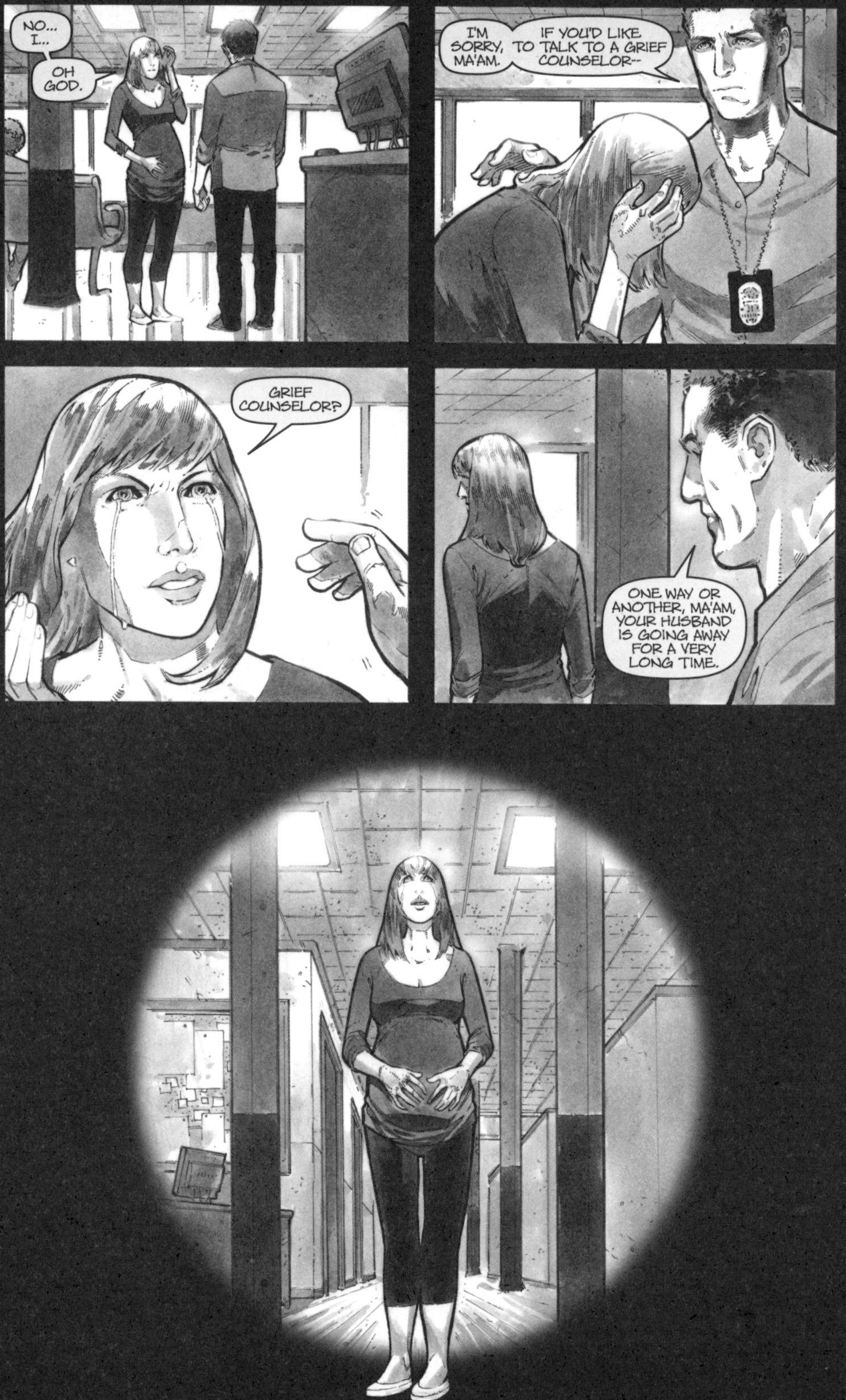
NO... I...
OH GOD.
I'M SORRY, MA'AM.
IF YOU'D LIKE TO TALK TO A GRIEF COUNSELOR--
GRIEF COUNSELOR?
ONE WAY OR ANOTHER, MA'AM, YOUR HUSBAND IS GOING AWAY FOR A VERY LONG TIME.

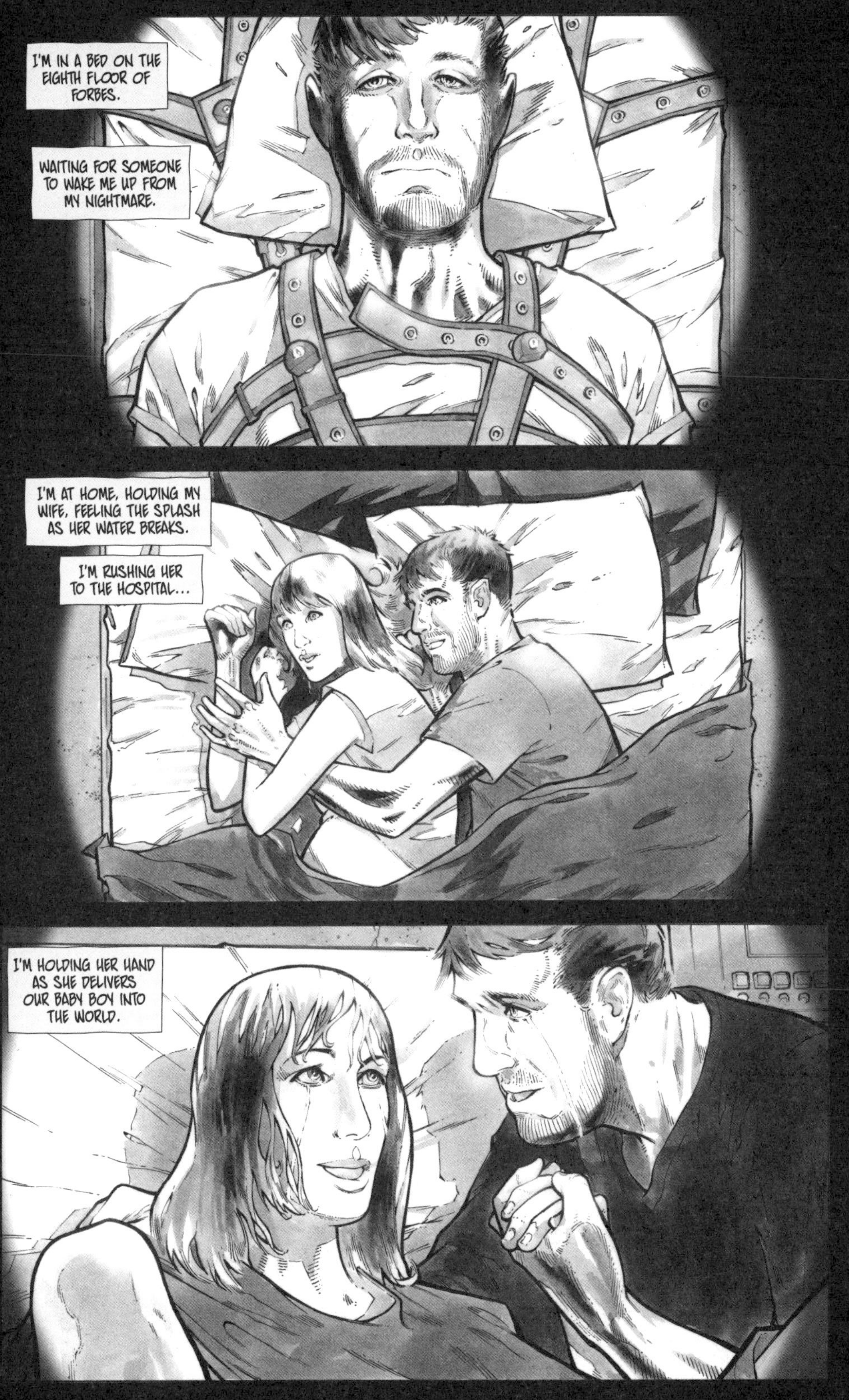
I'M IN A BED ON THE EIGHTH FLOOR OF FORBES.
WAITING FOR SOMEONE TO WAKE ME UP FROM MY NIGHTMARE.
I'M AT HOME, HOLDING MY WIFE, FEELING THE SPLASH AS HER WATER BREAKS.
I'M RUSHING HER TO THE HOSPITAL...
I'M HOLDING HER HAND AS SHE DELIVERS OUR BABY BOY INTO THE WORLD.

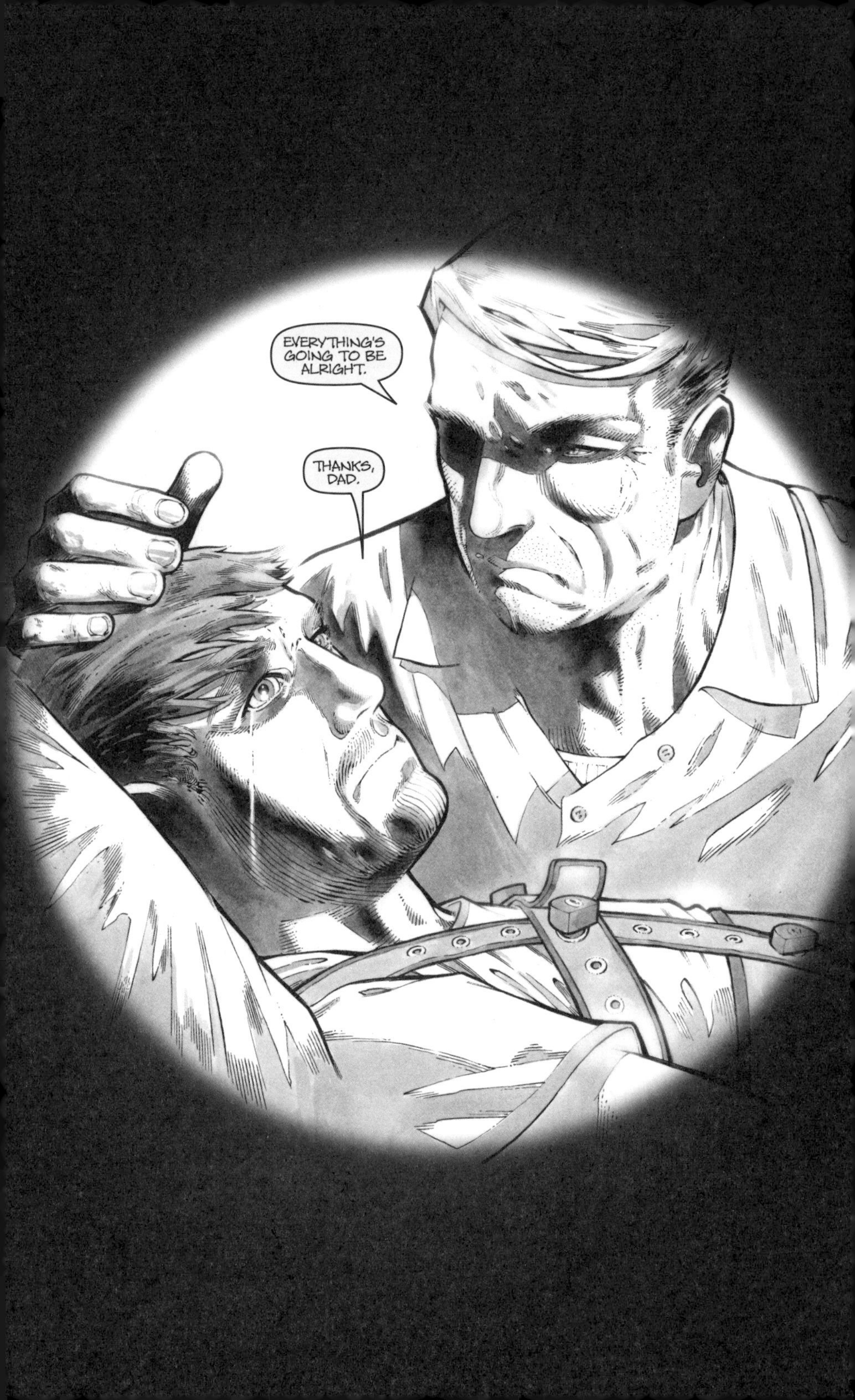
EVERYTHING'S GOING TO BE ALRIGHT.
THANKS, DAD.

ECHOES by Joshua Hale Fialkov and Rahsan Ekedal is one of those special creative endeavors you feel lucky to be part of. We felt strongly that it deserved a special presentation for the collected edition, which you've enjoyed thus far. An immense amount of work, thought, and love was poured into this project. Joshua and Rahsan have decided to share some behind-the-scenes extras to show their process.

- Filip Sablik
Publisher, Top Cow Productions, Inc.

Normally, my books change drastically between proposal and execution. I'll find something that I thought was just a detail that actually becomes a focal point for my writing. That thing will get stuck in my craw and upend the entire apple cart. This didn't happen with Echoes. Sitting here reading through the initial documents I used to pitch and develop the series, pretty much the only big change was to slightly more realistic use of schizophrenia, rather than some vague chemical imbalance.

It's extremely rare for an idea to come out this well formed out of the gate, so I figure I get bragging rights to show it all off.

- Joshua Hale Fialkov

ECHOES

An Original Graphic Novel in Five Parts
by Joshua Hale Fialkov

"I've killed three dozen girls over the past thirty years. I took pieces of their flesh and bone and made dolls of each one. I hid them under a house over on Haymaker. I need you to give them to the police, so that their families know what happened to them. It's my last wish."

These are the last words that Brian's father ever said. After years in an Alzheimer's induced near-coma, he had one moment of clarity, confessing this unthinkable crime to his son, with only his equally Alzheimer's afflicted roommate as a witness.

Brian and his father had a lot in common. They both haved a temper, an inability to get along with woman, and were both victims of abuse. They also share a chemical imbalance that they both treat with chemicals and psychotherapy. Brian is haunted by the thought that perhaps this is something they have in common, too. As Brian holds the metal box filled with dozens of tiny, grotesque dolls made of the bodies of his father's victims, and all he can do... is be impressed.

Brian's dad passes away, and Brian can't bring himself to turn him in. Instead, he takes the box to his own house and hides it from everybody, including his fiancee, Nicole. The day of his father's funeral, Brian and Nicole return home and find a small package on the front porch. When they open it they find another of the death dolls inside. This one is horrific, poorly made, but, seemingly made by the same hands as the others.

Brian's mental state is deteriorating, he hasn't seen his therapist in weeks, and his medication isn't working. He finds himself driving through the playgrounds of the local elementary schools looking at litte girls and imagining what they'd look like as dolls. One little girl in particular catches his eye. A few days later, another doll appears on his door step. It's the little girl. He adds it to the box, and promises himself that he's done with all of this.

Nicole notices the deterioration, and begs Brian to get help. He lies about going to see his doctor, and instead goes back to the elementary school to watch the children through the fence. That's when he meets Detective Allan Martin. He's seen him here before, and has done some research.

Martin takes Brian to a coffee shop, rather than to the station, putting Brian a little bit more at ease. Then he begins to interrogate him about both his late father and the missing girls. Brian cracks, he confesses that his father was the killer, and that he has the trophies. Martin enlists Brian to help find and capture the copycat killer.

As they follow the trail, Brian starts to lose control, realizing that he's investigating himself. Everything that made his father a monster, was alive in him. Martin drops him off at his car, and tells him that if anything else happens, to get in touch.

The next day, Martin returns to Brian's house, and tells him that he needs him to come along to lend a hand. Brian, confused, but, desperate to not be guilty, goes along. Among the stops they make, one is at the elementary school that Brian had visited earlier.

They talk to a little girl about what happened to her friend. The little girl describes a man, very similar in appearance to Brian having come to see the girl during the day. Martin suspects him and begins provoking him, unfolding the details, making it clear that he knows that it was Brian. Brian freaks out, and runs off, leaving Martin behind, as he goes back to the place this all started, his father's hospital room.

A new man has joined his father's roommate in the room. He stares at the bed that housed his father, and then goes to the roommate. He starts to talk, as he's the only other witness to his father's confession. When he talks, the other old man in the room repeats back what he says, perfectly. Same inflection, same voice. A nurse explains that this is called echolalia, and is one of the symptoms of late stage Alzheimer's. They can't control it, it just comes out.

Brian realizes what's been going on. He asks the nurse for the roommate's name. "Henry Martin." "What does his son do?" "He's a police officer."

And, a serial killer, realizes Brian.

Brian starts to panic as he leaves the home... Outside he finds himself face to face with Martin. With the killer. With all of his nightmares. Martin attacks him, and Brian struggles to fight him off. He manages to knock Martin out cold, and to get to the police for help.

He confesses everything, telling them the entire story from top to bottom. The cops listen quietly, and then walk out of the room. When they return it's with the trophy box. Which they found in his house. Each doll covered in his fingerprints. They show him photographs of him outside the elementary school the day before the last girl went missing. One by one they unveil pieces of evidence that Martin had corrupted to point to Brian as the killer. He begs them to listen, but the final piece of evidence is too much for even Brian.

They flip a switch on the wall that turns the mirror on the wall to a two way mirror. There's another little girl, wrapped in a blanket. It's the little girl that Martin had taken Brian to talk to earlier. She was found by Brian's fiancee locked up in the basement of their house. The little girl had said that a police man had asked her to go with him, and then he'd tied her up and locked her in his basement.

Brian's fiancee came to the police hours ago, with Detective Martin to tell what she knew about her fiancee and what she'd found in the basement with the little girl.

Brian sits silently in his cell when Martin comes to visit. He whispers in his ear, on behalf of his father and himself, two words. "Thank you."

ECHOES

WORK IN PROGRESS

CHARACTER DESIGNS

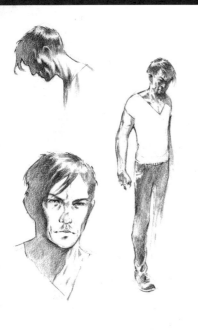

The earliest design of Brian. This version was quickly discarded as it simply didn't fit his character.

Pg:
Pg:
Pg:
Pg:
SANDY HAIR
PREPPY/ GEEK STYLE
OUT OF SHAPE DAVID BOREANAZ
Book:
Rahsan Ekedal

A later character design of Brian, closest to the version that finally materialized in the first finished pages.

- Rahsan Ekedal

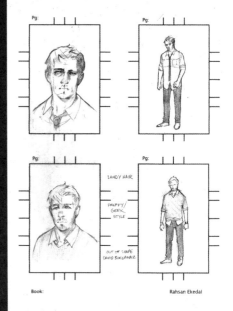

ECHOES™

WORK IN PROGRESS

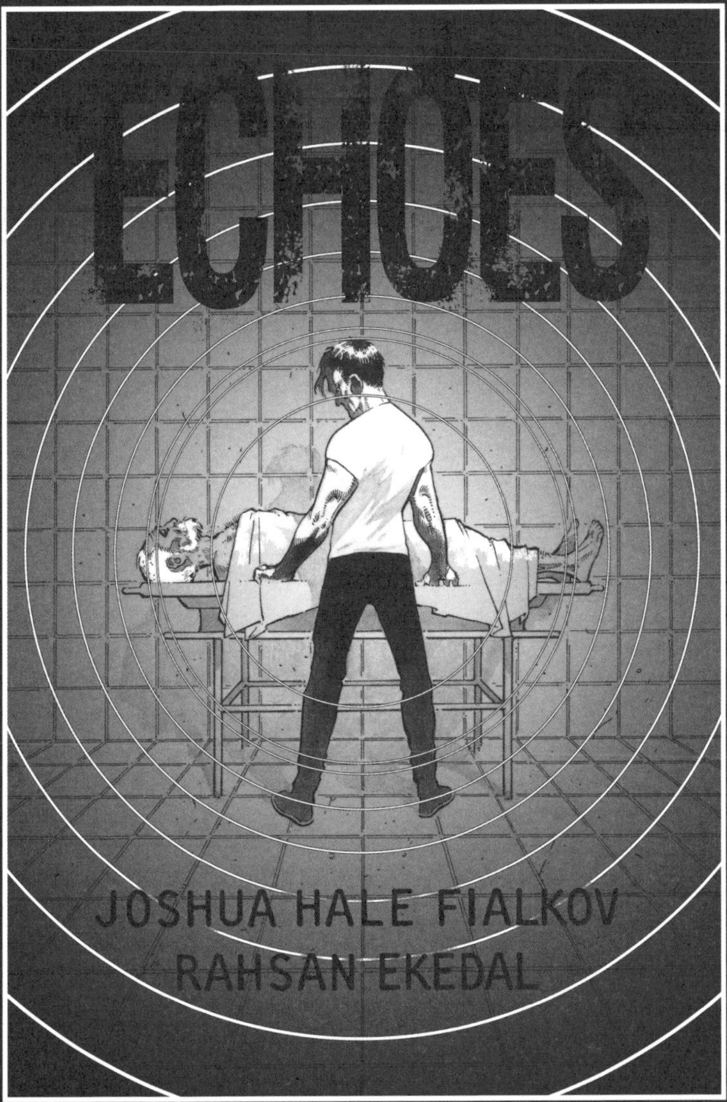
ECHOES
JOSHUA HALE FIALKOV
RAHSAN EKEDAL

An early teaser image that Josh used to pitch the book, before the first script was written. "Hero Brian" and "Bearded Father" made their first and last appearance in this image.

ECHOES

WORK IN PROGRESS

PROCESS PIECE

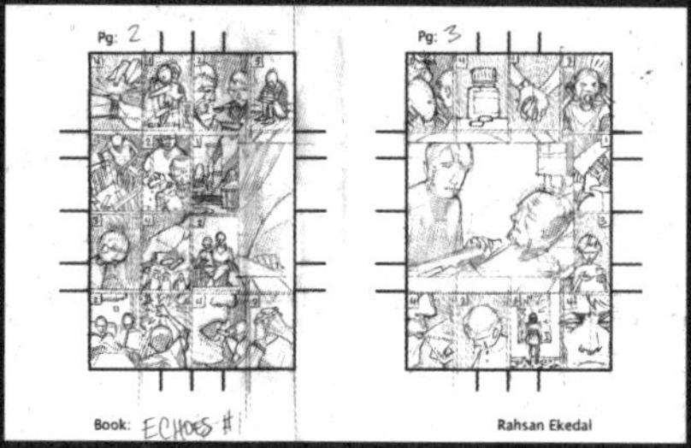
Pg: 2
Pg: 3
Book: ECHOES #
Rahsan Ekedal

The thumbnails for the big two-page spread from issue 1, the first of six spreads that were the visual anchor points for the entire story.

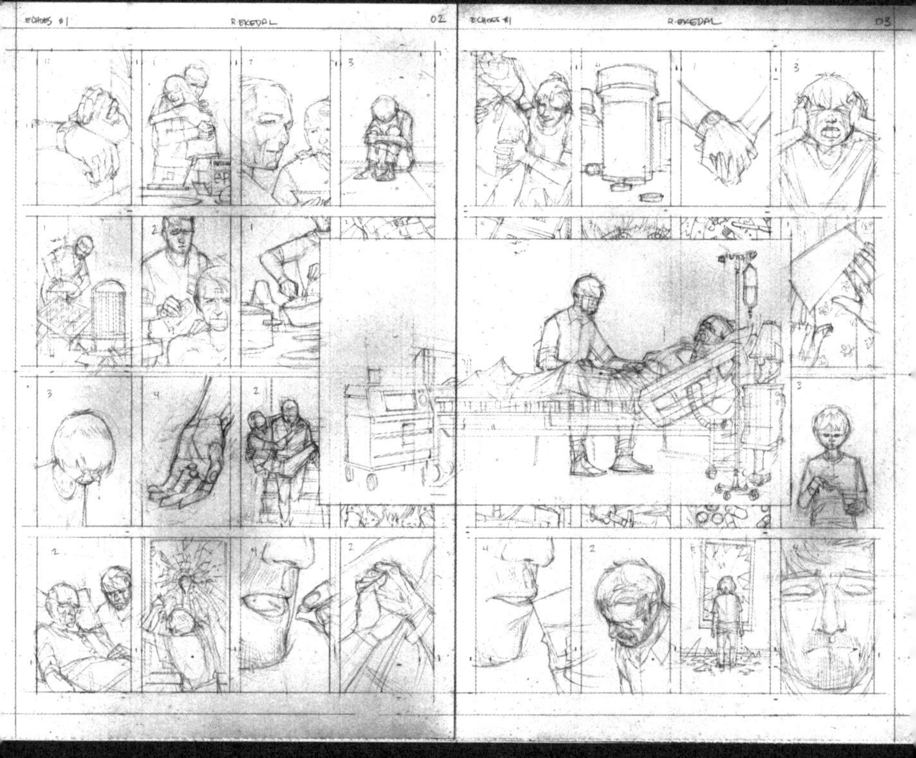
ECHOES #1
R.EKEDAL
02
ECHOES #1
R.EKEDAL
03

The full pencil layout, pages 2 and 3 of issue 1. Note the little numbers in each panel on this layout and the thumbnail of these pages. There were four different timelines running concurrently n alternating panels, and I played with bunch of different patterns before finally settling on the

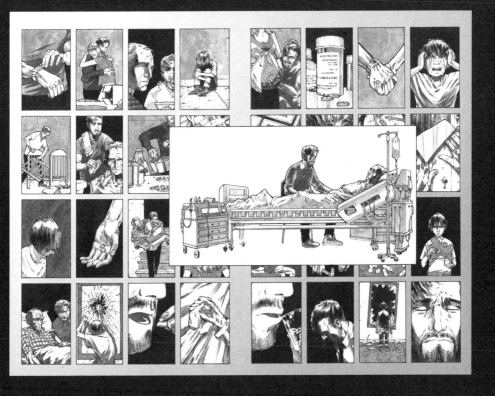

The final inks, pages 2 and 3, issue 1.

ECHOES™

ISSUE NO. 1 SCRIPTBOOK

In the following pages, we offer up Joshua Hale Fialkov's complete original script for Echoes #1, side by side with Rahsan Ekedal's layouts and pencils for a unique insight into the creative process. Additionally, courtesy of Comic Book Resources and Robot 6, each page is accompanied with annotations from Fialkov.

Echoes #1 Commentary
originally published: February 7th, 2011
http://www.comicbookresources.com
http://www.robot6.comicbookresources.com/echoescomic/2011/echoes-cover

CBR COMIC BOOK RESOURCES

Serialized story telling is about juggling. There's keeping the characters straight, as well as keeping the story momentum going, all while making sure there's a cliffhanger that keeps you coming back 30 days later. Through the years of working in comics, I've tried to hone some theories on all of those things, and hopefully, I'll get to talk about some of them here for you.

PAGE 1

PANEL 1
Wide Panel, XCU on Brian's eyes. They're sallow, sunken, and bloodshot. He looks like he's been crying.

BRIAN (CAPTION)
I'm in the Monroeville police station now, sitting with Officer Steve Davis, going over mystory for the 10th time.

PANEL 2
Wide panel, Brian sits next to his very pregnant wife as she gets an ultrasound.

BRIAN (CAPTION)
Now I'm at the Forbes regional Hospital hearing my son's heartbeat for the first time.

PANEL 3
Wide panel, Brian is holding a metal box that he stands in a grotty awful basement crawl space behind him filled with junk. The panel should center on the box of junk cutting Brian's head and his lower body off.

BRIAN (CAPTION)
Now I'm in the basement of the house 1/2 mile from where I grew up holding a box of my father's sins.

I spend a disproportionate amount of time working on my Page 1s. I want the reader to get into the rhythm of the book as quickly as possible, as well as the book's voice and tone. So what you see here is a tightly controlled visual story flow with the panels containing a repeating rhythm of dialogue, as well as one of the key narrative devices of the book.

By having just the three panels, and by having that dialogue with the repeating content, the reader is, in theory anyways, keyed into the pace of the book, and will feel the shock of what comes next with the right timing.

Now, here's why this pacing matters. In thirty days when you pick up number two, page 1 is going to match this page 1. The content will be new, but the style and format of the page is the same. This is to inspire a subconscious trigger for you, reminding you of the rhythm and pacing of the book last time. It lulls you back into the rhythm of the series in a subtle way, and requires less time for your mind to play catch up.

A note to young writers: This two page spread is a dick move for a writer. The original script read like this.

Okay, this is gonna be fun. Well, for me and the reader, not so much for you my poor put upon artist. The page is a 24 panel grid with an image floating in front of all of them. The front layer image is of Brian sitting next to his father's deathbed. We see all of Brian as he is he leaning forward sitting to the side of his father, Martin, who looks like he's about to go... He's gaunt, broken, and pale.

24 PANEL GRID

A series of small panels, details can be light as long as we get the gist of what the actions are. There's four storylines that you can alternate, each getting six panels. I'm leaving it up to you what the images are, instead I gave you the beats we need to see.

THREAD ONE
Brian finds out his wife is pregnant, Brian talking to his wife's belly, Brian holding his wife's hand, Brian building a crib, Brian cooking for his wife, Brian wallpapering the baby's room.

THREAD TWO
Brian feeds his father, Brian helps to carry his father up the stairs, Brian sponge bathing his father, Brian sitting next to his father in a hospital bed, Brian holding his father's hand, Brian crying gently.

THREAD THREE
The younger Brian sits with his arms around his legs, rocking gently. He's angry, he sat, he screaming, he's breaking she, he's taking his pills.

THREAD FOUR

This should follow the process of Brian taking his meds. So we see his dosage watch going off, the bottle of pills labelled _______, the pills in Brian's hand, Brian tossing the pills into his mouth, Brian's eyes shut tight as he swallows.

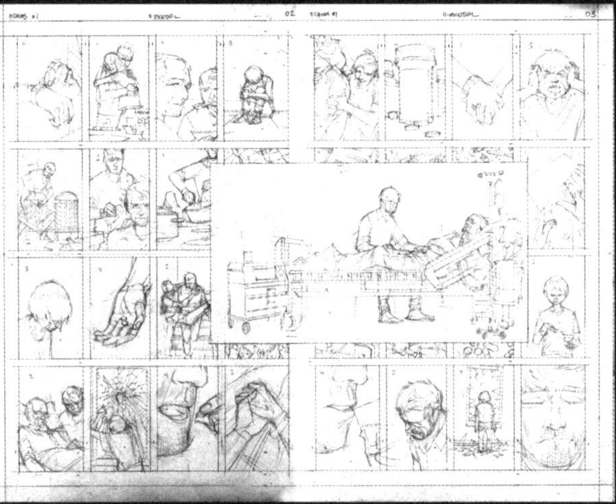

CAPTIONS SHOULD FLOW ACROSS THE PAGE

CAPTION
"Your father doesn't have long now Brian.
(Break)
You need to say goodbye.
(Break)
For what it's worth, he doesn't feel any pain anymore. The Alzheimer's has taken hold.
(break)
What you think of as your father is gone."
BRIAN
Hey dad, it's me.

CAPTION (OTHER PATIENT)
(faded and unreadable)
Everybody needs to know...
(break)
No one listens.
(break)
Everybody.
(break)
No one comes. Nobody cares.
(break)
No good for nothing son.

Now, in my defense, Rahsan added way more panels than I asked for, of his own freewill, and the spread is way more awesome than I could've ever imagined it. Secondly, I think these spreads will become one of the defining images of the series. Thus, going back to what we discussed yesterday with page 1. The first three pages of each issue are repeated throughout the series. Again, this is because of the familiarity as mentioned, and also because these pages represent exactly what our P.O.V. character is feeling in a hard, visual way. You understand when you look at this spread that his mind is a jumbled confused mess, as a thousand ideas race through them a mile a minute. So, Page 1 establishes how he thinks in a straight, easy to understand way, Pages 2 and 3 drive that point home.

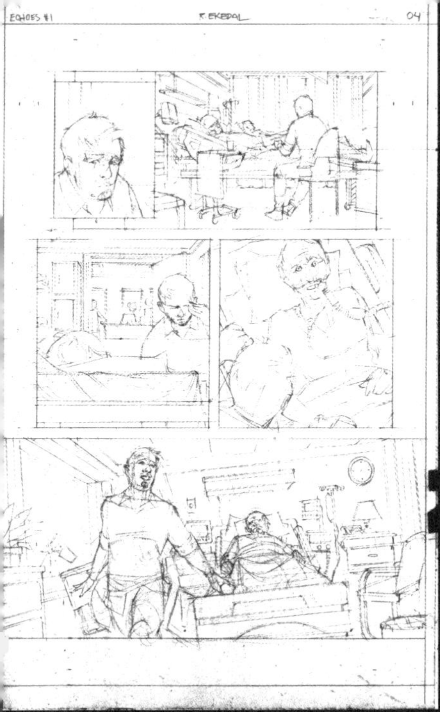
ECHOES #1
R. EKEDAL
04

PAGE 4

NOTE: AS MUCH AS POSSIBLE WE SHOULD MAKE IT CLEAR THAT THIS IS NOT A PRIVATE ROOM. THERE IS A CURTAIN DIVIDER BETWEEN MARTIN AND HIS NEIGHBOR.

PANEL ONE
Medium shot on Brian, tears in his eyes.

BRIAN
We saw the baby today, dad.

PANEL 2
OTHER PATIENT
(unreadable)
Always making trouble, never listening to me.
(break)

Good for nothing son of a-

BRIAN
I don't know how you put up with this guy, dad.

PANEL 3
From a three quarters angle, so that we see Brian's hand touching his father sand as well as both of their faces clearly. Martin's eyes are closed, like he's drifting to sleep. Through the curtain, we can see the shadow of another old man on another hospital bed.

BRIAN
We tried to get you a private room, but it was too-

MARTIN
(muttering)(off)
Mmm...the box...

PANEL FIVE
Brian stands up one hand on his father's body turned as though he's about to run out the door.

BRIAN
Just hold on dad I'll go get someone.

MARTIN
Dead girls... so many dead girls...

The hardest thing about horror in comics is that the reader's eye can see the scares coming. They can see the kick before they actually read the kick, and so therefore, the kick is more of a push. Rahsan and I spent a lot of time discussing how to combat this. How do we create a thriller where you can literally see the twists and turns coming. This page is the first example of how we combat that. You get a big shocking reveal that is hidden by how the page is weighted. What that means is that the bigger, more visually interesting moment on the page is the mundane moment, obscuring the shock of the words in the last few panels.

It's also a bit of cheating in that what's shocking isn't the action but the words spoken, so that you aren't seeing, y'know, blood and guts, but rather a sentence that is the twisty bit.

PAGE 5

PANEL ONE
Split focus shot, Brian freezes in place in the foreground, in the
background Martin looks to have more cognition than one would think
possible. Again, for the sake of foreshadowing, we can see at least a
part of the other patient.

BRIAN
What?

MARTIN
In the crawlspace... under the house on
Haymaker, you have to find the box
(break)
Thirteen thirty nine Haymaker.

PANEL TWO
Brian crosses to his father.

BRIAN
What box? I don't understand?

PANEL THREE
Wide thin panel - Silouette as Brian's car drives against the setting
sun through the suburban street. It's fall, the trees are nearly
bare, and the world is caught in that amber glow of old age. Filthy,
dying.

MARTIN (CAPTION)
"The bodies, the girls bodies..."

PANEL FOUR
Back in the hospital room, closer on Brian, he's freaking out. The
person in the next bed is there.

BRIAN
What bodies, dad?
(break)
What did you do?

PANEL FIVE
On Martin.

MARTIN
In the crawlspace... under the house on
Haymaker, you have to find the box
Thirteen thirty nine Haymaker.

PANEL SIX
Wide thin panel (like Pnl 3) - Brian stands in front of 1339
Haymaker. We see the mailbox number. The house is a two story,
cookie cutter mid 50's suburban home. With the useless shutters on
the windows, and a small concrete porch that leads to the front door.
There should be a few basement windows on one side, and a two car
garage on the other.

MARTIN (CAPTION)
In the crawlspace... under the house on
Haymaker, you have to find the box
(break)
Thirteen thirty nine Haymaker.

   Doing counterpoint, or juxtaposing two separate scenes, is something that, obviously exists in other
mediums, but, works especially well in comics. The effect is essentially the same as montage in film, but, as
here, allows your story to propel forward while getting important information (here, it's emotional rather than
plot based) out. Why I feel it works better in comics than anywhere else has to do again with how a page is
read. We look at the page as a unit first, so we see that there's these two different events occuring, Brian
trying desperately to understand his father, with finding and entering the house. What this does, in effect
is show that from the moment Brian hears this information, he's already out the door and across town. But
we also get to feel the emotional reverberation across time, as if Brian is still reliving that shocking moment
again and again.

   One of the more interesting side effects of this, is the appearance of a time jumble, when in fact, we're
simply just cross-cutting. It's slightly non-linear, but, an astute reader gets that the events are within minutes
of each other, so, we remain in a fully linear state, certainly in the POV of our protagonist.

PAGE 6

This page will be split in half. Left side is in the hospital, right side is at the house.

PANEL 1
On Martin, his eyes are slowly closing.

BRIAN (OFF)
Dad?

MARTIN
(weakly)
Thirteen Thirty-Nine Haymaker.

SFX
Beeeeeeeeeeeeeeep.

PANEL 2
From inside the house, as Brian tries to peer inside through a dirty window.

SFX (CONT FROM 1)
Beeeeeeeeeeeeeeeep.

PANEL 3
A nurse runs into the room.
NURSE
Out of the way, sir.

SFX
Beeeeeeeeeeeeeeeeeeep.

PANEL 4
Brian's hand on the door knob, trying it. We can see his dosage watch that reads "Clozapine 300mg Due."

SFX (CONT FROM 3)
Beeeeeeeeeeeeeeeeeeeep.

NURSE (CAPTION)
I'm sorry, sir. There's nothing we can do.

PANEL 5
The nurse's hand moves over Martin's eyes, closing them.

NURSE (OFF)
He wasn't in much pain at the end. You should take comfort in that.

PANEL 6
The door pushes open.

SFX
Click.

SFX
Beeeeeeeeeeeeeeep

BRIAN (CAPTION)
"Thank you."

BRIAN
Hello?
PANEL 7
Small Inset Panel - Brian pushes a button on his watch to "Snooze" the alarm.
SFX
Beeeee-
(break)
Beep-beep.

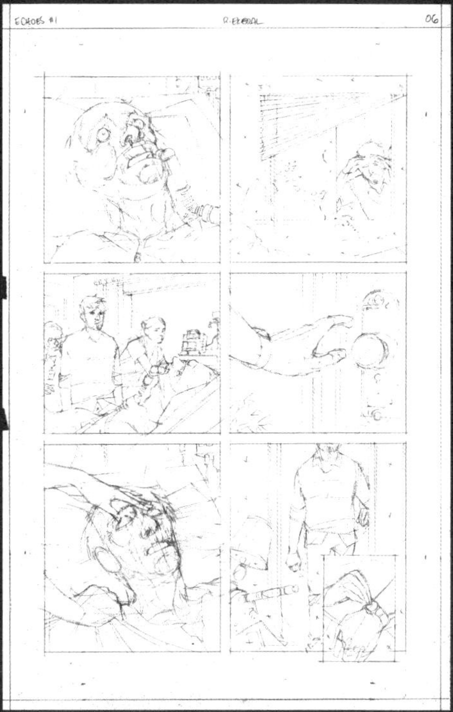

As I talked about before, the counterpoint technique allows you to instill information with double meaning extra weight. On this page we get one other little bonus. We don't have to waste time screwing around what happens in the moments after Brian's dad dies. We're quickly filling you in on what you need to w... as Brian's dad died, Brian was already anxious to leave. What happens in actuality between point a point b, clearly is unimportant, because we're not allowing that moment to hang. We're moving on to re the story has to go.

The idea for me is that we're showing a complete emotional scene, while letting you fill in the rest. The wardness, the tension, it's all inferred by Brian's clearly jumbled emotional state.

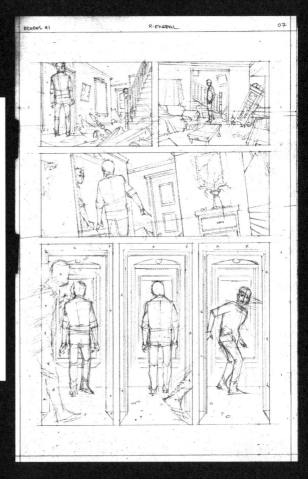

PAGE 7

PANEL 1
The house is a dusty mess, with canvas over the furniture, and a layer of filth on everything.

BRIAN
Uh. Hello? Anybody here?

PANEL 2
Brian walks into the room, leaving the door open behind him.

BRIAN
I'm sorry... I... uh...
(break)
The door was open...

PANEL 3
There's a mirror hanging in the back of the living room. Brian stares at himself in it.

PANEL 4
Same shot, a figure passes behind Brian, silently. Should be so close to us, that we just see a shadowy blur-

PANEL 5
That moves from right to left.

PANEL 6
Brian whips around.

BRIAN
Hello?

This page is a tribute to Rahsan Ekedal's amazing skill. The horror beat on this page is at the bottom half of the page, but, through design he manages to hide that scare until you're right up on it. Controlling a reader's eye is a far more difficult task then you would think, and Rah does it with style and confidence.

PAGE 8

PANEL 1
There looks to be... something... in that deep dark corner.

PANEL 2
Brian edges towards it.

PANEL 3
Brian crouches down, the darkness thick and heavy in front of him.

PANEL 4
He starts to slowly reach his hand into the darkness... (Don't forget
the watch on that hand.)

PANEL 5
On his hand, part of it swallowed by the darkness.

PANEL 6
Same shot, there's nothing there and then-
SFX (HUGE, JAGGED - LIKE A DISTORTION OF
THE HEART MONITOR BEEP IN THE HOSPITAL)
BEEEEEEEEEEEP BEEEEEEEEEEEP BEEEEEEEP!

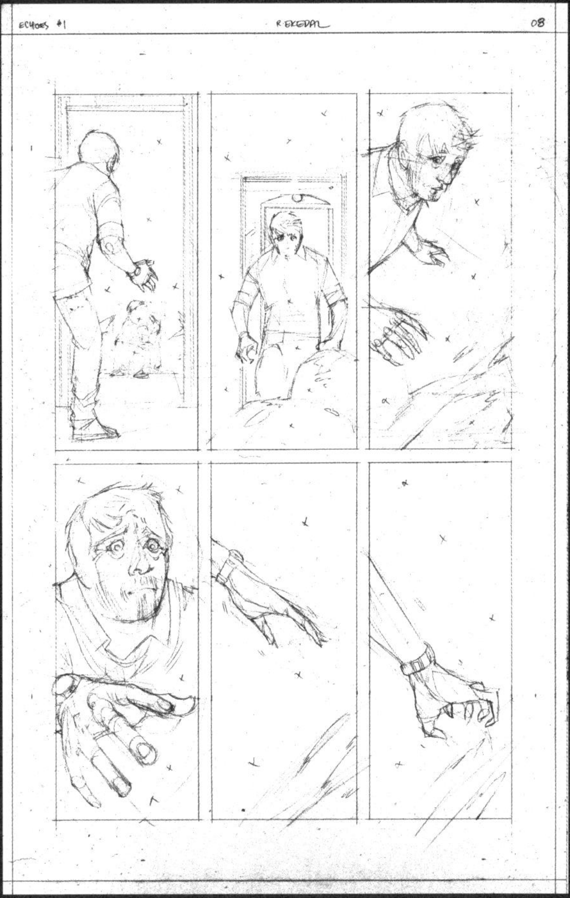
ECHOES #1
R EKEDAL
08

Another challenge of horror in comics is the lack of editing. Not, y'know, the expert work performed by Filip Sablik and Phil Smith, but, the control of pacing, the combination of sound and vision, shock cuts, jagged cuts, all of those things. What we attempt here, and kudos to Troy Peteri for pulling it off pretty well, is to get one of those shock cuts. We took an ordinary moment (a guy's watch alarm going off) and turn it into a scare. Again, Rahsan's brilliant design sense lets you see the shock that's coming, but, not know it's context, giving you an extra "Wah!" moment.

PAGE 9

PANEL 1
Brian jumps backwards, shrieking, as the BEEEEEP fills the air
around
him.

BRIAN
FUCK!

SFX
BEEEEEEEP BEEEEEEEEEP BEEEEEEEEEP

PANEL 2
On Brian, his eyes closed tight, trying to calm down.

BRIAN (MUTTERING)
Nothing --pant-- there --wheeze--, nothing-pantthere-
pant, nothing-wheeze-there.

SFX
BEEEEEEEEP BEEEEEEEEEP BEEEEEEEEEP

PANEL 3
Wider, we notice that Brian's watch is glowing and that the
beeping
is coming from his watch. The beeping should be much smaller,
the
tension and his condition were making it worse. Brian's eyes are
still closed.

SFX
Beeep beeep beeeep beeep.

PANEL 4
Brian opens his eyes.

BRIAN
Sigh.
(break)
I'm okay.
(break)
Just... shut up, I'll take the fucking pill,
jesus-

SFX
Beeep beeep beeep beeep beeep

PANEL 5
On his hand, we see that the watch is a dosage watch The
screen
reads "Clozapine 300mg OVERDUE."

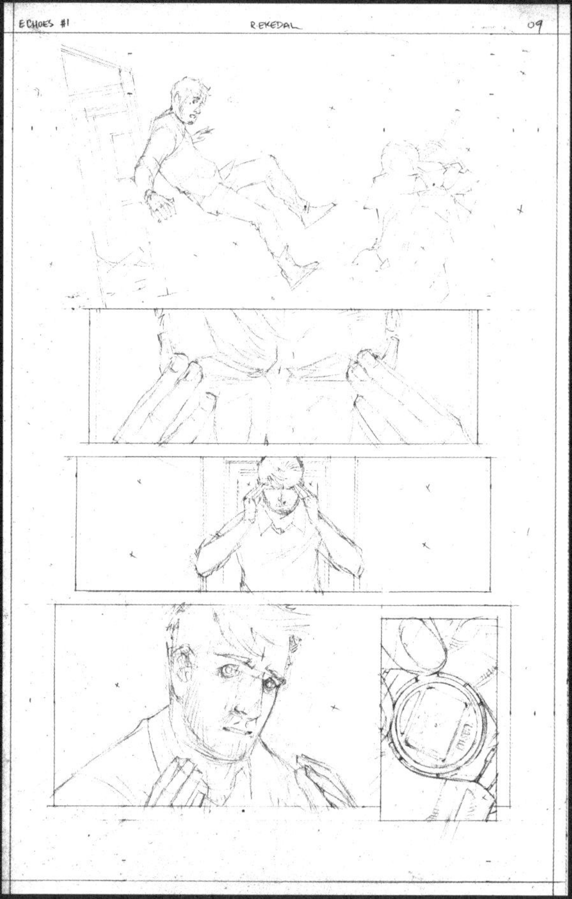

ECHOES #1
REKEDAL
09

Hours of research, long medical conversations, countless journal articles read, all culminating in this one page. Nay! In this one single panel! Now, if you haven't done all of that reading, you probably think it's totally weird that the guy has a wristwatch that yells at him to take his drugs, but, you're going to have to trust me that this is a (still relatively high end but) absolutely real thing. Alzheimer's patients as well as those with psychotic disorders who need to be strictly regimented use them.

In case you're wondering, the drug and dosage are both correct. Of course, no matter how in control or well balanced your drugs are, if you're a schizophrenic and you're under stress, like, say your father just confessed to being at least a pervert and at most a murderer and then dropped dead... Good luck staying in control.

PAGE 10

PANEL 1
Brian reaches into his pocket-

PANEL 2
Pulling out an elaborate pill case.

PANEL 3
He's got a pill in his hand-

SFX
De-de-de-do-de-de-de-do.

PANEL 4
He pulls his cell phone out of his pocket.

PANEL 5
Close on him, his cell phone in his shoulder.

BRIAN
Hey baby.
(break)
Yeah, I was about to-
(break)
Sweetheart, I'm not a baby. I can take my-
(break)
No, I'm fine. Just... It's dad...
(break)
He's gone, sweetheart.

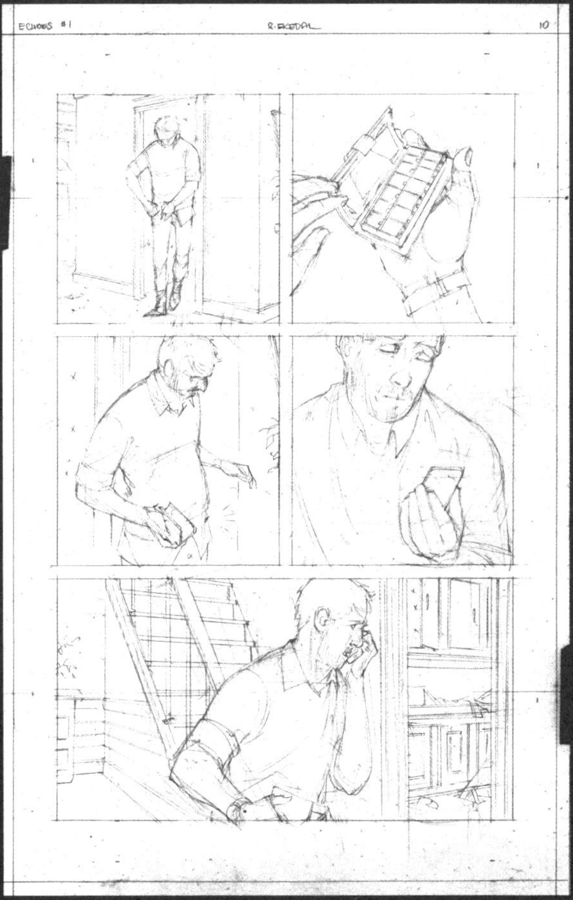
ECHOES #1
R. EKEDAL
10

Again, the sound effects interupting the silence, with hopefully very filmic results. The bigger issue here is using this little conversation to convey a ton of information as quickly as possible. Readers hate big expository chunks of dialogue or text. So, the idea is to convey a bunch of things as quickly as possible, i.e. wife, badgering him again about medication, dad's definitely dead in case you weren't sure, lying begins.

It's a lot of information conveyed in very few, non-descript words. And it's STILL really wordy.

PAGE 11

PANEL 1
Brian stands over the kitchen sink, trying to get some water poured.

BRIAN
I just needed some time to myself.
(break)
No. I'll be home, soon. I'll...
(break)
Yeah, I told you I'm taking it right now.

PANEL 2
Brian's hand turns the faucet, and the water comes out black and cruddy.

BRIAN
I'm under enough pressure without you-

SFX
Ch-ch-ch-ch-ch-ch-

BRIAN
Shit. I better pay attention. I love you and the turnip very much.

PANEL 3
Wide shot, Brian puts the phone back in his pocket. The water is still pouring, and still gross.

PANEL 4 - 6
Brian at three different sinks, each one pouring filth filled water.

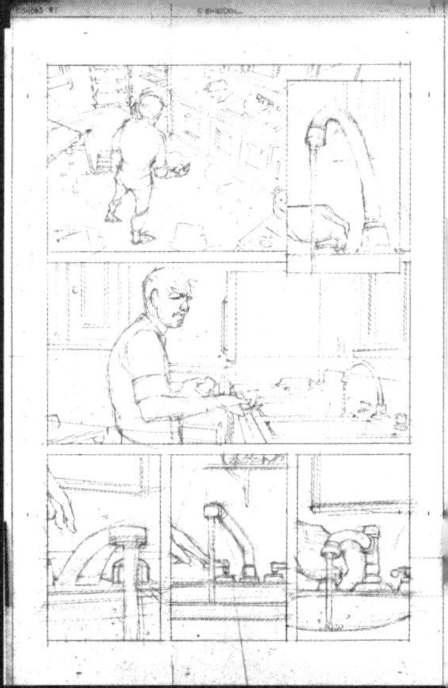

may sound ridiculous, but, this page is probably the most cinematic in the book. s is something that you generally can't do in comics... montage. As a reader, you c d waht the scene is. The water comes out brown, he goes and checks multiple fau ibly simple and clear, but, think about what comics normally do. Linear motion, o ional montage, meaning, change of scene or shift in narrative. What Rahsan has co ny money, is proof what an amazing storyteler he is. He concisely and clearly execute novie would just be a little bit of business, and instead he keeps the story and mooc nout losing a step.

PAGE 12

PANEL 1
Brian stares at himself in the mirror above the last sink. His reflection is taking it's own position, arms at it's side, indignant look on it's face.

BRIAN
Go look in the basement, find nothing, and then you can go drive to the CoGo's up the road and get a bottle of water and take your pills and everything will be normal.

BRIAN'S REFLECTION
You're still in control, right?

PANEL 2
On Brian, his eyes closed.

BRIAN
You're not there.

PANEL 3
Brian's eyes open, his reflection staring back at him is normal again.

PANEL 4
Brian turns and walks away, his reflection stays there, crazy Jack Nicholson in the Shining eyes staring after him.

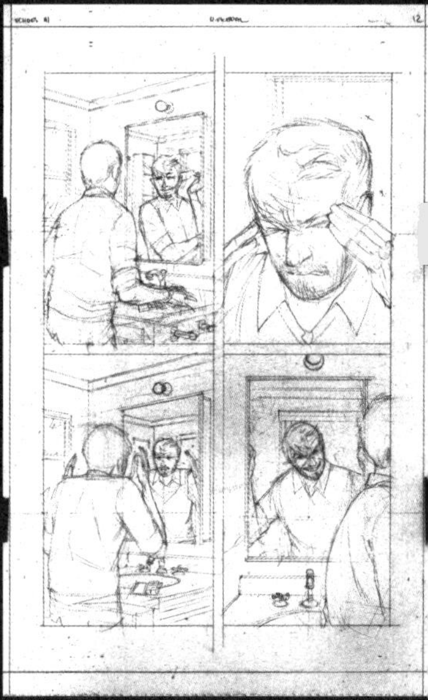

e you, Black Swan, for doing this bit and making it even better. Aronofsky's master ead on a lot of the same ground in terms of mental illness and the subtle art of g. Closer to the end of the series, I'll probably write a longer piece about the movie a

PAGE 13

PANEL 1
Left side of page - From the side we see the stairs to the basement, light spilling in from upstairs as Brian's legs are visible.

BRIAN
They're not real. It's just a chemical reaction in your brain that makes you extra anxious.
(break)
This is just an deserted house, with nothing going on. This is just my brain working against me.

PANEL 2
On the ground, Brian's foot in the foreground, still in darkness.

BRIAN (OFF)
This is just the meds wearing off, and the paranoia taking over.

PANEL 3
Same as 2, but the lights turn on.

BRIAN (OFF)
This is why you wear the watch. To remind you when you have to take your pill.
(break)
Otherwise you'd forget, and then you'd start to hallucinate and freak out and there's nothing here.

PANEL 4
Wide of the basement and Brian standing in it. It's dusty and dank, but there's not much to see. Bare drywall lines the top 1/2 of the walls, concrete runs below that to the ground. A few shelving units against the far wall, and a really grotty looking washer and dryer. Most importantly, there's no crawlspace.

BRIAN
Goddammit, dad. What the hell am I doing here?

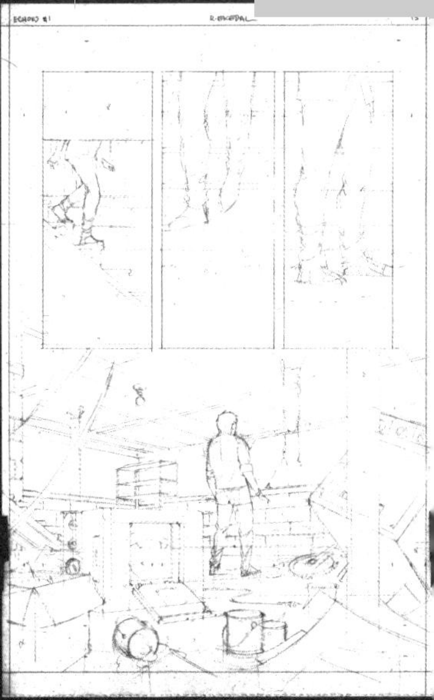

of our stranger storytelling choices. We don't see that he's turning on a light bulb, b changing lighting conditions. Also called a dick move for a writer. But, the one th t is camera placement, why is a shot from where it's from? A lot of the time that get but, on occasion, like on this weird ass shot, I have something specific in mind.

PAGE 14

PANEL 1
Brian stands at the far wall and stares intently at the bare drywall.

BRIAN
Hm.

PANEL 2
He digs his fingers into the dry wall.

PANEL 3
The dry wall coming up, his fingernails embedded in it.

PANEL 4
BIG PANEL - The dry wall's totally off, revealing a huge opening between the ceiling and the concrete. This is the crawlspace.

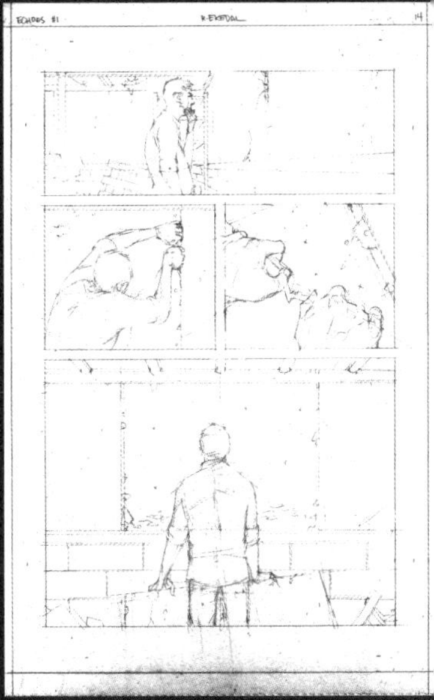

ably my favorite thing that Rahsan does, that's in abundance on this page, is th faces. We can clearly see that Brian is Brian, but, there's a tiny bit of our mind that our own. It's a subtle technique and one that really only works in comics, that allo d the character to merge with each other. It take subjective storytelling to the next le

PAGE 15

PANEL 1
Brian boosts himself up into the crawl space. It's pitch black aside from the light spilling in from the rest of the basement. The ground beneath him is chunky gravel. It's only high enough for him to crouch, so he goes at it on all fours.

PANEL 2
He's a few feet in, and cloaked in shadows-

PANEL 3
So he pulls out his cell phone...

PANEL 4
And it glows, illuminating the area around him... his face is pale. He's up on his haunches now.

PANEL 5
Reverse Shot, from Brian's POV... there's a rack covered in what looks like a 3 or 4 inch piece of leather. Next to it are a collection of knives displayed simply on a dirty towel. Opposite them is a bundle of something covered in a sheet. Next to that is a metallic box.

BRIAN
Jesus.

I could be wrong, but, I believe this is the first instance in a comic book of a person using their iPhone as a flashlight. As someone who's on their second wonder device, and who was writing for an artist who's just as glued to his, I think we've paid a fitting tribute to the weirdest use for an object ever that every person who owns one does.

Kudos to us!

PAGE 16

PANEL 1
Brians hand touches one of the knives.

BRIAN
Dad...

PANEL 2
Brian turns to the bundle of sheets.

BRIAN
You are in control, Brian.

PANEL 3
His hand reaches out for the sheet.

PANEL 4
His hand is getting closer...

PANEL 5
And closer... it's shaking a bit, speed lines to show it, maybe?

PANEL 6
His hand grabs the sheet and-

SFX
(from above)
Creeeeeeeeak.

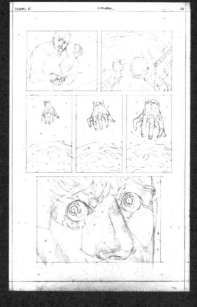

Ah, those three panels in the middle. Delightful. The feeling of both motion and stillness they convey is just... aching. That's another example of the tension building. The images are so subtly different that your brain forces your eye to slow down just to understand them. That allows the CREEEEEEAK in the last panel to actually startle you, or at least surprise you.

PAGE 17

PANEL 1
Brian falls backwards, terror on his face.

BRIAN
Gah!

PANEL 2
He lays down, frozen, listening intently.

PANEL 3
Same. Nothing.

PANEL 4
Same. Nothing.

BRIAN
You are in control. Not the chemicals, Brian,
you.

PANEL 5
He's back up on his knees...

PANEL 6
He pulls back the sheets-

By mirroring the page design here with the stutter panels again, Rahsan is masterfully guiding your pacing. Here we're reinstating the pace, after the shock to get the feeling of suspense back on track. Getting ready for...

PAGE 18

PANEL 1
Reveal - Under the sheets... just stacks of old porn magazines.

PANEL 2
Brian picks up a copy...

BRIAN
Shit dad...

PANEL 3
He flips through the withered old pages.

BRIAN
All this for some old porn magazines?
(break)
Hehheh.

PANEL 4
Brian starts to laugh...

BRIAN
Ha! Goddammit dad!

PANEL 5
Brian is losing control as he laughs harder and harder.

BRIAN
(sfx style)
HAHAHAHAHAHAHAHAHAHAHAHAHAHA!

PANEL 6
He falls backwards, to lay down and laugh.

BRIAN
(sfx style)
Hahahahahahahahahahahahahahahahaha!

A reversal. The opposite of what you were thinking was going to happen. This page manages to completely reveal the tension in such a beautiful way. The combination of the acting and the push in which gives us a sense of just where Brian is mentally. He's relieved, sure, but, he's already cracked at this point, or at least.. cracking. Those subtle tones are something that we really strived for in the book, moments of sheer subjectivity, where we're completely caught up in his reality rather than any other. That's important for what happens next...

PAGE 19

PANEL 1
Full Page Splash - From above, still tight, so that we understand the spacial constrictions of the room. We see that underneath Brian is not gravel pebbles like we thought... no... it's bones.

PANEL 2
Inset Panel - Brian's face turns to the side... The cellphone illuminating the skull right next to his head.

PANEL 3
Inset Panel - Brian's face turns to terror.

BRIAN
FUCK!

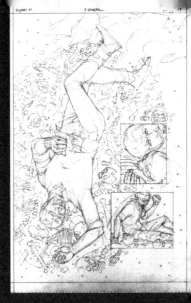

e's really nothing to say other than, goddamn. When I saw this page, I knew that
work. I knew that what we were trying to tell, the way we wanted to tell it, and the
l involved were going to deliver something amazing. This is probably my favorite
series.

PAGE 20

PANEL 1
Brian smacks his head on the ceiling as he gets up, trying to get away from the bones.

SFX
Thud.

PANEL 2
Brian holds his head, and tries to calm himself down.

BRIAN
You are in control. You are in control.

PANEL 3
Brian sees the box.

MARTIN (CAPTION)
"You have to find the box."

PANEL 4
Brian crawls over to the box and stares at it.

BRIAN
Goddammit, dad. What did you do?

PANEL 5
Brian unlatches the rusty bolt on the box.

implication, story wise of this page is that maybe, just maybe... Brian's imagining.
he sees what's around him, maybe he's so wrapped up in the moment that he's see
there... Including that box.   Probably the most satisfying aspect of working on this
various reactions. Some folks think that it's all a hallucination from here on out. Oth
completely real.   For me, that's part of the charm and the fun. What is reality? W
g sick and what is the world around him being sicker? That's important for wha

PAGE 21

PANEL 1
He reaches into the box...

PANEL 2
And pulls out a tiny doll made out of leather and bone and hair. It has a tiny note in it's shrivelled, leathery hand.

PANEL 3
Brian pulls out the note.

PANEL 4
XCU on the top half of the note -

TEXT
Marie Splotski - Age 9
(line break)
Born 7/18/85
(line break)
Died 9/15/94

PANEL 5
XCU on the bottom half of the note -

TEXT
Doll made from Skin, Flesh, and Bone
(line break)
In her memory.

PANEL 6
Brian looks like he's going to throw up...

dolls were one of the first images to come to me on the book. In fact, in the earliest e, Brian and his father were both dollmakers. It was sort of their thing that they shared to realize that it was something more for his dad. That went away fairly early on, bu naring something so grotesque is what led me down the road of telling the story.

or the design, I pretty much explained what I wanted and then Rahsan went right a m a thousand times cooler than I imagined. That's the joy of collaborating.

PAGE 22

PANEL 1
FULL PAGE SPLASH
Brian throws up next to the box. And we see inside that metal box... there's dozens... hell... at least a hundred more dolls inside.

PANEL 2
Inset Panel - Closer on the box.

PANEL 3
Inset Panel - Closer on the box.

PANEL 4
Inset Panel - On one of the dolls.

BELOW FRAME
CHAPTER TITLE
End Echoes Chapter One.

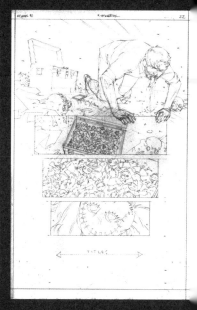

smile at the bottom of the page is just terrific. It's not the doll smiling at us, at all, i he world laughing and cackling at us. It's every nightmare you ever had pleased as and turned you into jelly.

best of all, it gets even better from here.

ECHOES™

COVER GALLERY

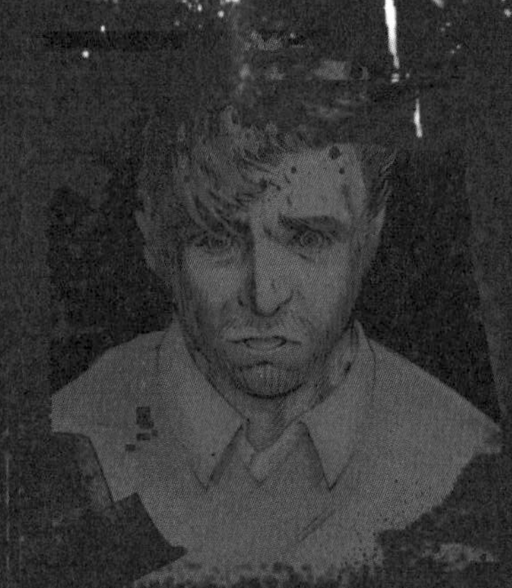

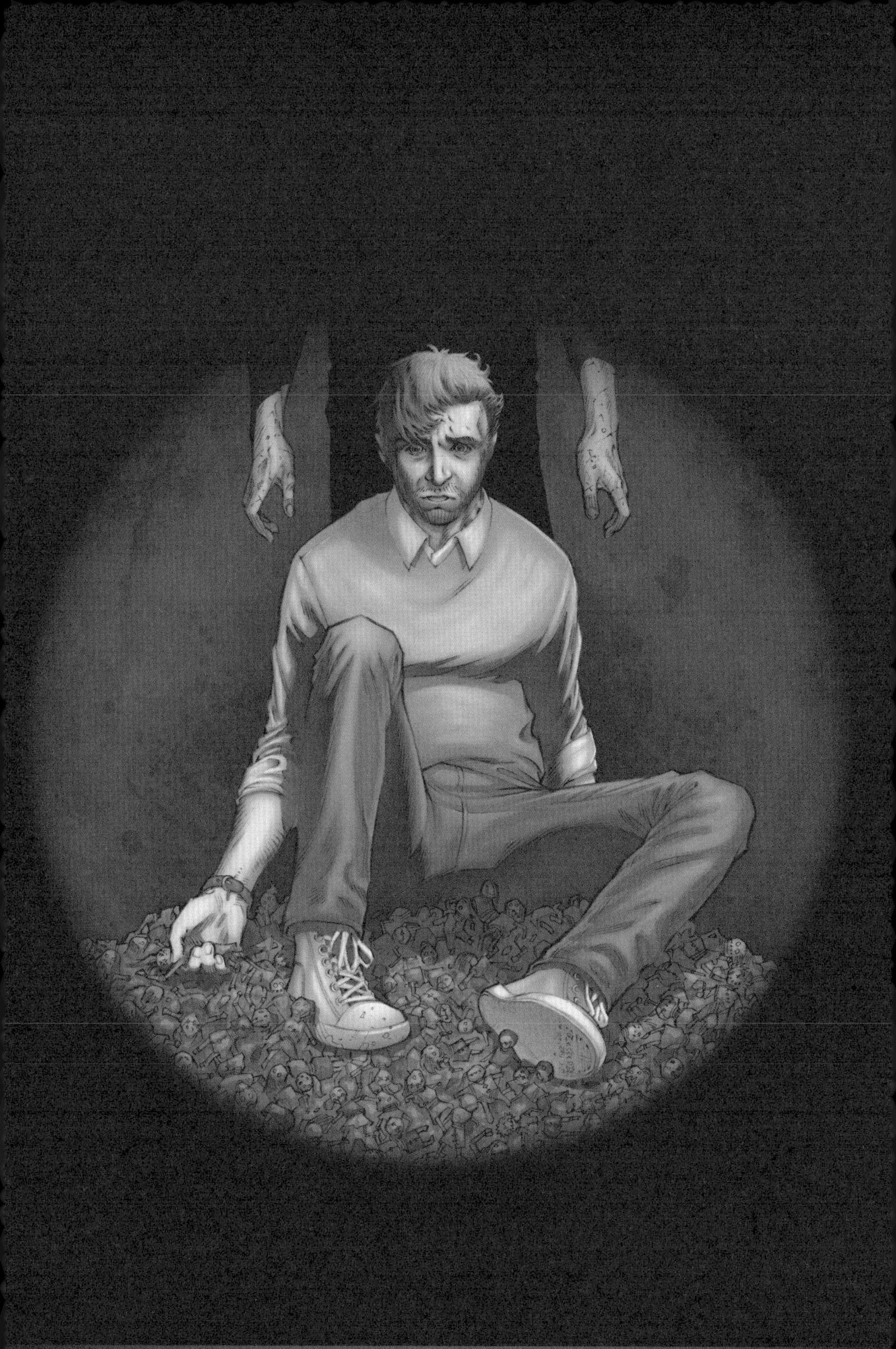

Line art by: Rahsan Ekedal
Colors by: Rob Schwager

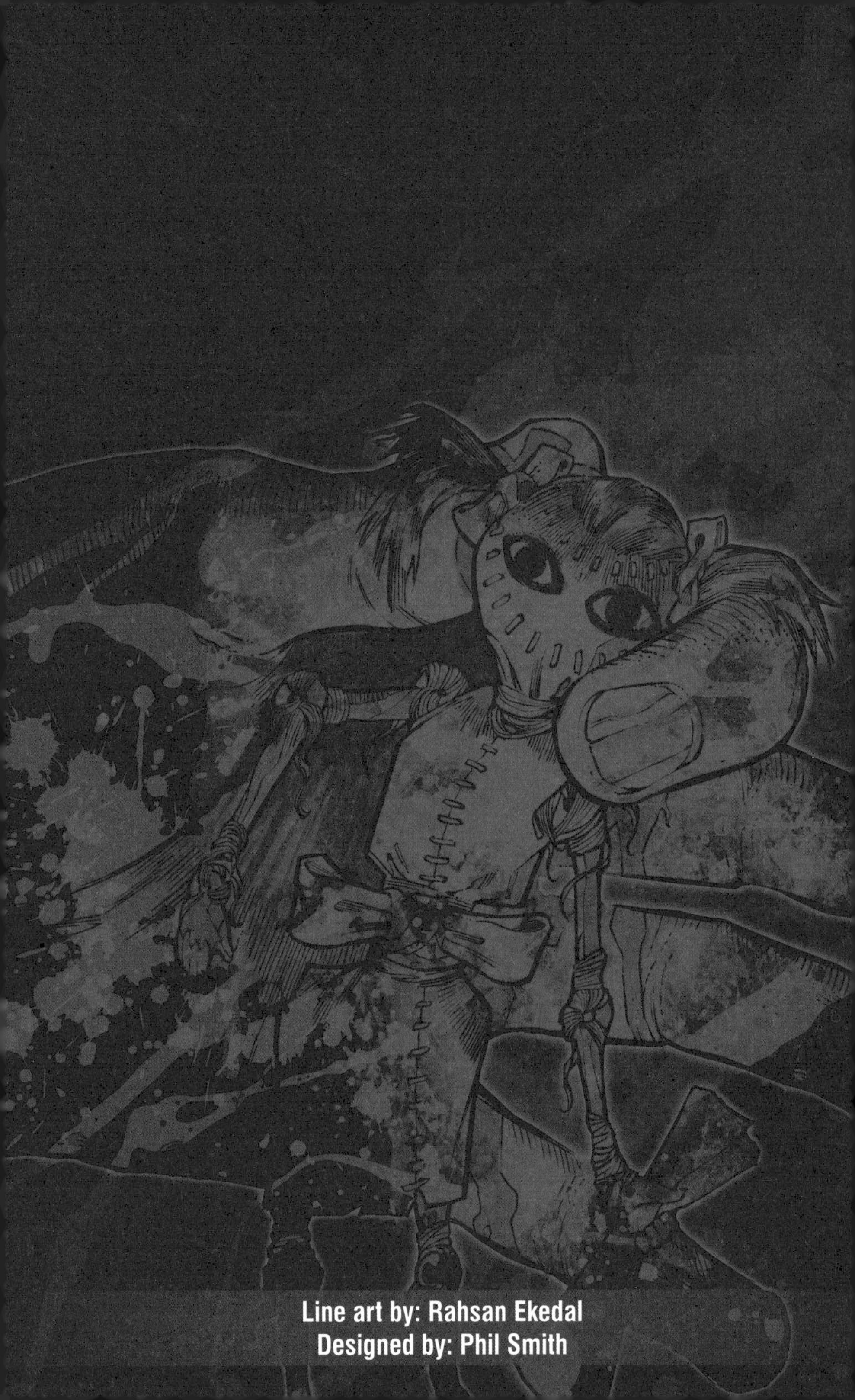

Line art by: Rahsan Ekedal
Designed by: Phil Smith

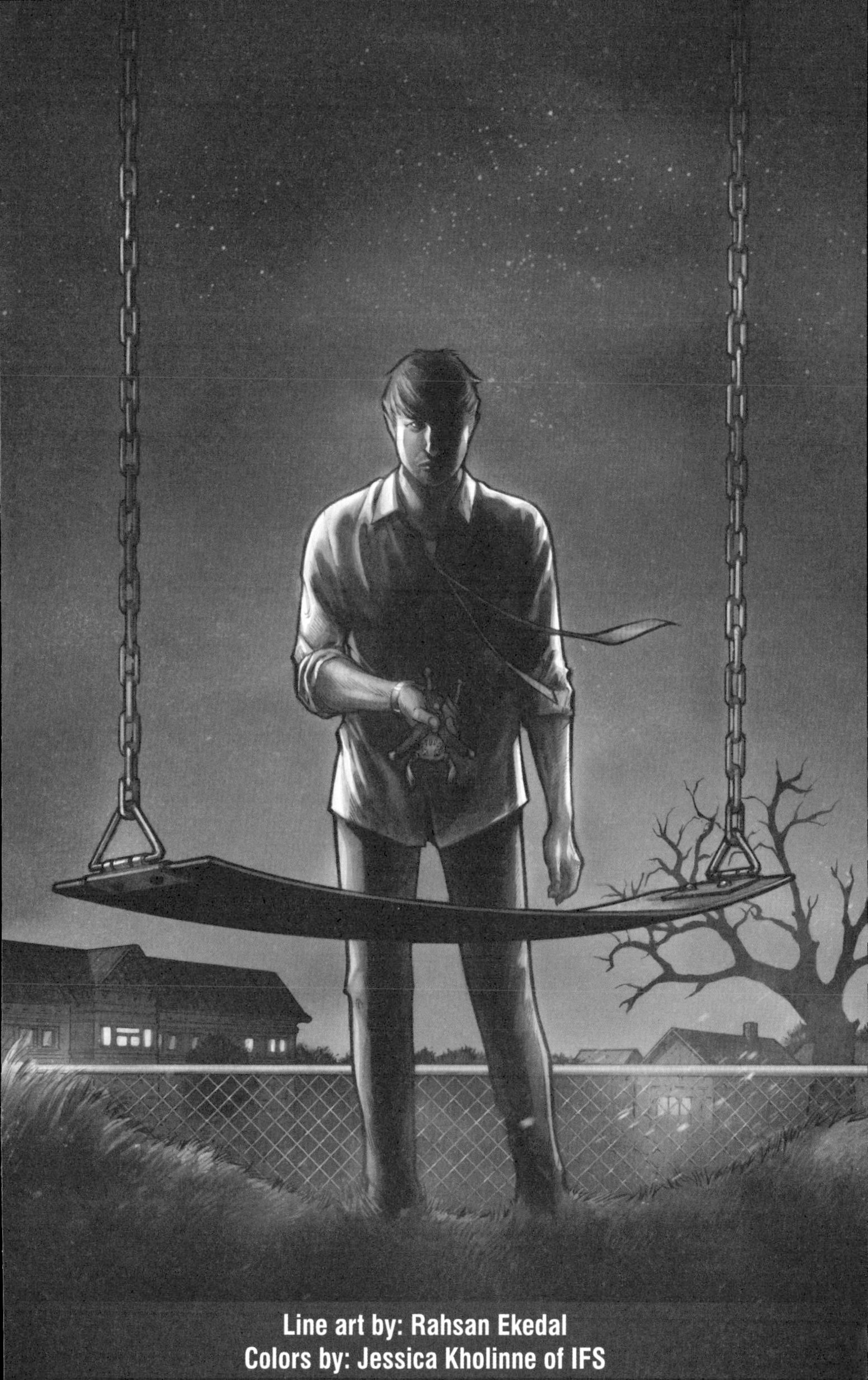

Line art by: Rahsan Ekedal
Colors by: Jessica Kholinne of IFS

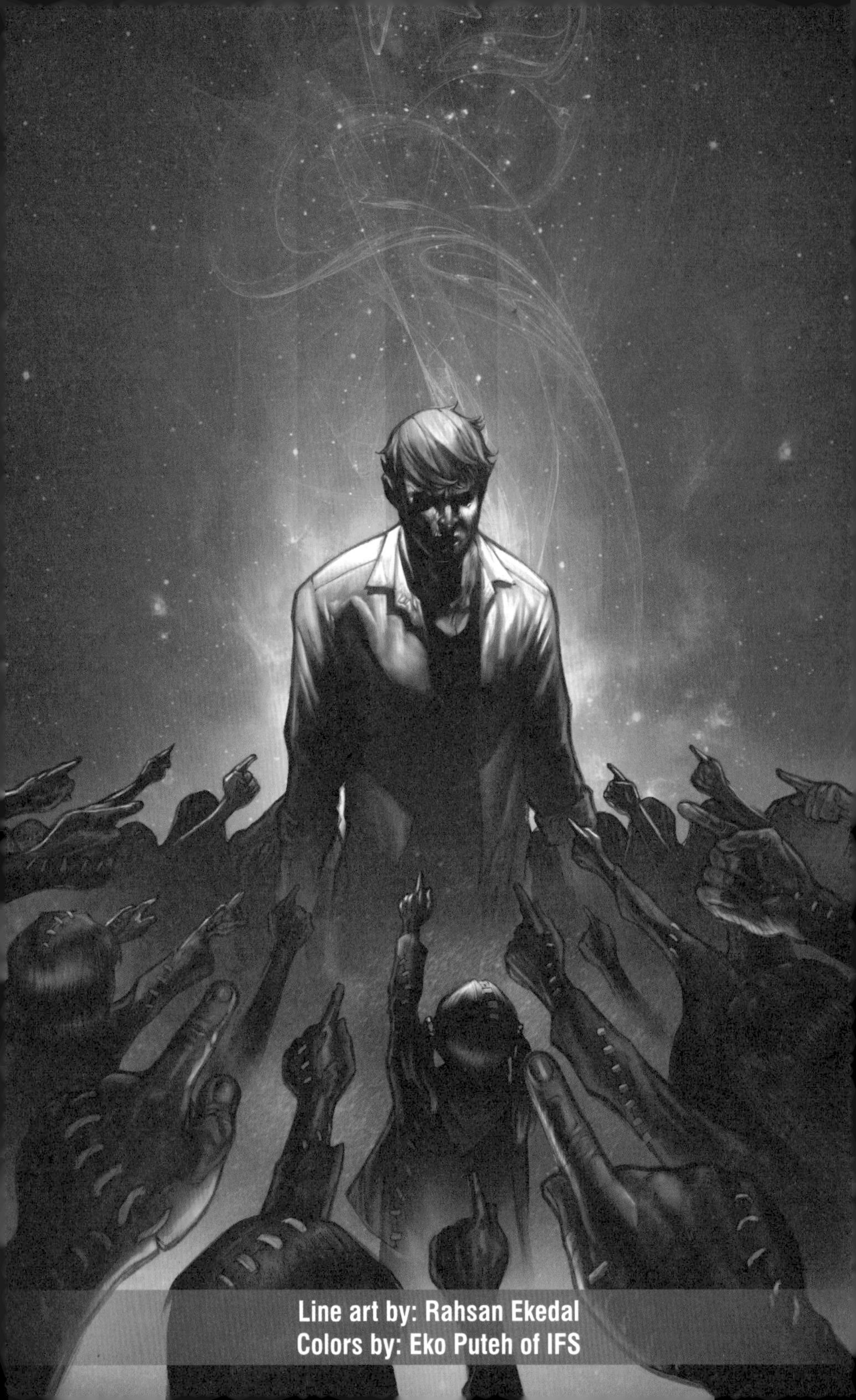

Line art by: Rahsan Ekedal
Colors by: Eko Puteh of IFS

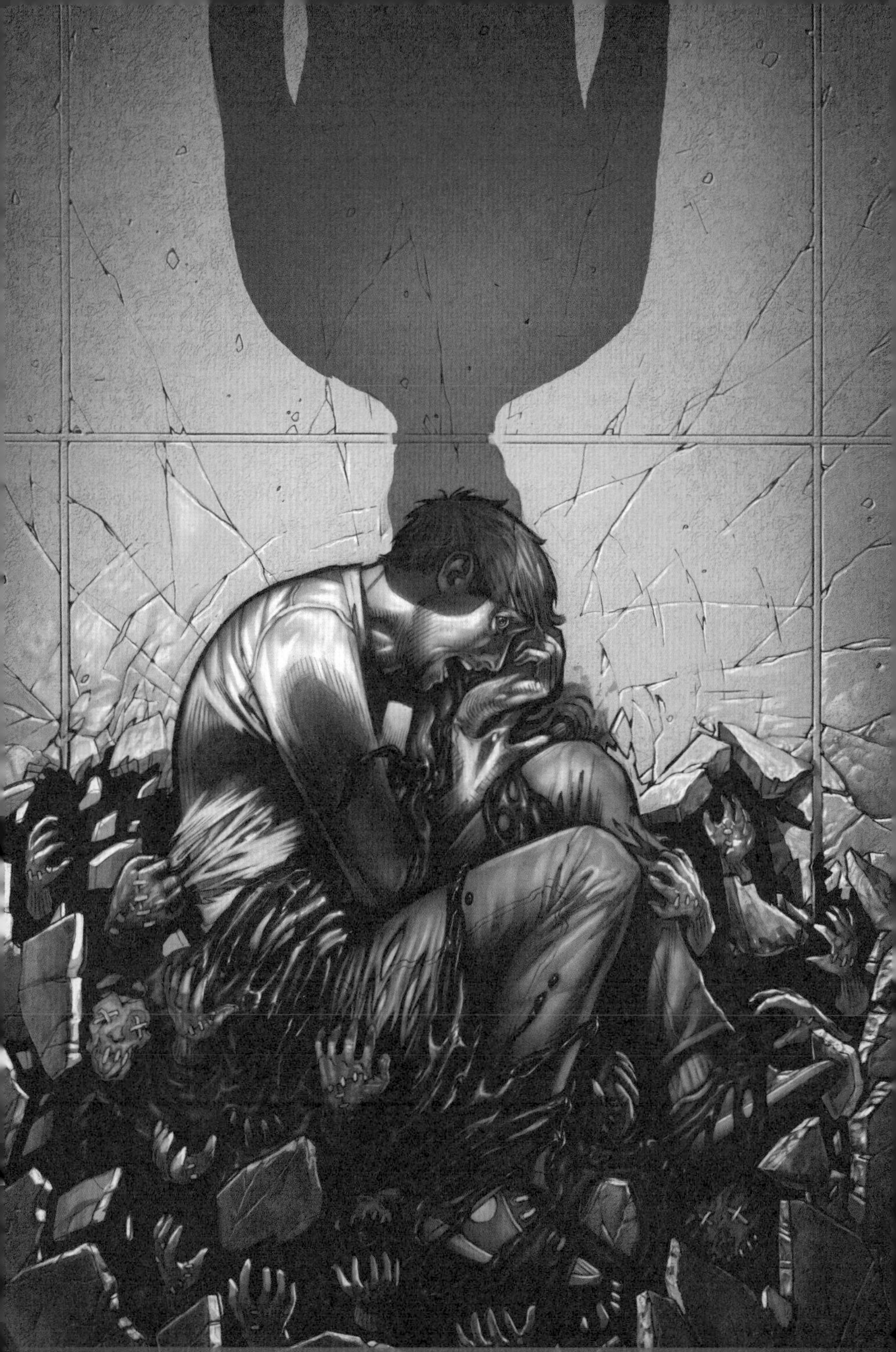

Line art by: Rahsan Ekedal
Colors [illegible]: Eko Puteh of IFS

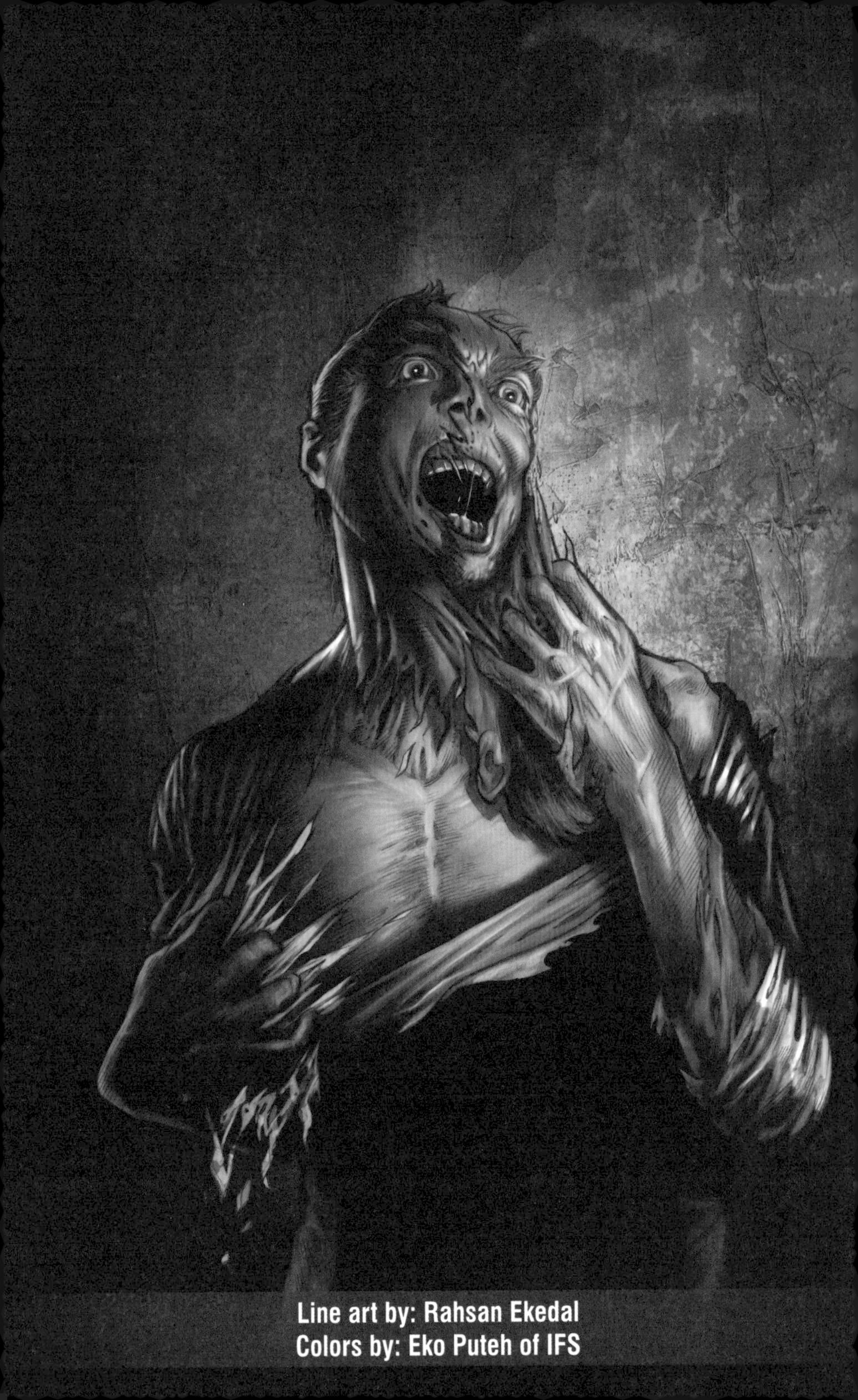

Line art by: Rahsan Ekedal
Colors by: Eko Puteh of IFS

ECHOES™

WORK IN PROGRESS

COVER PIECE

Pg: A
"MISSING" FLYERS SPIRAL AROUND THEM IN WIND
CIG SMOKE
ROBERT
BRIAN
CITY IN BG
MISSING
PAVEMENT (PARKING LOT?)
Pg: B
BLOOD-STAINED DIRTY, SCRATCHED TABLE TOP
NEEDLE AND "THREAD" (HAIR)
KNIFE POINT
Pg: C
MONROEVILLE IN BG
ROBERT LIGHTING CIG
"MISSING" FLYERS ON WOODEN FENCE
MISSING
Pg: D
BRIAN
ALL POINTING AT BRIAN
STITCHED LITTLE GIRLS
SHADOWED FACE
ZOOMING IN
Book: ECHOES #3
CRAZED TO OUT OF MIND TO DEAD INSIDE
4 - BUST W/ 3 HEADS?
Rahsan Ekedal

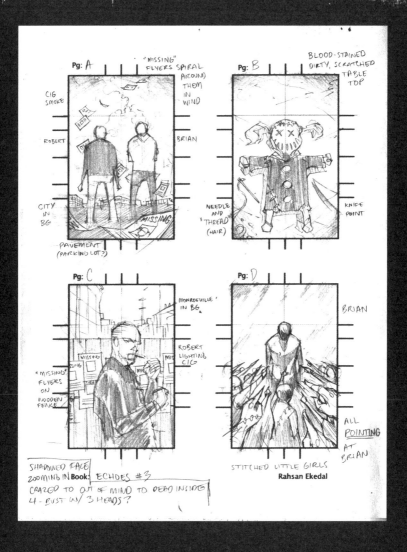

Thumbnail concepts for the cover to issue 3. The final image became my favorite of the series.

- Rahsan Ekedal

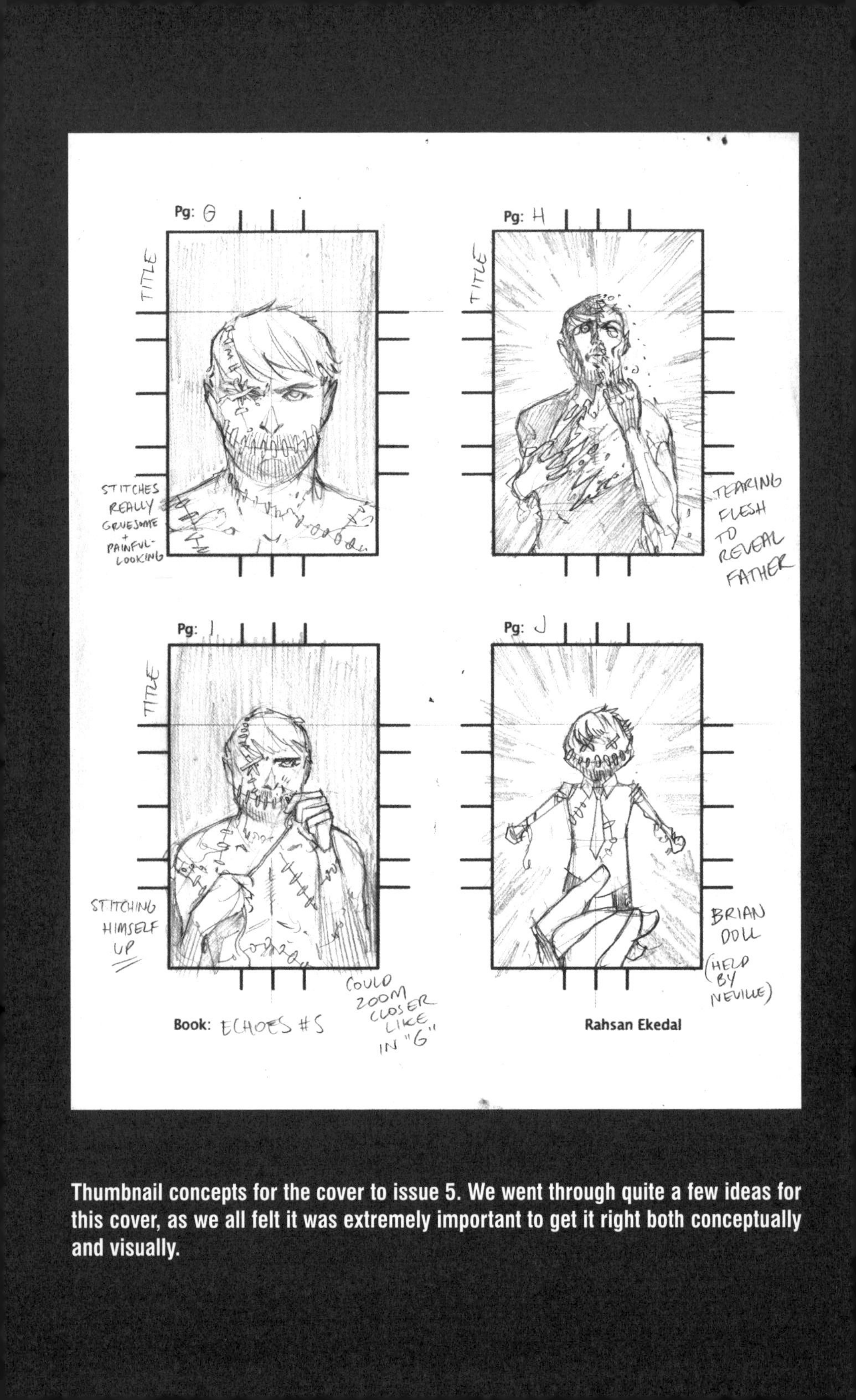
Pg: G
TITLE
STITCHES REALLY GRUESOME + PAINFUL-LOOKING
Pg: H
TITLE
TEARING FLESH TO REVEAL FATHER
Pg: I
TITLE
STITCHING HIMSELF UP
COULD ZOOM CLOSER LIKE IN "G"
Pg: J
BRIAN DOLL (HELD BY NEVILLE)
Book: ECHOES #5
Rahsan Ekedal

Thumbnail concepts for the cover to issue 5. We went through quite a few ideas for this cover, as we all felt it was extremely important to get it right both conceptually and visually.

Echoes snuck up on me.

Not unlike Detective Robert Neville himself, Echoes appeared friendly at first, a cool job on an interesting book, a chance to collaborate once again with a great writer and a great publisher. But pretty soon Echoes was sticking a fucking needle in my neck and dragging me off to its dark, sweaty crawlspace under the floorboards of emotional safety. I didn't realize that by the end of these 110 pages, I'd be sitting there literally crying over my bristol board, drawing the most personal and emotional work of my career.

My brother, Matteo Ekedal, suffered from an undiagnosed disorder that led to his accidental death in 2004 at the age of 31, during what was most likely an acute schizophrenic episode. In retrospect, all the signs were there - for years leading up to that episode, in fact - but I was completely ignorant and unprepared, as was everyone else around him. As are most families of loved ones who suffer from mental and emotional disorders. A lot of tragedy could be prevented if we educate ourselves and encourage others to talk about these issues. There is still a deep misunderstanding of the many forms mental illness can take, and a stigma surrounding those who suffer from it.

There shouldn't be. People with depression, schizophrenia, and mood disorders are not scary. They're wonderful people, often exceptionally so.

This book is for them. And for Matteo.

Rahsan Ekedal
Los Angeles
June 3, 2011

I always regret these fucking things. I've written two other afterwords for what will be considered my first two 'major works' meaning, the first two things worthy of getting deluxe collections with all sorts of bells and whistles. I reread the ones I wrote for TUMOR and ELK'S RUN (both of which are available for order, unless they've gone out of print, which is always possible) and there's so much I wish I could change to get right.

So, I figured I'd write something here that I hope I won't learn to regret down the road.

My father made me who I am today. My mother as well. I grew up with amazing, kind, supportive parents who didn't tell me to go screw when I said I wanted to take acting classes at a theater in downtown Pittsburgh, that I wanted to go to the extremely expensive Pre-College program at CMU, or go to that massively expensive fine arts college that would get me a degree without any actual intrinsic value.

My father balked, cause, well, he'd be paying for it. For a long, long time. But he let me go, and he made sure that I did my best, because that was all that could be expected and accepted.

My mother, no matter what I did, complimented me, supported me, told me that I was the best in the world. That gave me the confidence to do what I've done and the foolishness to think I could.

My father though... He didn't. He told me to do better. He famously told me after a screening of the film I worked around the clock on for the bulk of my senior year of college that he was "sure the next one would be better."

I hated him for it. Especially because he did it in front of other people.

But, here's the thing.

He was right. I could do better. I have done better. I will do better still.

What my father gave me, intentionally or not, was a complex. But, a complex of the very best kind. I strive to be the best at what I do, not the most successful, not the most beloved, but the very best, because of him. The reason that I can't just settle for good or okay or 'well, it's just a paycheck' will always be my father.

He's a man who's worked harder than any man I've ever known, fought to help more people than anyone could possibly be expected to, and done it at a great personal cost that few will ever understand.

This book is dedicated to my dad, and all that he did right and all that he did wrong.

Joshua Hale Fialkov
5-25-11
North Hollywod, CA

The Top Cow essentials checklist:

For more info , ISBN and ordering information on our latest collections go to:

www.topcow.com

Ask your retailer about our catalogue of our collected editions, digests and hard

covers or check the listings at:

Borders,
Barnes and Noble,
Amazon.com

and other fine retailers.

To find your nearest comic shop go to:

www.comicshoplocator.com